STUDY GUIDE

Carolyn J. Meyer

HUMAN DEVELOPMENT
NINTH EDITION

GRACE J. CRAIG
DON BAUCUM

PRENTICE HALL, UPPER SADDLE RIVER, NEW JERSEY 07458

©2002 by PEARSON EDUCATION, INC.
Upper Saddle River, New Jersey 07458

10 9 8 7 6 5 4 3

ISBN 0-13-061329-0

Printed in the United States of America

CONTENTS

Page

Chapter 1 - Perspectives, and Research Methods   1

Chapter 2 – Approaches to Understanding Human Development   15

Chapter 3 - Heredity and Environment   32

Chapter 4 - Prenatal Development and Childbirth   48

Chapter 5 - Infancy and Toddlerhood: Physical, Cognitive and Language Development   64

Chapter 6 - Infants and Toddlers: Personality Development and Socialization   81

Chapter 7 – Early Childhood: Physical, Cognitive, and Language Development   97

Chapter 8 – Early Childhood: Personality and Sociocultural Development   111

Chapter 9 - Middle Childhood: Physical and Cognitive Development   128

Chapter 10 - Middle Childhood: Personality and Sociocultural Development   143

Chapter 11 - Adolescence: Physical and Cognitive Development   158

Chapter 12 - Adolescence: Personality and Sociocultural Development   172

Chapter 13 - Young Adulthood: Physical and Cognitive Development   187

Chapter 14 - Young Adulthood: Personality and Sociocultural Development   201

Chapter 15 – Middle Adulthood: Physical and Cognitive Development   217

Chapter 16 – Middle Adulthood: Personality and Sociocultural Development   231

Chapter 17 - Older Adulthood: Physical and Cognitive Development   245

Chapter 18 - Older Adulthood: Personality and Sociocultural Development   260

Chapter 19 - Death and Dying   273

PREFACE

This Study Guide was written to accompany HUMAN DEVELOPMENT by Grace J. Craig. Its goal is to help you develop, in a planned sequence of steps, a full understanding of the subject matter covered in the text. However, a Study Guide can only help you if you USE it. I would recommend that you read the chapters in the text before they are covered in class, and then work through the corresponding chapter in this Study Guide. Set aside uninterrupted time to work on each chapter on your own. If you study with a group, discuss the Study Guide chapters <u>after</u> you have completed the chapter on your own.

Each chapter in the Study Guide is divided into sections. The first section is a brief outline of the subject matter that you should read over to get a general idea of the material covered in the chapter. The next two sections are Key Terms and Key Names. The key terms are listed for you but you must go back through the text and look up the definitions. This is a good way to become more familiar with the text material. The key names are people who have made a major contribution to the particular area of human development covered in the chapter. Try to match the names with their major contributions. The answers to this section are in the Answer Key at the end of the Study Guide chapter.

Each chapter also contains a Pretest and a Posttest with a Programmed Review of the chapter in between. Try to answer the questions in the Pretest without looking up the answers in the text. Check your answers with the Answer Key at the end of the Study Guide chapter and record the number correct. Then work your way through the Programmed Review. The answers are also in the Answer Key at the end of the chapter. Once you have finished the Programmed Review, try to answer the Posttest questions. Check your answers with the Answer Key and compare your Posttest score with your Pretest score. If you worked carefully through the Programmed Review, there should be a significant improvement in your score.

The last section in each chapter is a set of ten Essay Questions. It is a good idea to try to answer each question as fully as possible. Use the text as a source of material for your essays. Some of the questions deal with controversial topics and you are asked to write your opinion of the issue being covered. It is important that you carefully consider your answers so that you can sort out your opinions on these issues. The more time and thought you put into trying to answer these essay questions, the more thoroughly you will know the chapter.

Remember, your performance in any class is directly related to how much time and effort you put into the class material. If you read your text carefully, attend class and take careful notes, and work through this Study Guide, you should be able to achieve the grade you want. Good luck and good studying!

1
Perspectives and Research Methods

CHAPTER OUTLINE

Key Issues in the Study of Human Development
  Development in Context
  Developmental Domains
  The Scientific Study of Human Development
  Developmental Processes

Historical and Contemporary Perspectives on Human Development
  Images of Childhood
  Images of Adolescence
  Images of Adulthood
  Development in the Context of Changing Families

Studying Human Development: Descriptive Approaches
  Case Studies
  Systematic Observation
  Questionnaires and Surveys
  Psychological Testing
  Developmental Research Designs
  Correlation as a Descriptive Tool

Studying Human Development: Experimental Approaches
  The Search for Cause and Effect
  Experiments Focusing on Individuals
  Experiments Focusing on Groups

Ethics in Developmental Research
  Protection from Harm
  Informed Consent
  Privacy and Confidentiality
  Knowledge of Results
  Beneficial Treatments

KEY TERMS AND CONCEPTS

After reading the chapter in your text, try to write out the definition of each of the terms/concepts in this section. Then check your definitions with those in the text and make any necessary corrections. Most of these terms are key terms defined in the text. Some will require more effort to find the definition appropriate to this chapter.

Baby biography
Case study
Cognitive domain
Cohort effects
Collectivist culture
Conditioning
Confounding
Context
Contingency
Correlation
Critical period
Cross-sectional design
Culture
Dependent variable
Development
Enculturation
Ethnocentric bias
Experimental design
External validity
Imprinting
Independent variable
Individualist culture
Informed consent
Institutional review board

Internal validity
Laboratory observation
Learning
Longitudinal design
Naturalistic/field observation
Operational definition
Personality domain
Physical domain
Questionnaire
Random assignment
Random sample
Readiness
Reliability
Replication
Representative sample
Sensitive or optimal periods
Sequential/cohort design
Significant others
Single-subject design
Socialization
Society
Sociocultural domain
Standardization
Surveys
Validity

In most chapters, you will find the names of prominent people who have contributed to the field of psychology. This section presents a list of some of those people for you to match with their major contributions to the field. Put the letter of your choice in the space to the left of each name. Since you have already read the chapter, try to complete this section without looking up the names. You will find the correct answers in the Answer Key at the end of this chapter.

_____1. Mary Ainsworth　　　　　　　a. baby biographies

_____2. Albert Bandura　　　　　　　b. childhood agression

_____3. Charles Darwin　　　　　　　c. gifted children

_____4. Sigmund Freud　　　　　　　d. Little Albert experiment

_____5. G. Stanley Hall　　　　　　　e. psychoanalytic theory

_____6. B. F. Skinner　　　　　　　　f. single-subject design

_____7. Lewis Terman　　　　　　　　g. strange situation

_____8. J. B. Watson　　　　　　　　h. study of adolescence

In order to further test your knowledge of this chapter, try to answer each of the following questions without looking them up. Then check your answers with the Answer Key at the end of this chapter and record the number of correct answers in the space provided at the end of this section.

1. The definition of development includes changes which are the result of
   a. biology and experience.
   b. biology and heredity.
   c. genetics and heredity.
   d. experience and environment.

2. At what age does a child enter middle childhood?
   a. 4
   b. 5
   c. 6
   d. 7

3. Socialization and enculturation are part of what domain?
   a. physical
   b. cognitive
   c. sociocultural
   d. personality

4. Heredity vs. environment are the major issues in the debate over
   a. continuity vs. discontinuity.
   b. biology vs. experience.
   c. growth vs. maturation.
   d. collectivist vs. individualist.

5. An optimal period is
   a. the same as a critical period.
   b. an all-or-none time period.
   c. a sensitive period when development will be most efficient.
   d. the only time when a particular behavior will develop.

6. Childhood began to be considered a period of innocence in the
   a. ancient Greek culture.
   b. 1500s.
   c. the 18th and 19th centuries.
   d. the first part of the 20th century.

7. In the United States, _____ percent of parents spank their children at least occasionally.
   a. 80
   b. 60
   c. 40
   d. 20

8. Which of the following is true in collectivist cultures?
   a. The group takes priority over the individual.
   b. There is an emphasis on individuality.
   c. Competition is stressed over cooperation.
   d. Individual achievement is a high priority.

9. Who noted that adolescence was a separate period of dependency?
   a. Hall
   b. Skinner
   c. Erikson
   d. Freud

10. According to a United Nations study, _____ of the world's refugees and displaced persons are children.
    a. one-quarter
    b. one-third
    c. one-half
    d. two-thirds

11. Prolonged adolescence, as a distinct and major period of development, is
    a. a recent phenomenon.
    b. no longer of importance.
    c. characteristic only of agrarian societies.
    d. found only in literature from ancient Greece.

12. Which of the following used case studies?
    a. Bandura
    b. Freud
    c. Hall
    d. Watson

13. A test that yields similar scores from one testing to another is
    a. valid.
    b. longitudinal.
    c. reliable.
    d. sequential.

14. In which type of study are several overlapping cohorts studied longitudinally?
    a. cross-sectional
    b. longitudinal
    c. correlational
    d. cross-sequential

15. When a researcher tests the same group of people repeatedly at varying ages, she is conducting a(n) _____ study.
    a. cross-sectional
    b. longitudinal
    c. observational
    d. sequential/age cohort

16. In a research study on the effects of Head Start on children's later school performance, Head Start is the _____ variable.
    a. control
    b. dependent
    c. independent
    d. laboratory

17. Behavior modification is an example of what type of design?
    a. single subject
    b. longitudinal
    c. cross-sectional
    d. multiple-subject

18. Systematic repetitions of an experiment are called
    a. imitations.
    b. repetitions.
    c. replications.
    d. duplications.

19. Who conducted the "Little Albert" experiment?
    a. B. F. Skinner
    b. Charles Darwin
    c. Urie Bronfenbrenner
    d. J. B. Watson

20. Which of the following is part of research ethics?
    a. Participation is required to the end of the experiment.
    b. The names of all participants are released.
    c. All subjects are protected from harm.
    d. Confidentiality of results is maintained.

Pretest Score _____

This section is designed to give you a thorough review of the chapter. Try to fill in each of the blanks without referring back to the chapter in the book. Check your answers with the Answer Key at the end of the chapter and reread those sections of the chapter that cover any areas you missed.

1. Development refers to _____ over time in body and behavior due to biology and _____. It begins with _____ and continues throughout _____.

Key Issues in the Study of Human Development

2. Development is deeply embedded in _____, which refers to the immediate and extended settings in which it occurs. Examples include family, _____ (an organized group of interacting people), and _____ (the aspects of personal and group identity that interacting people share).

3. Human growth and change are divided into four _____: physical, _____, personality, and _____. But development is not piecemeal; it is _____.

4. Scientific inquiry is conducted as _____ and _____ as possible in order to overcome _____ bias.

5. Most development throughout the lifespan is a result of successive _____ between biology and experience, or _____ and _____. _____-oriented theorists assume that there are underlying biological structures, and _____ explanations focus on an individual's experiences and environmental factors.

6. Growth, maturation, and aging refer to _____ processes. Learning is change over time related to _____ or experience. When development is considered in terms of maturation and learning, the emphasis often shifts to _____.

7. The question of how maturation interacts with learning leads to the question of whether there are _____ periods during which certain types of development must occur or else will never occur. A sensitive or _____ period is the time when certain types of learning and development occur best and most efficiently. _____ refers to reaching a maturational point at which a specific behavior can be learned.

Historical and Contemporary Perspectives on Human Development

8. In agrarian societies of today, children are viewed as _____ and material contributors. In parts of ancient _____, strict obedience and harsh physical punishment were the norm; in ancient _____, undesirable or unwanted children were killed. By 1500, childhood was beginning to be considered a period of _____, and parents tried to _____ children from the excesses and evils of the adult world. By the eighteenth century, children were given a _____ of their own. Today, several nations have outlawed any use of _____ punishment.

9. In _____ cultures, the group takes priority over individuals and _____ is fostered. In _____ cultures, competition predominates over cooperation and _____ is valued.

10. In times of war, some societies use children as _____, and all children often suffer from _____ as a result of living in a war-torn country.

11. Prolonged adolescence as a distinct and major period of development is a recent phenomenon largely limited to _____ peoples. After World War I, advancing technology and rapid social change made it necessary for young people to stay in _____ longer. This modern view of adolescence as a separate period of dependency was first noted by _____. Adolescents tend to be highly sensitive to the _____ around them.

12. In industrialized nations, the adult years account for approximately _____ of the lifespan. Periods or stages in adulthood are determined in part by _____ status.

13. In the U. S. today, many children remain _____ dependent on their parents into their 20s. The high _____ of raising children to maturity, the widespread use of _____, and the growing number of _____ women have resulted in smaller families. Families develop their own _____ and childrearing patterns as a result of the _____ context in which they live.

Studying Human Development: Descriptive Approaches

14. In a _____ study, the researcher compiles large, intricate amounts of information on an individual, a family, or a community. An early example were the _____ biographies used by _____ in his study of evolution. Freud used case studies in developing his _____ theory and they are still important in _____ diagnosis and treatment.

15. Behavior can be observed and recorded in every day settings using _____ or field observation while being as unobtrusive as possible or by using _____ observation which is more controlled. An example is the _____ situation used by Ainsworth.

16. Questionnaires and _____ ask questions about past and present behavior. It is important that a _____ sample be selected and this is best achieved by selecting a _____ sample.

17. IQ tests are a form of _____ testing as are personality tests. In a _____ test, people are shown an ambiguous picture and asked to react to it. Tests should be _____(yielding similar scores from one testing occasion to the next), _____(measuring what they are supposed to measure); and _____ by administration to representative samples of people to establish _____.

18. In a _____ design, scientists study the same individuals over a period of time. These studies require a great deal of _____ from both researchers and participants, and the original _____ and _____ of the study may become outdated. Cross-sectional designs compare individuals of different _____, all at one point in _____. They are quicker, cheaper, and more _____, but they do require careful _____ of participants to avoid _____ because of _____ effects. Some researchers combine both approaches in a _____ design.

19. Researchers use a statistical technique called _____ to measure the relationship between variables. When variables change in the same direction, the correlation is _____; when they change in opposite directions the correlation is _____. This technique tells us nothing about _____.

Studying Human Development: Experimental Approaches

20. Skinner's work on conditioning was often a _____-subject design in which one subject at a time is exposed to _____ that are expected to alter behavior. Behavior _____ can be a highly effective method of eliminating problem behaviors.

21. In a laboratory setting, the researcher can systematically manipulate some of the conditions, or _____ variables, and observe the resultant behavior, or _____ variables. If what is done in the laboratory corresponds to what could happen in the real world, it has _____ validity. If it is clear that the experiment was conducted in a way that allows researchers to draw meaningful conclusions, it has _____ validity. Researchers use _____ definitions (concepts that can be defined in observable terms), and they also want to be able to repeat, or_____, the experiment.

Ethics in Developmental Research

22. The Society for _____ in Child Development and the American Psychological Association have suggested ethical principles to guide researchers. No treatment or experimental condition given to the individual should be _____ or _____ harmful. People should participate _____, and should give _____ consent. Children and adults should be free to _____ their participation in the research at any point. Privacy and _____ of the information obtained in the study must be preserved. Individuals have the right to be informed of the _____ of research in terms understandable to them and, in the case of children, the results may be shared with the _____. Each child participating in the study has the right to profit from _____ treatments provided to other participants in the study. Research organizations now have screening committees called Institutional _____ Boards.

Now that you have finished the programmed review, you should be able to answer the questions in this section. Check your answers with the Answer Key at the end of the chapter and also compare the number right in this section with the number you answered correctly in the Pretest. You should notice an improvement.

1. At what age does older adulthood begin?
    a. 50-55
    b. 55-60
    c. 60-65
    d. 65-70

2. The particular setting or situation in which development occurs is the
    a. domain.
    b. context.
    c. society.
    d. culture.

3. Thinking and perceiving are part of which domain?
    a. physical
    b. cognitive
    c. personality
    d. sociocultural

4. Which of the following does not belong with the others?
    a. aging
    b. growth
    c. learning
    d. maturation

5. The fact that rubella will affect prenatal development in the first months of pregnancy but not in later months is an example of a(n) _____ period.
    a. critical
    b. maturational
    c. optimal
    d. physical

6. The point at which a skill can be learned is
    a. a critical period.
    b. an optimal period.
    c. a sensitive period.
    d. readiness.

7. A culture in which competition predominates over cooperation is
   a. collectivist.
   b. medieval.
   c. agrarian.
   d. individualist.

8. All of the following have contributed to today's smaller family size EXCEPT
   a. the need for children to begin to work.
   b. the high cost of raising children to maturity.
   c. the widespread use of contraception.
   d. the growing number of working women.

9. The small, close-knit, "nuclear" family with mother at home and father at work
   a. is the predominant family type worldwide.
   b. only existed in ancient Greece and Rome.
   c. is more myth than reality.
   d. is more common in European homes.

10. Baby biographies are a form of
    a. case study.
    b. observational study.
    c. cross-sectional study.
    d. correlational study.

11. A researcher who is unobtrusively observing and recording behavior in everyday settings is conducting a
    a. correlational study.
    b. naturalistic observation.
    c. case study.
    d. survey.

12. In which research format are questions administered to a large number of people?
    a. projective test
    b. survey
    c. reliability test
    d. validity measure

13. A test that is valid
    a. measures what it intends to measure.
    b. is consistent and reliable.
    c. always proves the hypothesis.
    d. is repeatable.

14. When a researcher tests several groups of people at the same time, each group at a different age, he is conducting a(n) _____ study.
    a. cross-sectional
    b. longitudinal
    c. observational
    d. sequential/age cohort

15. When two variables change in the same direction, the correlation is
    a. negative.
    b. confounded.
    c. zero.
    d. positive.

16. Which of the following is the best correlation?
    a. -.86
    b. +.52
    c. -.32
    d. +.23

17. In an experiment to test the effects of sleep deprivation on school performance, school performance is the
    a. independent variable.
    b. dependent variable.
    c. control variable.
    d. experimental variable.

18. What type of definition translates general concepts into what is actually done in the experiment?
    a. independent
    b. operational
    c. correlational
    d. represenative

19. Which type of validity refers to whether an experiment is conducted in a way that allows researchers to draw meaningful conclusions about cause-and-effect relationships?
    a. external
    b. random
    c. replicable
    d. internal

20. The ethical principle of informed consent means all of the following EXCEPT
    a. people should participate voluntarily in the experiment.
    b. participants have a right to know the results.
    c. participants must be fully informed of the consequences of the research.
    d. participants should not be coerced into participating in the research.

Posttest score _____

Pretest score _____

Improvement _____

ESSAY QUESTIONS

The purpose of these essay questions is to give you a chance to consolidate your knowledge of the material in this chapter. Try to write complete and well-structured answers. You should refer to the text for material to support your ideas. No correct answers are given for this section because these questions should be answered in your own words and with your own ideas.

1. Summarize the research ethics that are used by all reputable researchers.

2. Explain why it is not easy for researchers to be objective and systematic when studying human development.

3. Compare longitudinal and cross-sectional research methods and explain how the sequential-cohort design relates to both.

4. Trace the changing views of childhood throughout history and describe the conditions that led to the origin of adolescence as a separate period of development.

5. Describe the trend in family size in the 20th century and explain the reasons for this trend.

6. Describe the nine periods of the human lifespan.

7. Heredity vs. environment and maturation vs. learning are processes in development. Describe each one and explain how they interact.

8. Describe the four developmental domains.

9. Describe and explain critical periods, sensitive periods, and readiness.

10. Compare collectivist and individualist cultures and give examples of each.

ANSWER KEY

Key Names

1. g	3. a	5. h	7. c
2. b	4. e	6. f	8. d

Pretest

1. a	5. c	9. a	13. c	17. a
2. c	6. b	10. c	14. d	18. c
3. c	7. a	11. a	15. b	19. d
4. b	8. a	12. b	16. c	20. c

Programmed Review

1. changes, experience, conception, life
2. context, society, culture
3. domains, cognitive, sociocultural, holistic
4. objectively, systematically, ethnocentric
5. interactions, heredity, environment, Heredity, environmental
6. biological, practice, timing
7. critical, optimal, Readiness
8. co-workers, Greece, Rome, innocence, protect, status, corporal
9. collectivist, interdependence, individualist, independence
10. soldiers, posttraumatic stress syndrome
11. industrialized, school, G. Stanley Hall, society
12. three-quarters, socioeconomic
13. financially, cost, contraception, working, identity, historical
14. case, baby, Darwin, psychoanalytic, clinical
15. naturalistic, laboratory, strange
16. surveys, representative, random
17. psychological, projective, reliable, valid, standardized, norms
18. longitudinal, time, purposes, methods, ages, time, manageable, selection, confounding, cohort, sequential-cohort
19. correlation, positive, negative, causation
20. single, contingencies, modification
21. independent, dependent, external, internal, operational, replicate
22. Research, physical, psychological, voluntarily, informed, discontinue, confidentiality, results, parents, beneficial, Review

Posttest

1. c	5. a	9. c	13. a	17. b
2. b	6. d	10. a	14. a	18. b
3. b	7. d	11. b	15. d	19. d
4. c	8. a	12. b	16. a	20. b

2
Approaches to Understanding Human Development

CHAPTER OUTLINE

Additional Questions About Development
    Active versus Passive Development
    Stages versus Continuity in Development

Psychodynamic Approaches
    Freud's Psychoanalytic Theory
    Erikson's Psychosocial Theory

Behaviorism and Learning Theories
    Pavlov's Classical Conditioning
    Thorndike's Law of Effect
    Classic Learning Theory
    Skinner's Operant Conditioning
    Social-learning Theory

Cognitive Approaches
    Piaget's Cognitive-Developmental Theory
    Vygotsky and Social-Cognitive Theory
    Information Processing Theory

Biological Approaches
    Evolution
    Ethology
    Evolutionary Psychology
    Developmental Neuroscience

Systems Approach
    Contextualism
    Ecological Systems Theories

Theories in Retrospect

KEY TERMS AND CONCEPTS

After reading the chapter in your text, try to write out the definition of each of the terms/concepts in this section. Then check your definitions with those in the text and make any necessary corrections. The terms in this chapter will be repeated throughout the text. Learning them now will provide a good foundation for later chapters.

Accommodation

Altruism

Artificial intelligence

Assimilation

Bioecological model

Castration anxiety

Catharsis

Chronosystem

Classical conditioning

Cognitive developmental theory

Conscience

Conscious mind

Contextualism

Covert behavior

Death instinct

Defense mechanisms

Developmental neuroscience

Direct fitness

Eclectic

Ecological systems theory

Ego

Ego ideal

Electra complex

Encoding

Epigenetic principle

Erogenous zones

Eros

Ethology

Evolution

Evolutionary psychology

Exosystem

Fixations

Free association

Guided participation

Id

Inclusive fitness

Indirect fitness

Information-processing theory

Instinct

Law of effect

Learning

Life instinct

Macrosystem

Mesosystem

Microsystem

Morality principle

Natural selection

Oedipus complex

Operant conditioning

Original sin

Overt behavior

Penis envy

Pleasure principle

Psychoanalysis

Psychodynamic approach

Psychosexual stages

Psychosocial theory

Reality principle

Repression

Resistance

Retrieval

Schemes or schema

Shared meanings

Social cognition

Sociobiology

Stages

Storage

Strict behaviorism

Structuralists

Superego

Tabula rasa

Thanatos

Unconscious mind

Zone of proximal development

KEY NAMES

In most chapters, you will find the names of prominent people who have contributed to the field of psychology. This section presents a list of some of those people for you to match with their major contributions to the field. Put the letter of your choice in the space to the left of each name. Since you have already read the chapter, try to complete this section without looking up the names. You will find the correct answers in the Answer Key at the end of this chapter.

_____ 1. Albert Bandura	a. attachment
_____ 2. John Bowlby	b. bioecological model
_____ 3. Urie Bronfenbrenner	c. classical conditioning
_____ 4. Charles Darwin	d. cognitive development
_____ 5. Erik Erikson	e. English empiricist
_____ 6. Sigmund Freud	f. evolution
_____ 7. Thomas Hobbes	g. imprinting
_____ 8. John Locke	h. inherent goodness
_____ 9. Konrad Lorenz	i. law of effect
_____ 10. Ivan Pavlov	j. operant conditioning
_____ 11. Jean Piaget	k. psychosexual stages
_____ 12. Jean Jacques Rousseau	l. psychosocial theory
_____ 13. B. F. Skinner	m. social learning theory
_____ 14. E. L. Thorndike	n. sociobiology
_____ 15. Lev Vygotsky	o. tabula rasa
_____ 16. E. O. Wilson	p. zone of Proximal Development

In order to further test your knowledge of this chapter, try to answer each of the following questions without looking them up. Then check your answers with the Answer Key at the end of this chapter and record the number of correct answers in the space provided at the end of this section.

1. Theorists from which of the following areas emphasize active development?
    a. organismic
    b. mechanistic
    c. reactionist
    d. interactionist

2. All of the following are related to psychoanalysis EXCEPT
    a. dream analysis.
    b. accommodation.
    c. free association.
    d. resistance.

3. According to Freud, arrestments in development are
    a. catharsis.
    b. fixations.
    c. gratifications.
    d. repressions.

4. Freud proposed that girls experience a(n) _____; whereas boys experience a(n) _____.
    a. castration anxiety; penis envy
    b. penis envy; castration anxiety
    c. Electra complex; Oedipus complex
    d. Oedipus complex; Electra complex

5. As 8-year-old boy would be in which of Freud's psychosexual stages?
    a. oral
    b. anal
    c. phallic
    d. latency

6. According to Freud
    a. the id operates on the pleasure principle.
    b. the ego contains the conscience.
    c. the superego operates on the reality principle.
    d. development is psychosocial.

7. The core concept of Erikson's theory is the acquisition of
   a. trust.
   b. autonomy.
   c. ego identity.
   d. generativity.

8. According to Erikson, a sense of self-confidence and self-control develops in the stage of
   a. autonomy vs. shame and doubt.
   b. initiative vs. guilt.
   c. industry vs. inferiority.
   d. intimacy vs. isolation.

9. Which of the following conditioning terms does NOT belong with the others?
   a. classical
   b. Pavlovian
   c. operant
   d. respondent

10. Who proposed the law of effect?
    a. Clark Hull
    b. E. L. Thorndike
    c. Ivan Pavlov
    d. B. F. Skinner

11. Who argued that each person is born tabula rasa?
    a. Piaget
    b. Hobbes
    c. Rousseau
    d. Locke

12. Piaget and other cognitive developmental psychologists have been called
    a. structuralists.
    b. sociologists.
    c. strict behaviorists.
    d. ecologists.

13. Who proposed the zone of proximal development?
    a. Clark Hull
    b. E. L. Thorndike
    c. Lev Vygotsky
    d. Jean Piaget

14. The human brain uses _____ processing; whereas computers use _____ processing.
    a. direct; indirect
    b. indirect; direct
    c. serial; parallel
    d. parallel; serial

15. Changing schemes when a new object or event does not fit in is
    a. assimilation.
    b. accommodation.
    c. fixation.
    d. allocation.

16. Children begin to use language in which stage of Piaget's cognitive theory?
    a. concrete operations
    b. formal operations
    c. preoperational
    d. sensorimotor

17. The initial processing of information is
    a. encoding.
    b. retrieval.
    c. storage.
    d. assimilation.

18. Which of the following theorists is an ethologist?
    a. E. L. Thorndike
    b. Lev Vygotsky
    c. Konrad Lorenz
    d. Urie Bronfenbrenner

19. Sociobiology is an extension of
    a. evolution.
    b. ethology.
    c. ecological theory.
    d. evolutionary neuroscience.

20. According to Bronfenbrenner, the immediate setting around a child is the
    a. exosystem.
    b. microsystem.
    c. mesosystem.
    d. macrosystem.

Pretest Score _____

This section is designed to give you a thorough review of the chapter. Try to fill in each of the blanks without referring back to the chapter in the book. Check your answers with the Answer Key at the end of the chapter and reread those sections of the chapter that cover any areas you missed.

1.   A good theory provides a framework and then _____ around it, offering _____, and providing testable _____.

Additional Questions About Development

2.   Theorists who emphasize active development are often referred to as _____ theorists. Those who view development more as a passive process are often referred to as _____ theorists. Mechanistic theorists claim that people are driven primarily by _____ drives and motivations in conjunction with _____ incentives and pressures provided by others and the environment in general. In reality, our active human minds _____ with the forces of society and nature.

3.   In general, _____ in development throughout the lifespan is the prevailing view. However, cognitive-developmental theorists view cognitive abilities as developing in discrete _____ during which children see the world in qualitatively _____ ways compared to adults.

Psychodynamic Approaches

4.   Freud used clinical _____ of his adult patients in developing psychoanalysis, a theory referring to analysis of the "psyche" with its origins in the Greek word for _____.

5.   Freud experimented with various techniques but wound up emphasizing his method of free _____. He also used _____ analysis, and when therapy reached a certain point, would begin to make his own _____. Any confrontation, avoidance, or lack of acceptance on the patient's part was deemed to be _____.

6.   From birth, the infant is dominated by the _____, the primitive component of personality. It generates biologically based impulses or _____ wishes that constitute the _____ instinct, which Freud called _____. The life instinct operates according to the _____ principle and seeks immediate _____. The _____ instinct called _____ accounts for processes involved in death, aggression, and destructiveness. The id is part of the _____ mind.

7.   As development proceeds, the _____ gradually evolves. It serves as the _____ agent for dealing with impulses, and is the _____ mind. The ego operates according to the _____ principle. It is responsible for _____ mechanisms which are ways of reducing or at least disguising _____. The most basic of these is _____.

8. During early childhood, the _____ begins to evolve from the ego and consists of the _____ and the ego _____. It operates according to the _____ principle.

9. According to Freud, the personality develops through _____ stages with a focus on _____ zones of the body. The first stage occurring in _____ and centering around the lips and mouth is the _____ stage. The _____ stage erogenous zone is the region around the anus and _____ training usually occurs. Next is the _____ stage in which the erogenous zone is the _____. This is followed by the _____ stage during middle childhood when sexual urges become _____ and finally the _____ stage, which begins at puberty when sexual feelings again become prominent.

10. Freud also proposed that _____ or arrestments in development can occur during the psychosexual stages and cause the adult to continue to seek _____ in ways that are appropriate only for children.

11. Freud proposed that all children experience what he called the _____ complex. The boy develops lustful desires for his _____, becomes afraid that his father will castrate him for those desires (_____ anxiety), and _____ with his father. Girls experience the _____ complex. The girl develops lustful desires for her _____ in conjunction with _____ envy, and eventually resolves the conflict by either _____ with the mother or through hopes of having a _____ child.

12. Freud's greatest error originated in his _____ from a very restricted sample of case studies to all humans. Classical psychoanalytic theory revolutionized how we look at _____ and _____. Freud's lasting contributions include his idea of the _____ mind and ideas about ego _____ mechanisms.

13. Erikson is called a _____ because his theory has a different emphasis from that of Freud. Erikson focused mainly on the effects of _____ interactions in shaping personality and his approach is therefore called a _____ theory. The theory includes developmental stages throughout the human _____. Underlying the developmental stages are what Erikson called the _____ principle, a biological concept.

14. In the stage of _____, infants form a global impression of the world as a _____ place. In the stage of autonomy versus shame and doubt, toddlers discover their own _____ and how to _____ it. They gain a sense of _____ and _____. In the stage of _____, children discover how the world works. In _____, children develop numerous _____ and _____ in school, at home, and in the outside world. In the stage of _____, adolescents seek basic _____ and _____ that cut across their various roles. In the late adolescent and young adulthood stage of _____, the person develops an ability to share _____ with another person of either sex without fear of losing personal _____. Success in resolving this stage is affected by the resolution of the five earlier _____. The stage of _____ occurs in adulthood and the person is now free to direct attention more fully to the _____ of others. During _____, it is typical for individuals to look back over their lives and judge themselves.

15. The core concept of Erikson's theory is ego _____. The theory is strongly oriented toward understanding personality development in Western and other cultures that stress _____ over _____ identity.

Behaviorism and Learning Theories

16. True experimentation began in the late _____ century with the _____ behaviorists and _____ - response or S-R behaviorism. They studied only what was directly _____. Thinking, feeling, and knowing, are _____ behaviors that can't be seen or measured with instrumentation. The premise is that behavioral researchers limit themselves to studying _____ behavior, meaning that which can be observed and measured objectively.

17. In Pavlov's _____ conditioning, also called _____ conditioning, two or more stimuli are paired and become _____ with each other in the subject's brain.

18. Thorndike's law of _____ states that when behavior is followed by satisfying or pleasurable consequences, it tends to be repeated, and when it is followed by unsatisfying or unpleasurable consequences, it tends not to be repeated. Thorndike formulated his law on the basis of research with animals, typically _____. He called this _____ and error learning.

19. Learning refers to a relatively _____ change in behavioral potential as a result of practice or _____. Early learning theorists focused on _____ behaviors that are involved in producing _____. The learning theorists looked at drives, motivation, incentives, and inhibitions, which are _____ behaviors; but _____ argued that such terms are scientific to the extent that they can be defined in terms of _____ operations.

20. Skinner maintained that an animal's behavior operates on its _____ and is repeated or not repeated because of its _____. In the lab, Skinner studied operant conditioning primarily with _____ and _____.

21. Locke argued that each person is born a _____, or blank slate. His view follows logically from the _____ position that everything we know and are derives from our experience via the senses. In the 20th century, _____ elaborated Locke's on views. Hobbes proposed that people are inherently _____ and consequently in need of strict molding and ongoing _____ if they are to become cooperative members of society. A very similar position underlies Freud's _____ theory. These views are also highly consistent with the Christian doctrine of original _____. Rousseau held that people are born inherently _____ but are often corrupted by the evils of _____. Abraham _____ and Carl _____ argued that our inner core is basically good with positive motives toward both self and others.

22. Social-learning theorists such as Albert _____ recognize that children and adults _____ their own behavior, the behavior of others, and also the _____ of those behaviors.

23. Social-learning theory has roots in _____ psychology and related disciplines. Its limitation is that it tends to approach learning as a _____ street, without allowance for ongoing _____ and give-and-take between observer and model.

Cognitive Approaches

24. Piaget and other cognitive-developmental psychologists have been called _____ because they are concerned with the structure of thought and the way in which the mind _____ on information. Piaget's investigations grew out of his studies in _____ and _____ and his early work on _____ tests. Children's _____ gave him insights into how children think. He saw consistent patterns indicating that children's thinking is _____ different from that of adults.

25. A key feature of Piaget's theory is that the mind is an _____ participant in the learning process. If information or an experience the person encounters fits with an existing mental framework, it is _____. If it does not fit, the mind may _____ the new information or experience. Assimilation consists of interpreting new experiences in terms of existing mental structures called schemes or _____ without changing them significantly. Accommodation means _____ existing schemes to integrate new experiences. Most learning situations involve an _____ between both processes.

26. According to Piaget, from birth to approximately 2 years of age, the child is in the _____ stage, in which intelligence relies on the _____ and on bodily _____. From 2 to 7 years, the child is in the Preoperational stage, in which concepts and symbols are limited to personal immediate _____. From 7 through 11 or 12 years of age, the child is in the _____ stage and can begin to think _____. From 11 or 12 years of age on, the person is in the _____ stage, and can explore all the logical _____ to form both concrete and abstract concepts. They can think _____ about all possibilities and come up with logical solutions; they can project into the _____ or recall the past in solving problems; and they can reason by _____ and _____.

27. According to Piaget, the child is an _____ scientist who interacts with the physical _____ and develops increasingly complex thought _____. But developmentalists are also emphasizing that the child is a _____ being.

28. Lev Vygotsky was the first to emphasize the _____ context in which most of children's cognitive development takes place, as well as the _____ development of the community's knowledge and understanding. He concluded that we understand our world only by learning the _____ meanings of others around us. We develop understanding and expertise mainly through _____ with more knowledgeable learners. This _____ participation enables us to understand more about our world. The first level of cognitive development is the child's _____ developmental level as determined by independent problem solving. The second is the child's level of _____ development. The distance between the two is the zone of _____ development. Social _____ emphasizes beliefs and attitudes and other units of knowledge, and social-cognitive theories tend to be much more circumscribed and _____ on specific aspects of development and behavior.

29. Artificial _____ refers to programming computers to think like humans. The information processing theorists use _____ analogies in developing models of how memory and other aspects of cognition work. However, computer processing is _____, and humans use _____ processing. The computer model has generated research on child-adult differences in _____, the initial processing of information; _____, the temporary or permanent retention of information; and _____, the remembering of information at a later time.

Biological Approaches

30. The process by which species change across generations is _____. Darwin proposed the theory of _____ selection, which centers around _____ of the fittest. If one species is better than another at obtaining limited resources, the other species will die out if it doesn't find a different environmental _____.

31. Ethologists study evolved patterns of behavior with emphasis on behavior that is guided by _____. For a behavior to be considered instinctive, it must occur in all _____ members of a species; it must always occur under the same _____; and it must occur in essentially the _____ way every time.

32. _____ is an extension of ethology oriented toward the study of evolutionarily based human social behaviors. A central tenet is the concept of _____ fitness in which evolutionary survival of the fittest comes about as _____ fitness (the survival of the individual long enough to pass adaptive characteristics to the next generation), or _____ fitness (based on the biological relatedness of relatives). Our primary motive in life is to pass along our characteristics to the next _____.

33. The field of evolutionary developmental psychology has its origins in the research of _____. Modern evolutionary developmental psychologists are taking a broader look at the adaptive value of _____ in and of itself, cognitive and physical _____ during childhood, and the extended period of _____ in humans.

34. _____ neuroscience and _____ neuroscience seek to establish links between the functioning of brain structures, overt behaviors, and the mind. A primary area of interest has been the development of brain structures associated with different kinds of _____.

Systems Approaches

35. A system is an organized and _____ set of components which operate according to certain _____ and serve some _____.

36. The systems view that development and behavior always occur in a specific physical and sociocultural context is called _____. Historically, the contextual approach relied on _____ comparisons and the effects of different _____ practices on the child. Contextual approaches emphasize how cultural practices and the child or adult _____ over the course of development.

37. The ecological _____ theory approaches hold that human development cannot be understood in a simple _____ or cause-and-effect way.

38. The _____ model of Bronfenbrenner emphasizes that human development is a dynamic reciprocal process that begins with _____ endowment and unfolds as a result of interactions with the immediate _____. The sociocultural environment is pictured as a nested arrangement of four _____ systems, the interactions of which yield a fifth system called the _____.

39. The _____ refers to the activities, roles, and interactions of an individual and his or her immediate setting. The _____ is formed by the interrelationships among two or more microsystems. The _____ refers to social settings or organizations beyond the child's immediate experience that affect the child. The _____ consists of the values, laws, and customs of the society in which the individual lives.

Theories in Retrospect

40. The need to be _____ means accepting and using those parts of a theory that work.

POSTTEST

Now that you have finished the programmed review, you should be able to answer the questions in this section. Check your answers with the Answer Key at the end of the chapter and also compare the number right in this section with the number you answered correctly in the Pretest. You should notice an improvement.

1. Theorists who believe people primarily react to events in the environment are
   a. organismic.
   b. mechanistic.
   c. realistic.
   d. pessimistic.

2. Who founded the psychodynamic approach?
   a. Sigmund Freud
   b. Erik Erikson
   c. E. L. Thorndike
   d. Urie Bronfenbrenner

3. According to Freud, the ego operates on what principle?
   a. pleasure
   b. reality
   c. morality
   d. unconscious

4. The ego ideal and conscience are part of which part of the personality?
   a. ego
   b. superego
   c. id
   d. conscious

5. Venting negative emotions in a socially accepted way is
   a. association.
   b. repression.
   c. resistance.
   d. catharsis.

6. From age 12 on, a person is in which psychosexual stage?
   a. genital
   b. latency
   c. phallic
   d. anal

7. According to Freud, the mouth is the major erogenous zone in the _____ stage.
   a. anal
   b. latency
   c. oral
   d. phallic

8. Who developed a psychosocial theory of development?
   a. Freud
   b. Erikson
   c. Piaget
   d. Skinner

9. According to Erikson, the final stage of development should result in a sense of
   a. autonomy.
   b. integrity.
   c. intimacy.
   d. trust.

10. Whose theory is based on an epigenetic principle?
    a. Erik Erikson
    b. Sigmund Freud
    c. Clark Hull
    d. Ivan Pavlov

11. A relatively permanent change in behavior potential as a result of practice or experience is the definition of
    a. learning.
    b. accommodation.
    c. catharsis.
    d. assimilation.

12. Skinner developed his theory of operant conditioning based primarily on research on
    a. infants.
    b. human adults.
    c. dogs and cats.
    d. rats and pigeons.

13. Which of the following is a social learning theorist?
    a. Bandura
    b. Skinner
    c. Pavlov
    d. Thorndike

14. Who argued that people are born inherently good?
    a. Hobbes
    b. Rousseau
    c. Freud
    d. Erikson

15. A child is raised on a dairy farm and sees many cows. At age three, the child sees his first horse and calls it a cow. The child has just demonstrated
    a. accommodation.
    b. assimilation.
    c. conservation.
    d. equilibration.

16. Piaget's stage for infancy is
    a. concrete operations.
    b. formal operations.
    c. preoperational.
    d. sensorimotor.

17. Piaget would place adolescents in the _____ stage.
    a. concrete operations
    b. formal operations
    c. preoperational
    d. sensorimotor

18. Which of the following does not belong with the others?
    a. survival of the fittest
    b. natural selection
    c. ethology
    d. evolution

19. Which field emerged from the work of Bowlby?
    a. evolutionary developmental psychology
    b. ethology
    c. developmental neuroscience
    d. evolution

20. According to Bronfenbrenner, the values, laws, and customs of society are the
    a. microsystem.
    b. exosystem.
    c. mesosystem.
    d. macrosystem.

Posttest score _____

Pretest score _____

Improvement _____

ESSAY QUESTIONS

The purpose of these essay questions is to give you a chance to consolidate your knowledge of the material in this chapter. Try to write complete and well-structured answers. You should refer to the text for material to support your ideas. No correct answers are given for this section because these questions should be answered in your own words and with your own ideas.

1. Describe and compare classical and operant conditioning giving concrete developmental examples of each.

2. Describe social learning theory and give examples of its application to development.

3. Describe the biological approaches to human development and give examples of each.

4. What is meant by a systems approach to developmental psychology?

5. Describe and give examples of each level of Bronfenbrenner's bioecological model of development.

6. Describe the positive and negatives aspects of psychoanalytic theory. Suggest ways that this theory might be changed to make it more useful for psychology today.

7. Stage vs. continuity and active vs. passive development are two areas of debate in developmental theories. Describe each one and explain your views of each.

8. Compare and contrast the work of Piaget, Vygotsky, and the information-processing theorists.

9. Compare and contrast the theories of Erikson and Freud.

10. If you were a developmental psychologist, which of the theories covered in this chapter would you use in your work? Explain your answer.

ANSWER KEY

Key Names

1. m	5. l	9. g	13. j
2. a	6. k	10. c	14. i
3. b	7. e	11. d	15. p
4. f	8. o	12. h	16. n

Pretest

1. a	5. d	9. c	13. c	17. a
2. b	6. a	10. b	14. d	18. c
3. b	7. c	11. d	15. b	19. b
4. b	8. a	12. a	16. c	20. b

Programmed Review

1. organizes, explanations, predictions
2. organismic, mechanistic, internal, external, interact
3. continuity, stages, different
4. case studies, soul
5. association, dream, interpretations, resistance
6. id, instinctual, life, eros, pleasure, gratification, death, Thanatos, unconscious
7. ego, executive, conscious, reality, defense, anxiety, repression
8. superego, conscience, ego ideal, morality
9. psychosexual, erogenous, infancy, oral, anal, toilet, phallic, genitals, latency, dormant, genital
10. fixations, gratifications
11. Oedipus, mother, castration, identifies, Electra, father, penis, identifying, male
12. generalizing, personality, motivation, unconscious, defense
13. neoFreudian, social, psychosocial, lifespan, epigenetic
14. trust vs. mistrust, safe, body, control, self-confidence, self-control, initiative vs. guilt, industry vs. inferiority, skills, competencies, ego identity vs. ego diffusion, values, attitudes, intimacy vs. isolation, oneself, identity, conflicts, generativity vs. self-absorption, assistance, integrity vs. despair
15. identity, individual, collective
16. 19th, strict, stimulus, observable, covert, overt
17. classical, respondent, associated

18. effect, cats, trial
19. permanent, experience, instrumental, consequences, covert, Hull, observable
20. environment, consequences, rats, pigeons
21. tabula rasa, empiricist, Watson, selfish, control, psychoanalytic, sin, good, society, Maslow, Rogers
22. Bandura, observe, consequences
23. social, one-way, interactions
24. structuralists, operated, biology, philosophy, intelligence, errors, qualitatively
25. active, assimilated, accommodate, schemas, changing, interaction
26. sensorimotor, senses, motion, experience, concrete operations, logically, formal operations, solutions, systematically, future, analogy, metaphor
27. active, environment, strategies, social
28. social, historical, shared, apprenticeship, guided, actual, potential, proximal, cognition, focused
29. intelligence, computer, serial, parallel, encoding, storage, retrieval
30. evolution, natural, survival, niche
31. instinct, normal, conditions, same
32. Sociobiology, inclusive, direct, indirect, generation
33. Bowlby, attachment, immaturity, childhood
34. Behavioral, cognitive, memory
35. interactive principles, function
36. contextualism, cross-cultural, childcare, interact
37. systems, mechanistic
38. bioecological, genetic, environment, concentric, chronosystem
39. microsystem, mesosystem, exosystem, macrosystem
40. eclectic

Posttest

1. b	5. d	9. b	13. a	17. b
2. a	6. a	10. a	14. b	18. c
3. b	7. c	11. a	15. b	19. a
4. b	8. b	12. d	16. c	20. d

3
Heredity and Environment

CHAPTER OUTLINE

Molecular Genetics
Human Cells
Genes and Protein Synthesis

Genes, Chromosomes, and Cell Division
Cell Division and Reproduction
Mutation
From Genotype to Phenotype

Genetic and Chromosomal Disorders
Sex-Linked Disorders
Autosomal Disorders
Genetic Counseling

Advances in Genetic Research and Treatment
Gene Therapy
Cloning Entire Organisms

Behavior Genetics
Adoption Studies
Twin Studies

Environmental Influences and Contexts

Processes Within the Microsystem
Habituation
Classical Conditioning
Operant Conditioning
Social Learning and the Evolving Self-concept

Processes that Transcend the Microsystem
The Developmental Niche
Family Systems
The Family as Transmitter of Culture
Sociocultural Influences on Development Across the Lifespan

A Tale of the Interaction Between Heredity and Environment

KEY NAMES

Match the following individuals with their major contributions to the field of psychology and check your answers with the Answer Key at the end of the chapter. There will be one answer that will apply to two names.

_____1. Paul Baltes   a. classical conditioning

_____2 Albert Bandura   b. cloning

_____3. Urie Bronfenbrenner   c. identity

_____4. Francis Crick   d. law of effect

_____5. Erik Erikson   e. microsystem

_____6. Ivan Pavlov   f. normative influences

_____7. B. F. Skinner   g. operant conditioning

_____8. E. L. Thorndike   h. self-efficacy

_____9. James Watson   i. structure of DNA

____10. Ian Wilmut

Classification of Disorders

Classify the following disorders as: a. autosomal dominant, b. autosomal recessive, c. autosomal chromosomal, d. incomplete dominance, e. sex-linked genetic, f. sex-linked chromosomal, or g. gene imprinting.

_____ 1. Angleman's syndrome   _____ 8. Colorblindness

_____ 2. Cystic Fibrosis   _____ 9. Down syndrome

_____ 3. Fragile X syndrome   _____ 10. Homophilia

_____ 4. Huntington disease   _____ 11. Klinefelter syndrome

_____ 5. Phenylketonuria (PKU)   _____ 12. Prader Willi syndrome

_____ 6. Sickle-cell anemia   _____ 13. Sickle-cell effect

_____ 7. Tay-Sachs disease   _____ 14. Turner's syndrome

KEY TERMS AND CONCEPTS

After you have read Chapter 3 in the text, try to write out the definitions for each of the following key terms and concepts and then check your answers with the definitions in the text and make any necessary corrections. Because there is such a long list of new terms for this chapter, key terms mentioned in previous chapters have been omitted. It would be a good idea to review the terms from Chapters 1 and 2 as well.

Alleles
Amino acids
Autosomes
Base pairs
Bases
Behavior modification
Behavior genetics
Bioinformatics
Cell membrane
Cells
Chromosome
Codominance
Codon
Collagen
Concordance
Congenital anomalies
Cytoplasm
Cytoskeleton
DNA (deoxyribonucleic acid)
Developmental niche
Dominant
Endoplasmic reticulum
Enzymes
Ethnocentrism
Gametes
Genes
Gene imprinting
Gene therapy
Genetic counseling
Genotype
Golgi apparatus
Habituation
Hemoglobin
Heritability
Heterozygous
Homozygous

Hormones
Human genome
Incomplete dominance
Independent assortment
Karyotype
Meiosis
Metabolic pathways
Mitochondria
Mitosis
Negative punishment
Negative reinforcement
Nonnormative influences
Normative age-graded influences
Normative history-graded influences
Nucleotides
Nucleus
Partial reinforcement
Phenotype
Phobia
Polygenic inheritance
Polypeptide chain
Positive punishment
Positive reinforcement
Proteins
Recessive
Recombinant DNA technology
Ribosomes
RNA (ribonucleic acid)
Self-concept
Self-efficacy
Sex-linked inheritance
Sex chromosomes
Shaping
Single nucleotide polymorphism (SNPs)
Transcription

In order to test your knowledge of this chapter, try to answer each of the pretest questions without looking up the answers, then check your answers with the Answer Key at the end of this chapter and record the number correct at the end of this section.

1. The "powerhouse" of the cell is the
   a. enzyme.
   b. Golgi apparatus.
   c. ribosome.
   d. mitochondria.

2. Which of the following DNA base pairs is correct?
   a. cytosine - adenine
   b. uracil - adenine
   c. guanine - thymine
   d. adenine - thymine

3. An ova or sperm contains _____ chromosomes.
   a. 23
   b. 46
   c. 23 pairs of
   d. 46 pairs of

4. Collagen is the protein found in
   a. bones and connective tissue.
   b. red blood cells.
   c. muscles.
   d. hormones.

5. The normal male has _____ on the 23rd chromosome pair.
   a. XX
   b. XY
   c. YO
   d. YY

6. Cell division in all but the reproductive cells is called
   a. meiosis.
   b. mitosis.
   c. mutation.
   d. reproduction.

7. An individual's biochemical makeup is the person's _____ and the expressed traits are the person's _____.
   a. autosome; genotype
   b. genotype; phenotype
   c. phenotype; chromosome
   d. chromosome; karyotype

8. One of the Supermale Syndrome chromosome patterns is
   a. XX.
   b. XXY.
   c. XO.
   d. XYY.

9. Two sex-linked disorders are
   a. Turner's syndrome and sickle cell disease.
   b. fragile X and Tay Sachs.
   c. color blindness and hemophilia.
   d. Down syndrome and fragile X.

10. Down syndrome occurs in persons with an extra chromosome on pair
    a. 2.
    b. 12.
    c. 17.
    d. 21.

11. All of the following are recessive disorders EXCEPT
    a. cystic fibrosis.
    b. Huntington's chorea.
    c. phenylketonuria.
    d. Tay-Sachs disease.

12. If the two alleles for a trait are the same, the individual is _____; if the alleles differ, the individual is _____.
    a. phenotypic; genotypic
    b. homozygous; heterozygous
    c. heterozygous; homozygous
    d. genotypic; phenotypic

13. Which of the following diseases is an example of incomplete dominance?
    a. cystic fibrosis
    b. sickle-cell anemia
    c. Turner's syndrome
    d. Down syndrome

14. The study of patterns of inheritance at the behavioral level is
    a. behavior genetics.
    b. behavior modification.
    c. the ecological systems approach.
    d. bioinformatics.

15. Research with twins shows that the EAS traits are frequently inherited. EAS stands for
    a. eagerness, aggressiveness, sociability.
    b. energy, activity level, stubbornness.
    c. emotionality, activity level, sociability.
    d. emotionality, anxiety, suspiciousness.

16. In Pavlov's classical conditioning research, he conditioned a dog to salivate to the sound of a bell. The bell was the
    a. conditioned response.
    b. conditioned stimulus.
    c. unconditioned response.
    d. unconditioned stimulus.

17. The law of effect was suggested by
    a. Bandura.
    b. Pavlov.
    c. Thorndike.
    d. Watson.

18. Escape training is
    a. negative reinforcement.
    b. negative punishment.
    c. positive punishment.
    d. positive reinforcement.

19. The tendency to assume that our culture's beliefs, perceptions, and values are true, correct, and factual, and those of others are not is called
    a. cultural diversity.
    b. ethnocentrism.
    c. multiculturalism.
    d. socialization.

20. Which of the following is a history-graded influence?
    a. high school graduation
    b. the Vietnam War
    c. marriage
    d. a hurricane

Pretest Score _____

PROGRAMMED REVIEW

To see how much you remember of this chapter, try to fill in each of the blanks in the following chapter review without looking up the answers. Check your answers with the Answer Key at the end of the chapter, and reread any sections in the chapter with which you had problems.

1. In June, 2000, it was announced that the correct alphabetical order of the 3.12 billion letters of the human _____ had been mapped.

Molecular Genetics

2. The human body is comprised of over 200 different kinds of _____, which are the smallest self-contained structures. The outside layer is the cell _____, and within the cell is the _____ comprised of specialized structures held together by a _____. _____ process nutrients and provide the cell's _____. The _____ reticulum, the _____ apparatus, and the _____ are components that produce the many kinds of proteins. The inner part of the cell is the nucleus which is most of the _____ (DNA).

3. The structure of DNA was discovered by James _____ and Francis _____.

4. The building blocks of DNA are called _____ which consist of a _____ molecule and a _____ molecule, and one of four nitrogen-carbon-hydrogen _____. Which two bases bond to form base _____ cannot vary. Adenine can only pair with _____, and cytosine can only pair with _____. Three things can vary: which _____ of the ladder each base comes from, the _____ in which the base pairs occur along the ladder, and the overall _____ of base pairs.

5. Genome research has found that a much more useful term than race in describing and understanding peoples is _____, a concept that incorporates social, religious, linguistic, dietary, and other variables to identify individual persons and populations.

6. The DNA of each normal human being is about _____ the same as every other normal human being. At the molecular level, a large portion of the .1% individual difference takes the form of single nucleotide _____.

7. A _____ is a delineated segment of DNA that may be several hundred to several million base pairs long. The most significant thing genes do is _____ synthesis. _____ are the most common kind of protein, serving as catalysts in biochemical reactions. The _____ in red blood cells is a protein that binds with oxygen. Muscles are made up of special _____ protein; bones and connective tissues include _____, and another class of proteins is _____ that regulate physical growth and development.

8. Protein synthesis begins when a nuclear enzyme attaches to the appropriate segment of DNA and causes the nucleotide bonds to _____. One side then serves as a template and begins attracting free nucleotides in a process called _____ that will result in _____. The pre-mRNA strand separates and the DNA strands _____. The pre-mRNA then undergoes further processing in the nucleus of the cell turning it into _____ mRNA. Each triplet of nucleotides is called a _____, each of which will be translated into specific _____ through a process initiated by _____. A _____ starts at one end of the mRNA-tRNA strand and moves along it. Adjacent amino acids are bonded into a string called a _____ chain.

Genes, Chromosomes, and Cell Division

9. When a cell prepares to divide, the DNA assembles into _____. Abnormalities at the chromosomal level can be detected by studying an individual's _____. In normal humans, most cells contain exactly _____ chromosomes arranged in _____ pairs. Twenty-two of the pairs are called _____. The 23rd pair are the _____ chromosomes. There are two _____ chromosomes in a normal female and an _____ pattern in a normal male.

10. In the process termed _____, each cell divides and duplicates itself. The process of cell division that creates reproductive cells is called _____, which creates _____ with only 23 chromosomes. In males, meiosis takes place in the _____ and involves two rounds of division, resulting in four fertile _____ cells. Meiosis in females begins in the _____ before birth and only partly completes all of the roughly 400,000 _____ a woman will ever have. The final stage occurs at _____.

11. _____ is the primary reason why children are not exactly like their parents. When the parents' chromosomes separate at the beginning of meiotic division, genetic material randomly _____ over and is exchanged between chromosomes. There is also a possibility of _____. Which chromosomes go into which sperm or ovum is determined by _____, a process called independent _____, and which sperm and ovum unite is also determined by _____.

12. At the molecular level, a mutation is an alternation in the _____ that typically occurs during mitosis or meiosis. In most cases mutation is _____, but a small number of mutations are _____ and the cell survives. In _____ cell division, if a viable mutation occurs early in development, it will be passed on to all cells replicated in subsequent divisions. Mutations primarily occur at the molecular level, usually during _____. Base _____ are the most common type; others include _____ (the loss of nucleotides) and _____ (the addition of nucleotides). Mutations can also occur at the _____ level.

13. Alternate versions of a gene that perform the same function are called _____. All the pairs of alleles constitute a person's _____. When an allele is _____, its presence in a gene pair will cause that specific trait to be expressed as the _____.

14. If the two alleles for a simple dominant-recessive trait are the same, the individual is said to be _____ for that trait. If the alleles differ, the individual is _____.

15. The sickle cell trait is an example of _____ dominance in that people with a single recessive gene for the trait have a marked percentage of abnormal, sickle-shaped red blood cells that interfere with _____ transport, but have normal blood cells as well. In _____, neither allele is dominant resulting in a phenotype that is an equal blend of the two. The overall system of interactions among genes and gene pairs is called _____ inheritance. The 23rd chromosome pair determines _____ inheritance. Because the _____ chromosome contains many more genes than the _____ chromosome, _____ are much more likely than females to display recessive traits.

Genetic and Chromosomal Disorders

16. In the United States, about _____ percent of births produce babies with congenital anomalies that typically involve problems with specific _____ pathways. Sex-linked disorders can occur either at the _____ or the _____ level.

17. Hemophilia is an example of a _____ disorder that is more likely to occur in _____. It has also been associated with _____.

18. Extra or missing sex chromosomes occur in a variety of ways such as chromosomal _____ that can occur in males and females. An example is _____ syndrome that is now the most common hereditary disorder associated with mental _____. Because it involves a recessive gene on the X chromosome, _____ tend to be more severely affected.

19. _____ syndrome is the most common autosomal anomaly and the most frequent type is _____, in which an extra chromosome is attached to the 21st pair.

20. Gene _____ refers to a phenomenon in which gene expression and phenotype depend upon which parent the gene or genes came from. For example, if the _____ genes are expressed the result is Prader Willi syndrome and if the _____ genes are expressed, the result is _____ syndrome. This can happen if one parent's genes are _____, leaving the others to determine the phenotype. Another way is uniparental _____ in which both of the chromosomes containing the defective genes come from only one parent.

21. Genetic _____ includes analysis of parental medical records and family histories to construct a genetic pedigree, maternal and perhaps paternal _____ screening, and _____ screening of the developing child.

Advances in Genetic Research and Treatment

22. Within the emergent discipline called _____, the mesh of biology and computer science, the basis for most advances in genetic research and treatment is _____ DNA technology in which DNA is extracted from cell nuclei and initially cleaved into segments by selected _____. The resulting fragments are then joined to one of an assortment of self-_____ elements and combined with the DNA to form functional gene _____ capable of producing proteins.

23. In the _____ approach to gene therapy, missing genes are cloned and inserted into a bacterial growth medium and their _____ are harvested and introduced into the patient's system. In _____ gene therapy, treatment begins with the removal of defective cells from a patient and these cells are then infused with _____ of normal genes, cultured, and reinstated in the patient. _____ gene therapy takes advantage of benign _____ to penetrate cells and deliver the normal gene.

24. It is now well established that we can clone animals from the DNA of a _____ cell. Numerous _____ clonings have been accomplished and conservationists are now attempting to clone _____ species as a way of keeping them from becoming extinct. It is also possible that human _____ for replacement could eventually be cloned without producing an entire human.

Behavior Genetics

25. Behavior _____ is an approach that assesses patterns of inheritance at the behavioral level and incorporates the accepted view that complex traits are determined by _____ and _____. The field also takes the view that what is inherited are genetic _____. The primary tool of behavior genetics is correlation, which translates into _____, the extent to which biologically related people show similar characteristics. Concordance rates give rise to estimates of _____.

26. Numerous adoption studies have found at least a _____ degree of heritability for a large variety of psychological traits and characteristics. In _____ genotype/environment interaction, besides providing their children with _____, parents also provide their children with living _____ consistent with the parents' own genes.

27. Repeatedly, studies of twins show a _____ concordance in intellectual abilities, and that identical twins show _____ concordance than nonidentical twins. Twin studies have also found that a wide range of specific _____ traits are at least partially heritable. Three such characteristics are called the EAS traits which include _____, the tendency to become aroused easily to fear or anger, _____, the extent to which individuals prefer to do things with others rather than alone, and _____level. The estimate is a genetic contribution to personality of about _____ percent. Twin studies are unable to tell us how genes _____ with the environment.

Environmental Influences and Contexts

28. The developing child's environment consists of multiple settings that _____ and change over time.

Processes Within the Microsystem

29. Habituation means _____ to attend or respond to irrelevant stimuli. It enables us to stay _____, and to attend to things that are important.

30. Classical conditioning starts with an _____ stimulus that elicits an _____ response and is repeatedly paired with a _____ stimulus that becomes a _____ stimulus that produces a _____ response. Classical conditioning works best if the CS slightly _____ the UCS. The learning theory explanation of phobias is that they are acquired by _____ conditioning.

31. Skinner used different terminology in applying the law of _____. The first part of the law in which behavior is performed in order to achieve pleasant or satisfying consequences is called _____ and the second part in which behavior is not performed because the consequence is unpleasant or unsatisfying is called _____. In _____reinforcement or reward training, the subject receives rewards and the behavior predictably _____. In _____ reinforcement or escape training or active avoidance training, something unpleasant is taken away and again the behavior _____. In positive punishment, sometimes called _____ avoidance, behavior results in something aversive being presented. Negative punishment is also called _____ training. Shaping is accomplished by means of _____ approximations. In _____ reinforcement, only some instances of a behavior are reinforced, and the most powerful version is a _____ schedule. Programs that shape human behavior for therapeutic goals are called behavior _____. We always need to consider the active _____ part of human nature in the learning of behaviors.

32. Albert Bandura pointed out that in daily life people notice the _____ of their own actions. Observational _____ and conscious _____ of what we see in our social environment play a major role in learning and development. Self-_____ refers to what we are actually capable of doing in a given situation. Self-_____ is one's aggregate of beliefs and feelings about oneself.

33. In expressing self-concept, children demonstrate their capabilities, preferences and _____. During middle childhood, self-knowledge expands to include a range of _____ labels. In adolescence, self-knowledge becomes more _____ and adolescents develop a sense of ego _____, a coherent, unified idea of self as in Erikson's definition.

Processes that Transcend the Microsystem

34. The developmental _____ includes everyday physical and social settings, child-care and child-rearing customs, and the overall _____ of the caregivers.

35. The family systems approach deals with the network of _____ and expectations within the family. Members of the same family do not necessarily experience the same _____. The more _____ the social fabric, the more pressure the family system experiences, and it also becomes more difficult to transmit values when they are _____ and in _____. The tendency to assume that one's own culture's beliefs, perceptions, and values are true, correct, and factual, and that those of other people are not is called _____. Parental influences are just one element in the larger process of _____, the lifelong process by which individuals learn to become members of a social group.

36. Baltes proposed that three basic factors interact. Normative _____ influences are the biological and social changes that happen at predictable ages. Normative _____ influences affect large numbers of people at the same time. _____ influences are not predictable. Factors like race, sex, social class _____ both the type and the effects of these influences. The impact of these influences also differs according to _____.

POSTTEST

Answer the following questions without looking them up in the book. Check your answers with the Answer Key at the end of this chapter, record the number correct, and subtract your pretest score. You should see an improvement in your score.

1. What is the most common type of protein?
   a. hormones
   b. collagen
   c. hemoglobin
   d. enzymes

2. An alteration of DNA that typically occurs during mitosis or meiosis is
   a. crossing over.
   b. mutation.
   c. independent assortment.
   d. meiosis.

3. Chromosome pairs 1 through 22 are called
   a. autosomes.
   b. karyotypes.
   c. mutations.
   d. sex chromosomes.

4. Females have a 23rd chromosome pattern of _____ and males of _____.
    a. XX; YY
    b. XX; XY
    c. YY; XY
    d. YY; XX

5. Reproductive cells are formed by
    a. meiosis.
    b. mitosis.
    c. mutation.
    d. reproduction.

6. Mutation occurs by all of the following EXCEPT
    a. base substitutions.
    b. additions.
    c. crossing over.
    d. deletions.

7. Which of the following has an XXY chromosome pattern?
    a. Down syndrome
    b. Turner syndrome
    c. Supermale syndrome
    d. Klinefelter syndrome

8. All of the following are true about fragile X syndrome EXCEPT
    a. it is often more severe in females than in males.
    b. a small portion of the tip of the X chromosome seems to be susceptible to breakage.
    c. it is associated with mental retardation.
    d. 20% of males who carry the fragile X chromosome do not experience the syndrome.

9. Which of the following disorders is associated with AIDS?
    a. cystic fibrosis
    b. hemophilia
    c. PKU
    d. Tay Sachs disease

10. Mental retardation is likely to occur in all of the following disorders EXCEPT
    a. Down syndrome.
    b. fragile X syndrome.
    c. hemophilia.
    d. Klinefelter syndrome.

11. A mandatory screening for _____ is given to all newborns in the United States.
    a. PKU
    b. Huntington's chorea
    c. hemophilia
    d. cystic fibrosis

12. Candidates for genetic counseling include
    a. all women under 21 years of age.
    b. couples who do not know their grandparents.
    c. women who work in factories.
    d. a couple in which the man is over age 55.

13. Ceasing to attend or respond to irrelevant stimuli is
    a. passive avoidance.
    b. active avoidance.
    c. extinction.
    d. habituation.

14. Clinical trials of gene therapy are being used for people suffering from
    a. Down syndrome.
    b. hemophilia.
    c. PKU.
    d. Tay Sachs.

15. Research on behavioral genetics has provided an estimate of the genetic contribution to personality of
    a. 20 percent.
    b. 40 percent.
    c. 60 percent.
    d. 80 percent.

16. In Pavlov's classical conditioning research, he conditioned a dog to salivate to the sound of a bell. Salivation to the meat was the
    a. conditioned response.
    b. conditioned stimulus.
    c. unconditioned response.
    d. unconditioned stimulus.

17. Successive approximations of a behavior are rewarded in
    a. shaping.
    b. generalization.
    c. discrimination.
    d. classical conditioning.

18. What an individual believes about himself is
    a. identity.
    b. self-efficacy.
    c. self-concept.
    d. ethnocentrism.

19. Which of the following is a nonnormative influence?
    a. puberty
    b. unemployment
    c. marriage
    d. retirement

20. The Baby Boomers were born in what period?
    a. Pre-World War I
    b. Depression
    c. Post-World War II
    d. Post-Vietnam

Posttest Score _____

Pretest Score _____

Improvement _____

ESSAY QUESTIONS

The following essay questions will test your grasp of the concepts included in this chapter. Try to write detailed and well-structured answers to each of the questions referring to the text for material to support your answers.

1. Summarize the process of protein synthesis in human cells.

2. Describe classical and operant conditioning and give practical examples of each.

3. Describe the difference between autosomes and sex chromosomes.

4. Explain mitosis and meiosis and how they are related.

5. Describe the transmission of sex-linked disorders. Cite some examples.

6. Explain the difference between dominant and recessive genetic disorders and give some examples of each.

7. What is meant by incomplete dominance, codominance, and polygenic inheritance?

8. Describe the process of genetic counseling and discuss the possible advantages and disadvantages of its use.

9. Describe the latest developments in gene therapy and how they are being used. Do you see any problems in the future with this new technology? Explain your answer.

10. Discuss the problem of ethics that has arisen with the new techniques of gene therapy such as cloning.

ANSWER KEY

Key Names

1. f	3. e	5. c	7. g	9. i
2. h	4. i	6. a	8. d	10. b

Classification of disorders

1. g	4. a	7. b	10. e	13. d
2. b	5. b	8. e	11. f	14. f
3. f	6. d	9. c	12. g	

Pretest

1. d	6. b	11. b	16. b
2. d	7. b	12. b	17. c
3. a	8. d	13. b	18. a
4. a	9. c	14. a	19. b
5. b	10. d	15. c	20. b

Programmed Review

1. genome
2. cells, membrane, cytoplasm, cytoskeleton, mitochondria, energy, endoplasmic, Golgi, ribosomes, DNA
3. Watson, Crick
4. nucleotides, phosphate, sugar, bases, pairs, thymine, guanine, side, order, number
5. ethnicity
6. 99.9%, polymorphisms
7. gene, protein, enzymes, hemoglobin, contractile, collagen, hormones
8. separate, transcription, messenger RNA, reunite, mature, codon, amino acids, transfer RNA, ribosomes, polypeptide
9. chromosomes, karyotype, 46, 23, autosomes, sex, XX, XY
10. mitosis, meiosis, gametes, testes, sperm, ovaries, ova, puberty
11. meiosis, crosses, mutations, chance, assortment, chance
12. DNA, maladaptive, viable, mitotic, replication, substitutions, deletions, insertions, chromosomal
13. alleles, genotype, dominant, phenotype
14. homozygous, heterozygous
15. incomplete, oxygen, codominance, polygenic, sex-linked, X, Y, males
16. 3%, metabolic, genetic, chromosomal
17. sex-linked, males, AIDS
18. breakage, Fragile X, retardation, males
19. Down, trisomy 21

20. imprinting, mother's, father's, Angelman's, defective, disomy
21. counseling, blood, prenatal
22. bioinformatics, recombinant, enzymes, replicating, clones
23. indirect, proteins, ex vivo, clones, in vivo, retroviruses
24. single, mammal, endangered, organs
25. genetics, heredity, environment, predispositions, correlation, concordance, heritability
26. moderate, passive, genes, environments
27. high, higher, personality, emotionality, sociability, activity, 40%, interact
28. interact
29. ceasing, focused
30. unconditioned, unconditioned, novel, conditioned, conditioned, precedes, classical
31. effect, reinforcement, punishment, positive, increases, negative, increases, passive, omission, successive, partial, variable-ratio, modification, thinking
32. consequences, learning, imitation, efficacy, concept
33. possessions, trait, abstract, identity
34. niche, psychology
35. interrelationship, environment, diverse, unfocused, transition, ethnocentrism, socialization
36. age-graded, history-graded, Nonnormative, mediate, age

Posttest

1. d	6. c	11. a	16. c
2. a	7. d	12. d	17. a
3. a	8. a	13. d	18. c
4. b	9. b	14. b	19. b
5. a	10. c	15. b	20. c

4

Prenatal Development and Childbirth

CHAPTER OUTLINE

Prenatal Growth and Development
　Periods and Trimesters
　Conception and the Germinal Period
　The Embryonic Period
　The Fetal Period
　Developmental Trends

Prenatal Environmental Influences
　Maternal Age
　Maternal Health and Nutrition
　Prenatal Health Care
　Critical Periods in Prenatal Development
　Teratogens and Their Effects

Childbirth
　Stages of Childbirth
　Approaches to Childbirth
　Prenatal Screening and Perinatology
　Complications in Childbirth

Premature and High-Risk Infants
　Prematurity
　High-Risk Infants

The Evolving Family
　First Impressions
　The Beginnings of Attachment
　The Transition to Parenthood

KEY TERMS AND CONCEPTS

Read the entire chapter in your text and then write out the definitions of each of the following terms and check your answers with the definitions in the text.

Afterbirth
Age of viability
Amniocentesis
Amniotic fluid
Amniotic sac
Anoxia
Apgar scoring system
Attachment
Beta-endorphins
Birthing centers
Blastula
Breech presentation
Cephalocaudal trend
Cesarean section
Chorionic villus sampling (CVS)
Colostrum
Differentiation
Dizygotic (fraternal) twins
Ectoderm
Embryo
Embryonic period
Endoderm
Episiotomy
Fallopian tubes
False labor
Fetal alcohol effects (FAE)
Fetal alcohol syndrome (FAS)
Fetal period
Fetal monitor
Fetus
Fontanelles
Germinal period

Gross-to-specific trend
Human chorionic gonadotrophin
Initial labor
Lanugo
Mesoderm
Microcephaly
Midwife
Molding
Monozygotic (identical) twins
Natural or prepared childbirth
Neonate
Neural tube
Oxytocin
Ovulation
Perinatology
Perineum
Placenta
Posterior presentation
Preterm status
Prolactin
Proximodistal trend
Showing
Small-for-date
Sonogram
Spontaneous abortions
Teratogen
Traditional childbirth
Ultrasound
Umbilical cord
Uterus
Vacuum extraction
Vernix caseosa
Zygote

KEY NAMES

There are only two new names in this chapter to add to your list of key names. It is a good idea to take this opportunity to review terms from previous chapters. Try to match the names with their contributions to psychology and then check your answers with the Answer Key at the end of this chapter.

_____1. Virginia Apgar   a. newborn screening tests

_____2. Fernand Lamaze   b. prepared childbirth

PRETEST

Try to answer the following questions and then check your answers with the Answer Key at the end of this chapter and record the number of correct answers in the space at the end of this section.

1. Release of an ovum from an ovary is called
   a. gestation.
   b. ovulation.
   c. implantation.
   d. fertilization.

2. Fertilization of an ovum by a sperm takes place in the
   a. Fallopian tubes.
   b. ovaries.
   c. uterus.
   d. vagina.

3. The first two weeks of pregnancy are called the _____ period.
   a. conception
   b. embryonic
   c. fetal
   d. germinal

4. Fraternal twins are created by
   a. a single egg and sperm.
   b. one egg fertilized by two sperm.
   c. two eggs both fertilized by the same sperm.
   d. two eggs and two sperm.

5. What percent of blastulas never successfully implant?
   a. less than 10%
   b. 20%
   c. 30%
   d. over 50%

6. The embryo or fetus receives nourishment by means of an organ called the
   a. amniotic sac.
   b. embryonic disc.
   c. placenta.
   d. umbilical cord.

7. The embryo's muscles and blood develop from a layer called the
   a. ectoderm.
   b. embryonic disc.
   c. endoderm.
   d. mesoderm.

8. The fetus is considered to be viable after _____ weeks.
   a. 6
   b. 12
   c. 18
   d. 24

9. Head to foot growth is the _____ developmental trend.
   a. cephalocaudal
   b. gross-to-specific
   c. prenatal
   d. proximodistal

10. Which of the following is least likely to cross the placental barrier?
    a. viruses
    b. alcohol
    c. nicotine
    d. bacteria

11. How much alcohol can a pregnant woman consume without harming the embryo or fetus?
    a. seven or more drinks a week
    b. five drinks per occasion
    c. two ounces daily
    d. none

12. The third largest cause of mental retardation in the United States is
    a. brain damage.
    b. Down syndrome.
    c. FAS.
    d. fragile X syndrome.

13. Which of the following taken in large doses while pregnant can cause excessive bleeding?
    a. aspirin
    b. tobacco
    c. amphetamines
    d. marijuana

14. The only dangerous Rh factor combination is
    a. positive mother/positive baby.
    b. positive mother/negative baby.
    c. negative mother/ positive baby.
    d. negative mother/negative baby.

15. The branch of medicine that focuses on the period from conception to the first few months of life is
    a. gynecology.
    b. obstetrics.
    c. pediatrics.
    d. perinatology.

16. An incision to enlarge the vaginal opening is a(n)
    a. neonate.
    b. fontanelle.
    c. episiotomy.
    d. perinatology.

17. The newborn has high levels of all of these EXCEPT
    a. adrenalin.
    b. beta-endorphins.
    c. noradrenalin.
    d. oxytocin.

18. The lowest score on the Apgar Test at which a newborn is considered normal is
    a. 3.
    b. 5.
    c. 7.
    d. 9.

19. What prenatal screening technique produces a sonogram?
    a. ultrasound
    b. fetoscopy
    c. amniocentesis
    d. CVS

20. The average newborn is _____ long.
    a. 10-15 inches
    b. 19-22 inches
    c. one foot
    d. two feet

Pretest Score _____

PROGRAMMED REVIEW

In order to test your knowledge of this chapter, fill in the blanks in the following programmed review without looking up the answers in the text. Check your answers with the Answer Key at the end of this chapter, and then go back to your text and review the areas that gave you difficulties.

1. In the United States, about _____ percent of all pregnancies are unintended. Childbirth is a _____ programmed sequence of events, but the reality of a specific child's birth is strongly defined by the _____, _____ and _____ contexts of that birth.

Prenatal Growth and Development

2. It is estimated that _____ percent of all fertilized eggs are lost within the first two weeks. Of the survivors, another _____ percent may be lost through miscarriage later in the pregnancy.

3. About the tenth day after the beginning of a regular menstrual period, an _____ is stimulated by hormones and enters a the final stage of meiosis. By the end of the 13th or 14th day of growth, the _____ surrounding the ovum breaks, and the ovum is released to begin its journey down one of two _____. This release of the mature ovum is called _____.

4. The mature ovum survives for _____, and the male's sperm survive for as long as _____. If the ovum is not fertilized , it continues to the uterus where it _____.

5. After the ovum is united with the sperm, it is called a _____ and enters the _____ period, a time of very rapid cell division and _____ that lasts for about two weeks.

6. In some cases, the first division of the zygote produces two identical cells, which then separate and develop into two individuals called _____ or _____ twins. These twins are always the same _____ and they share the same physical _____. In other cases, two ova are released and each unites with a sperm to produce _____ or _____ twins. These twins may be of the same or opposite _____ because the ova are fertilized by two separate sperm.

7. By the end of the first week, the dividing cells have formed a _____, a ball of cells with a fluid filled center, that moves into the _____. The cells begin a process of _____, separating into groups according to their future function. Some of the cells move to one side of the hollow sphere and form the _____ from which the child will develop. The other group begins to develop into the _____ structures. Human _____ gonadotrophin is secreted to shut down _____ and prevent the next _____ period. The blastula begins to burrow into the lining of the _____ and within a few days, it becomes embedded in the uterine wall in a process called _____. Over _____ percent of blastulas never successfully implant.

8. Generally, the _____ period is considered to extend to two months after conception. From the _____ layer of cells, all tissues and structures that will house, nurture, and protect the developing child for the remainder of the nine months are formed. From the _____ disc, development begins of the _____ itself.

9. The embryo develops within an _____ filled with fluid; it is nourished through the _____, which is a disk-shaped mass of tissue growing from the wall of the _____, that serves as a partial filter. The _____, containing two _____ and one _____, connects the mother to the child. The placenta provides for an _____ of materials between mother and embryo. It is important to note that the mother and child do not actually share the same _____ system.

10. Immediately after implantation, the embryo develops into _____ distinct layers. They are the _____ or outer layer, which becomes skin and the nervous system; the _____, or middle layer, which becomes muscles, blood, and the excretory system; and the _____, or inner layer, which becomes the digestive system, lungs, and glands. Simultaneously, the _____ tube starts to develop. _____, or spontaneous abortions, occur during the embryonic period, usually caused by inadequate development of the _____, the _____ cord, or the _____ itself.

11. The fetal period lasts for about _____ months and it is during this period that the organs and systems _____ and become _____.

12. At the end of the second trimester, the fetus reaches the age of _____ and as many as _____ percent of fetuses born at this time survive. Yet over half of these have serious _____. The third trimester is a time of extensive _____ maturation, and system _____.

13. In the eighth month, brain scans show periods that look like _____ sleep and as the fetus moves into the ninth month, it develops daily cycles of _____ and _____. During the ninth month, the fetus begins to shift to a _____ position in preparation for the trip through the birth canal. The _____, a cheese-like protective coating, starts to fall away, and the special fine body hair called _____ dissolves. _____ to protect against disease pass from the mother to the fetus. Approximately one to two weeks before birth, the baby _____ as the uterus settles lower into the _____ area.

14. Usually development proceeds from the top of the body downward, which is called the _____ trend, and from the middle of the body outward in the _____ trend. At birth and later, the movements become more localized and specific due to the _____ trend.

Prenatal Environmental Influences

15. In the United States, every year about _____ percent of babies are born with congenital anomalies. The majority of birth defects are caused by _____ influences during the prenatal period or during _____.

16. The age of the mother _____ with the prenatal development of the child. Teenage mothers and mothers over 35-40 are at greater risk for having _____, stillbirths, or children with congenital anomalies. The incidence of Down Syndrome increases steadily with maternal _____.

17. Fetal malnutrition may be caused by a mother's unbalanced _____, a _____ or protein deficiency, or deficiencies in the overall _____ of the mother. The most notable symptoms are low _____, smaller _____ size, and smaller _____ overall. Malnourished pregnant women also often have _____, give birth _____, or lose their babies shortly after _____. Malnutrition can cause reduced _____ development. Many brain and spinal abnormalities could be prevented if the mother consumed sufficient _____ before and during the early weeks of pregnancy.

18. One of the best predictors of a full term healthy baby is _____ or more visits to a doctor or health care facility beginning in the first _____ of pregnancy.

19. During critical periods of prenatal development, the child is at greatest risk for different kinds of defects as a result of _____. The timing and nature of these periods can be seen in the range of effects of the drug _____, a mild tranquilizer given to relieve nausea. If the mother took the drug between the 34th and 38th days after her last menstrual period, the child had no _____, between the 38th and 47th days, the child had missing or stunted _____, and in the latter part of that time range, the child had missing or stunted _____. Often a drug or chemical agent must reach a certain concentration or _____ level in an organ or tissue layer in order to have any impact.

20. Most kinds of bacteria do not cross the _____ barrier but many _____ do. Rubella may cause blindness, _____ abnormalities, deafness, _____ damage, or _____ deformity. Diseases may produce infections that gain entry to the fetus through the _____ (HIV and rubella) and through the _____ fluid (syphilis and gonorrhea), or during _____ and _____.

21. Prescription drugs such as tetracycline cause _____ anomalies. Some anticonvulsive medications given to epileptic mothers can cause _____ malformations, _____ delays, _____ abnormalities, or even mild mental _____ or _____ irregularities. Use of DES causes _____ cancer or _____ abnormalities in daughters and _____ cancer in sons.

22. More than one-third of infants born to heavy drinkers show _____ abnormalities. A recent study showed that as little as two ounces of alcohol daily taken early in pregnancy would produce _____ deformities. These abnormalities have been identified as _____ syndrome. FAS children have distinct facial characteristics, such as a thin upper _____ with a poorly developed _____ above, a wide space between the margins of the _____, and flat _____. FAS is the _____ leading cause of mental retardation in the U. S. Milder abnormalities occur with fetal alcohol _____. The more alcohol consumed during pregnancy, the _____ the risk of damage to the child.

23. Among mothers who smoke heavily, there is an increased risk of spontaneous _____, _____, and _____. Babies born to heavy smokers tend to weigh _____ at birth and have delayed _____. It appears that high doses of marijuana during pregnancy affect the _____ system.

24. Mothers using cocaine experience more _____ complications. Their infants have a high risk of _____, _____ retardation, _____ retardation, and _____ dysfunction. Many exposed newborn infants have difficulty establishing _____ coordination, orienting to _____ objects or sounds, and achieving the normal regulation of _____ and _____. They have great difficulty controlling their _____ system. These infants _____ frantically and seem unable to _____. Years later, there is a much higher rate of _____ disorder, _____ delays, and _____ disabilities. The majority of expectant mothers who abuse drugs are _____ users.

Childbirth

25. The first stage, or initial _____, is the period during which the cervical opening of the uterus begins to _____ to allow passage of the baby. It typically takes _____ hours for the first child and _____ hours for later children. The muscular contractions of this stage are _____. Some mothers experience _____ labor called Braxton-Hicks contractions. During labor, a mucous plug that covers the cervix is released in a process called _____ and the _____ may break.

26. The second stage of childbirth begins with stronger, more regular _____ and ends with the actual _____ of the baby. The head _____, or becomes visible and emerges causing the mother's _____ to stretch considerably. In order to avoid tearing, doctors may make an incision called an _____. Obstetricians may use _____ or a _____ extractor should complications arise. The baby should be born in a _____ position. The expulsion of the _____ is the third stage of childbirth, sometimes called _____.

27. Today, _____ childbirth means hospital childbirth by a medical team. Lamaze developed the technique of natural or _____ childbirth. Labor is shorter and less stressful for both the mother and infant if the mother and coach have accurate _____, if only limited _____ is used, and if the mother is able to actively _____.

28. _____ centers seek to combine the privacy, serenity, and intimacy of a _____ birth with the safety and backup of _____ technology. The delivery is most often performed by a certified _____ and these centers encourage _____ childbirth, an early return _____, and infants with the mothers to promote early _____. Birthing centers are not equipped to handle such high risk women as those over _____ having their _____ baby, women having _____, suffering from _____ or _____ problems, and those who have previously had _____ deliveries.

29. The least invasive and most widely used method of providing information about the growth and health of the fetus is _____, which produces a picture called a _____ to detect _____ problems. In _____, fluid is withdrawn from the amniotic sac and discarded fetal _____ are analyzed. Chorionic _____ sampling can be conducted at around 8 to 12 weeks after conception and draws cells from the _____ surrounding the fetus.

30. A branch of medicine known as _____, considers childbirth as a span of time from conception through the first few months of life. The _____ is a specialist in the management of high-risk pregnancies and deliveries. She uses prenatal screening procedures such as _____ and the _____. Many hospitals use either internal or external fetal _____, but their use is discouraged because they lead to increased use of _____ sections. More difficult births occur when the baby is positioned in a _____ presentation (buttocks first) or a _____ presentation (facing the mother's abdomen) and may have to be delivered by Cesarean. The psychological reaction of mothers to Cesarean childbirth can be _____ with a higher rate of postpartum _____.

31. The _____ score is taken at one minute and five minutes after birth and includes observation of _____, _____, muscle _____, general _____ response, and general skin _____. A perfect score is _____ and a score of _____ or more is considered normal.

Premature and High-Risk Infants

32. An infant born before a gestation period of 35 weeks is _____. A full-term newborn who is low birth weight is considered _____. The most common cause of prematurity is _____ birth. _____ control is a common problem in premature infants. Prematurity is often a _____ of an abnormality rather than a _____. The consequences of limited early _____ due to prematurity can be seen throughout infancy. Some of the detrimental effects of prematurity may be offset by an enriched _____ during the first year of life.

33. High risk infants are those born with _____ disabilities. Parents of these infants frequently need to go through a period of _____ for the perfect child that did not arrive.

The Evolving Family

34. Newborns to about one month of age are called _____. At birth, the average full-term baby weighs between _____ and _____ pounds and is between _____ and _____ inches long. The baby's skin may be covered with _____, and _____ hair may be present and will drop off during the first month. The head may be misshapen by a process called _____ and external _____ of both boys and girls may be enlarged because of maternal hormones.

35. Childbirth is a _____ event for the newborn. In the last few moments of birth, the infant produces a major surge of _____ and _____. This counteracts any _____ deficiency and prepares the baby for breathing through the _____. The newborn has relatively high levels of the natural painkiller, _____, as well.

36. Immediately after birth, the lungs inflate and begin to work as the basic organ of the child's _____ system. The baby's heart no longer needs to pump blood to the _____ and the blood now circulates to the _____. The infant's _____ system takes a longer time to adapt, as does _____ regulation.

37. Attachment is an emotional _____ between parents and children. The baby's physical responses trigger _____ processes in the mother's body. The baby's licking or sucking at the breast causes increased secretion of _____, a hormone important in nursing, and _____, a hormone that contracts the uterus and reduces bleeding, and the mother produces a substance called _____ which appears to help the infant's digestion.

38. The pregnant woman may feel _____ or experience a fullness in her _____, suffer _____ and emotional _____ early in pregnancy, but in the middle stage she may experience a sense of heightened _____. In the last stages, there is some _____ discomfort. She must come to terms with a new body _____.

39. Some fathers report feelings of _____ and _____ with the coming child, an increased sense of _____, some feelings of _____ of their wives, or feelings of being a _____. Both parent's attitudes are shaped by their _____.

POSTTEST

Now try the following questions and check your answers with the Answer Key at the end of this chapter and record your score at the end of this section. You should see a significant improvement over your Pretest scores.

1. It is estimated that _____ percent of all fertilized eggs are lost within the first two weeks.
   a. 10-30
   b. 30-50
   c. 50-70
   d. 70-90

2. After the ovum is united with a sperm, it is called a(n)
   a. embryo.
   b. fetus.
   c. ova.
   d. zygote.

3. Identical twins are created by
   a. a single egg and sperm.
   b. one egg fertilized by two sperm.
   c. two eggs both fertilized by the same sperm.
   d. two eggs and two sperm.

4. The embryo develops within protective membranes in the fluid-filled
   a. amniotic sac.
   b. embryonic disc.
   c. placenta.
   d. umbilical cord.

5. The embryo's skin and nervous system develop from the
   a. ectoderm.
   b. embryonic disc.
   c. endoderm.
   d. mesoderm.

6. Research on prenatal hearing indicates that
   a. the fetus does not hear a thing.
   b. the fetus hears everything the mother hears.
   c. hearing is nonfunctional until birth.
   d. the fetus can hear sounds muffled by noise from the prenatal environment.

7. Near-to-far development is the _____ trend.
   a. cephalocaudal
   b. gross-to-specific
   c. prenatal
   d. proximodistal

8. Fetal respiration may be depressed by exposure to all of the following EXCEPT
   a. caffeine.
   b. heroin.
   c. methadone.
   d. morphine.

9. Research into the effects of maternal smoking on prenatal development has revealed that
   a. there is no relationship between amount of cigarettes smoked and newborn weight.
   b. children of mothers who smoke during pregnancy may do poorly in school.
   c. smoking during pregnancy may lead to a higher rate of newborn mortality.
   d. nicotine exposure leads to excessive weight gain prenatally.

10. The majority of expectant mothers who abuse drugs are
    a. heroin users.
    b. polydrug users.
    c. cocaine users.
    d. marijuana users.

11. Which stage of childbirth lasts the longest?
    a. afterbirth
    b. birth
    c. labor
    d. placental expulsion

12. What is the correct order of steps in childbirth?
    a. false labor, initial labor, afterbirth
    b. initial labor, delivery, afterbirth
    c. afterbirth, delivery, labor
    d. initial labor, delivery, episiotomy

13. The release of the mucous plug covering the cervix is
    a. afterbirth.
    b. crowning.
    c. molding.
    d. showing.

14. When a baby is born facing toward the mother's abdomen, the birth is
    a. a breech presentation.
    b. normal.
    c. a posterior presentation.
    d. a spontaneous abortion.

15. Most premature infants weigh less than
    a. 1 pound.
    b. 2-1/2 pounds.
    c. 3 pounds.
    d. 5-1/2 pounds.

16. During the first year of life the infant is called a
    a. neonate.
    b. fetus.
    c. zygote.
    d. embryo.

17. Birthing centers encourage all of the following EXCEPT
    a. prepared childbirth.
    b. the presence of an obstetrician at all births.
    c. early return home.
    d. rooms shared by mother and infant.

18. Which substance clears the infant's digestive system?
    a. colostrum
    b. estrogen
    c. nicotine
    d. adrenaline

19. Inspection for fetal limb and facial abnormalities is done with
    a. ultrasound.
    b. CVS.
    c. fetoscopy.
    d. amniocentesis.

20. The newborn's head appears to be misshapen because of
    a. episiotomies.
    b. CVS.
    c. crowning.
    d. molding.

Posttest Score _____

Pretest Score _____

Improvement _____

ESSAY QUESTIONS

The following essay questions will test your grasp of the concepts included in this chapter. Try to write detailed answers to each question and then check in the text to be sure you have included everything.

1. Describe the various ways mothers and fathers may react to the birth of a child.

2. Discuss the pros and cons of the use of fetal monitoring.

3. Briefly describe the three stages of prenatal development and indicate the most important aspects of each.

4. Briefly describe the three trimesters of pregnancy and contrast them with the three stages of prenatal development.

5. Explain how the critical period concept applies to prenatal development.

6. If you were an obstetrician, what would you advise a woman who has just become pregnant about her behavior during her pregnancy?

7. What is the difference between fetal alcohol syndrome and fetal alcohol effect?

8. Your friend is having her first baby and is worried about what will happen when she gives birth. What could you tell her about the birth process so that she knows what to expect?

9. Outline an idea for a media campaign to convince pregnant women that they should seek prenatal care throughout their pregnancies.

10. Describe the various methods of prenatal diagnosis and explain the strengths and weaknesss of each.

ANSWER KEY

Key Names

1. a	2. b

Pretest

1. b	5. d	9. a	13. a	17. b
2. a	6. c	10. d	14. c	18. c
3. d	7. d	11. d	15. d	19. a
4. d	8. d	12. c	16. c	20. b

Programmed Review

1. 50 percent, biologically, cultural, historical, family
2. 50-70, 25
3. ovum, follicle, fallopian tubes, ovulation
4. 3-5 days, 2-3 days, disintegrates
5. zygote, germinal, organization
6. identical, monozygotic, sex, traits, fraternal, dizygotic, sex
7. blastula, uterus, differentiation, embryonic disc, supportive, chorionic, ovulation, menstrual, uterus, implantation, 50
8. embryonic, outer, embryonic, embryo
9. amniotic sac, placenta, uterus, umbilical cord, arteries, vein, exchange, blood
10. three, ectoderm, mesoderm, endoderm, neural, Miscarriages, placenta, umbilical, embryo
11. seven, mature, functional
12. viability, 50, anomalies, brain, rehearsal
13. dream, activity, sleep, head-down, vernix caseosa, lanugo, Antibodies, drops, pelvic
14. cephalocaudal, proximodistal, gross-to-specific
15. 5-8, environmental, childbirth
16. interacts, miscarriages, age
17. diet, vitamin, metabolism, spontaneous abortions, prematurely, birth, brain, folic acid
18. five, trimester
19. teratogens, thalidomide, ears, arms, legs, threshold
20. placental, viruses, heart, brain, limb, placenta, amniotic, labor, delivery
21. congenital, structural, growth, heart, retardation, speech, vaginal, cervical, testicular
22. congenital, facial, fetal alcohol, lip, indentation, eyelids, cheekbones, third, Effect, greater
23. abortion, stillbirth, prematurity, less, growth, central nervous
24. labor, prematurity, growth, mental, neuromotor, motor, visual, waking, sleeping, nervous, cry, sleep, attention-deficit, language, learning, polydrug
25. labor, dilate, 12-15, 6-8, involuntary, false, showing, amniotic sac
26. contractions, birth, crowns, perineum, episiotomy, forceps, vacuum, face down, placenta, afterbirth
27. traditional, prepared, knowledge, medication, participate
28. Birthing, home, medical, nurse-midwife, prepared, home, attachment, 35, first, twins, diseases, cardiac, Cesarean
29. Ultrasound, sonogram, structural, amniocentesis, cells, villus, membranes
30. perinatology, perinatologist, amniocentesis, fetoscope, monitors, cesarean, breech, posterior, negative, depression
31. Apgar, pulse, breathing, tone, reflex, tone, 10, 7
32. preterm, small-for-date, multiple, Temperature, symptom, cause, contact, environment
33. physical, mourning
34. neonates, 5-1/2, 9-1/2, 19, 22, vernix caseosa, lanugo, molding, genitalia
35. stressful, adrenalin, noradrenalin, oxygen, lungs, beta-endorphin
36. respiratory, placenta, lungs, digestive, temperature
37. bond, physical, prolactin, oxytocin, colostrum
38. nauseated, breasts, fatigue, hypersensitivity, well-being, physical, image
39. rivalry, responsibility, envy, bystander, culture

Posttest

1. c	5. a	9. b	13. d	17. b
2. d	6. d	10. b	14. c	18. a
3. a	7. d	11. c	15. d	19. c
4. a	8. a	12. b	16. a	20. d

5

Infancy and Toddlerhood: Physical, Cognitive, and Language Development

CHAPTER OUTLINE

Neonates
    States of Arousal
    Reflexes
    Neonatal Assessment
    Learning and Habituation

Physical and Motor Development
    Maturation or a Dynamic System?
    An Overview of the First Two Years
    Infant Nutrition and Malnutrition

Sensory and Perceptual Development
    Studying Infant Perceptual Capabilities
    Vision and Visual Perception
    Audition and Auditory Perception
    Taste, Smell and Touch
    Sensory Integration and Intermodal Perception

Cognitive Development
    The Active Mind
    The Sensorimotor Period
    Closing Thoughts on Piaget's Sensorimotor Stage
    Perceptual Organization and Categories

Language Development
    Elements of Language
    The Beginnings of Language
    Words and Sentences
    Processes of Language Learning

After reading the chapter in your text, try to write out the definition of each of the terms/concepts in this section. Then check your definitions with those in the text and make any necessary corrections.

Adaptation	Marasmus
Affordances	Novelty paradigm
Apnea monitors	Object permanence
Circular reactions	Open words
Cognition	Overextensions
Cognitive development	Perception
Deferred imitation	Pincer grasp
Content	Pivot grammar
Contentives	Pivot words
Electroencephalograph	Preference method
Event-related potential method	Primitive reflexes
Expressive jargon	Productive language
Fine motor skills	Receptive language
Form	Sensation
Functors/function words	Sensorimotor period
Gross motor skills	Surprise paradigm
Habituation method	Survival reflexes
Holophrastic speech	Symbolic representation
Iteration	Telegraphic speech
Kwashiorkor	Use
Language acquisition device	Visually guided reach

KEY NAMES

Now try to match each of the following names with the person's contribution to the field of development and check your answers with the Answer Key at the end of this chapter. Note, one name has two contributions.

_____1. T. Brazelton   a. affordances

_____2. Roger Brown   b. language acquisition device

_____3. N. Chomsky   c. language learning styles

_____4. Arnold Gesell   d. maturational markers

_____5. Eleanor Gibson   e. Neonatal Behavioral Assessment Scale

_____6. Katherine Nelsen   f. newborn behavioral states

_____7. Jean Piaget   g. sensorimotor stage

_____8. P. H. Wolff   h. visual cliff

                                i. telegraphic speech

PRETEST

Try to answer the following questions without referring to the text and then check your answers with the Answer Key at the end of this chapter. Record your score at the end of this section so that you can compare it with your Posttest score. If you missed more than two or three questions, it might be a good idea to reread the parts of the text that gave you difficulty.

1. All of the following have been identified as infant states EXCEPT
   a. irregular sleep.
   b. nervous agitation.
   c. drowsiness.
   d. alert inactivity.

2. The infant's startle reaction is the _____ reflex.
   a. grasping
   b. Moro
   c. stepping
   d. tonic

3. Becoming accustomed to certain kinds of stimuli and no longer responding to them is called
   a. learning.
   b. accustomization.
   c. habituation.
   d. relaxation.

4. The Neonatal Behavioral Assessment scale measures all of the following EXCEPT
   a. autonomic stability.
   b. habituation.
   c. physical growth.
   d. reflexes.

5. At birth, the infant's head represents about _____ of total body length.
   a. one-half
   b. one-quarter
   c. one-eighth
   d. one-tenth

6. SIDS is sometimes called
   a. crib death.
   b. marasmus.
   c. kwashiorkor.
   d. sleep apnea.

7. SIDS occurs more often in the
   a. fall.
   b. spring.
   c. summer.
   d. winter.

8. Moving on hands and feet is called
   a. bearwalking.
   b. creeping.
   c. cruising.
   d. scooting.

9. In 1992, _____ percent of American infants suffered from iron deficiency anemia.
   a. 1-5
   b. 5-10
   c. 10-20
   d. 20-24

10. Which of the following diseases is the result of insufficient protein?
    a. hemophilia
    b. kwashiorkor
    c. marasmus
    d. SCID

11. Which of the following is least common in the United States?
    a. severe malnutrition
    b. protein deficiencies
    c. iron deficiencies
    d. empty calories

12. The research technique for studying infant perceptual abilities that is based on the infant's preference for new stimuli is the _____ paradigm.
    a. habituation
    b. novelty
    c. perceptual
    d. surprise

13. Infants demonstrate well-controlled, visually guided reach by the age of
    a. 1 month.
    b. 3 months.
    c. 4 months.
    d. 5 months.

14. Research on infant hearing has shown that
    a. hearing is probably muffled for the first few weeks.
    b. infants are soothed by a high pitched voice.
    c. infants are not usually startled.
    d. infants cannot distinguish speech from other sounds.

15. Infants focus best at a distance of
    a. 1-10 inches.
    b. 7-10 inches.
    c. 12-18 inches.
    d. 1-2 feet.

16. According to Gibson, the potential uses of objects are
    a. affordances.
    b. schemes.
    c. acquisition devices.
    d. phonemes.

17. In language, the meaning of any written or spoken message is its
    a. use.
    b. scheme.
    c. form.
    d. content.

18. A child's understanding of the spoken or written word is
    a. grammar.
    b. syntax.
    c. receptive language.
    d. productive language.

19. Use of single words to convey complete thoughts is
    a. holophrastic speech.
    b. pivot grammar.
    c. babbling.
    d. telegraphic speech.

20. Which of the following is a function word?
    a. verb
    b. adjective
    c. article
    d. noun

PROGRAMMED REVIEW

To test your knowledge of all the information in this chapter, fill in the blanks in the following programmed review without looking back in the text and check your answers with the Answer Key at the end of the chapter. Then go back to the text and go over any sections that you missed in the review.

Neonates

1. The first month is a period of _____ from the birth process and _____ of vital functions. It is also a time for developing a _____ between over- and under-stimulation. However, recent experiments have shown that we had grossly _____ newborn capabilities. They have definite _____, and a striking ability to _____, and deliberately attract _____ to their needs.

2. Peter Wolff identified _____ newborn behavioral states. These states are regular and seem to follow a predictable daily _____. Infants in a state of alert inactivity are easily _____ and react to a sound or sight with increased _____. Infants who are already in an active state tend to _____ down when stimulated. At first, newborns spend most of the day in either regular or irregular _____.

3. Infants enter the world with _____ reflexes necessary for adaptation and survival and _____ reflexes which may have been important in our evolutionary history. The _____ reflex is the newborn's startle reaction.

4. During the first few days of a baby's life, hospitals perform an extensive evaluation usually including a _____ examination and a _____ assessment. _____ Neonatal Behavioral Assessment Scale has been used increasingly by many hospitals. It measures seven clusters of behaviors: habituation, orientation, _____ tone and activity, _____ of state, _____ of state, _____ stability, and reflexes.

5. _____ is the ability to become accustomed to certain kinds of stimuli and no longer respond to them. The habituation _____ is used in infant research as is the high amplitude _____ procedure.

Physical and Motor Development

6. Arnold Gesell found that the capabilities of average children emerged in an _____ and _____ sequence. He concluded that development does not primarily depend on the _____, and that normally, most achievements result from an internal _____ timetable, as a function of _____. However, Gesell's findings must be taken cautiously because the children he studied all came from one _____ class and shared _____.

7. By four months, most infants have nearly _____ in weight. Their eyes now _____, they _____ contentedly, and _____ in response to pleasant stimulation. At birth, an infant's head represents _____ of the total body length, but by young adulthood, it will be only _____ the body's total length. The first tooth erupts at about _____ months. Many bones are still soft _____ and tend to be _____ under stress and rarely _____. Muscles, however, may _____ easily.

8. The most common cause of death among U. S. infants during the first year of life is _____, defined as the death of an apparently _____ infant in whom no _____ cause can be found. It is sometimes called _____ since it tends to happen while the child is _____. SIDS is more common in children of mothers who were _____ during pregnancy or did not receive _____ care. The American Academy of Pediatrics recommends putting babies to sleep on their _____ or propped on their _____ against pillows. SIDS seems to occur most often in _____. Vestibular stimulation by rocking has been shown to be beneficial for premature babies in reducing _____, which can be associated with SIDS.

9. By eight months, the baby's legs are oriented so that the _____ of their feet no longer face each other. At about five months, most infants achieve visually _____ reach and systematic _____ of objects begins. Use of hands is a _____ motor skill. Most eight-month-old babies are able to pass _____ from hand to hand and some are able to use the _____ and _____ to grasp.

10. Gross motor skills involve the larger _____ or the whole _____. Most eight-month-olds can get themselves into a _____ position and nearly all can sit without _____. Many can _____ while holding on to some support. Some may be _____ by using furniture for support. Babies may learn to _____ with the body on the floor, _____ on hands and knees, _____ on hands and feet, or _____ in a sitting position. Many eight-month-old babies begin to play _____ games such as peekaboo.

11. At 12 months, most infants are about _____ times heavier than they were at birth. Girls tend to weigh slightly _____ than boys. The ability to stand and walk gives the toddler a new _____ perspective and locomotion allows for more active _____. Twelve-month-olds actively _____ the environment and their newly developed _____ grasp, where the thumb opposes the forefinger, allows them to pick up many things. Many children now begin to feed themselves, using a _____ and holding their own _____ for drinking.

12. At 18 months, children may be stacking from two to four _____ to build a tower and they can often manage to _____ with crayon or pencil. Many of their actions _____ what they see others doing. Two-year-olds can usually pedal a _____, _____ in place on both feet, _____ briefly on one foot, and throw a _____.

13. In 1992, a national program serving low-income families reported 20% to 24% of poor infants suffered from _____. In 2000, UNICEF estimated that worldwide _____ of children under 5 suffer moderate to severe _____ as a result of malnutrition. Infant malnutrition also leads to delays in _____ and _____. Long-term deficits in _____ size, together with deficits in _____ and _____ processing also occur.

14. Starvation or severe lack of food results in a condition called _____, in which _____ wastes away and stored _____ is depleted. If the condition lasts for a relatively _____ period of time, there will be no long-term negative effects. An insufficiency of protein results in _____. In the United States, _____ and _____ deficiencies are quite common. Many people consume food high in _____ but low in _____, vitamins, and _____.

15. The breast milk of a well-fed mother contains a well-balanced combination of _____. Unless the mother is very _____, has an inadequate _____, or uses _____ or other _____, breast milk is better for a baby's health. The shift to commercial infant formula has resulted in widespread _____ in lower income nations because people lack the money to buy expensive _____ substitutes and many babies die when the commercial formula is diluted with contaminated _____, thereby transmitting _____ diseases to the infants. At about _____ of age, infants gradually start to accept some strained foods. _____ is a crucial time for the onset of malnutrition.

Sensory and Perceptual Development

16. The translation of external stimulation into neural impulses is _____, and the active process of interpreting information from the senses is _____.

17. Classical conditioning, operant conditioning, and habituation have been used to assess infant _____ and _____ capabilities. An infant cannot be conditioned to _____ to stimuli that the infant cannot perceive.

18. The _____ paradigm uses infants' preferences for new stimuli over familiar ones in order to investigate their ability to detect small _____ in sound, pattern, or color. In the _____ method, infants are given a choice between stimuli to look at or listen to in order to determine if they can perceive a _____. The _____ paradigm is a research technique used to test infants' memory and expectations on the assumption that if something happens that they don't _____, they respond with surprise. The event-related _____ method uses electrodes to obtain the equivalent of an _____.

19. Infants are born with a full, intact set of _____ structures. Newborns' eyes are sensitive to _____. They have some control over eye _____ and can visually _____ an object that moves within their field of vision. Newborns are able to focus optimally on objects within a range of _____ inches, with objects beyond this appearing _____. Newborns lack fine _____ of the eyes; that is, they are unable to focus both eyes on the same point. Newborns prefer to look at moderately _____ patterns, the _____ and _____ of objects, and especially _____. They are also exceptionally responsive to the human _____.

20. Three- to four-month olds _____ almost as well as do adults and by _____, color perception is nearly equal to that of adults. By two months infants look at the _____features of a face, by four months infants prefer a _____ arranged face over a _____ one. By five months infants look at the _____ of a person who is talking and by seven months respond to facial _____. Older infants are better able to control their eye _____ and spend more time _____ and _____their environment.

21. In _____ vision, the left-eye view and the right-eye view are slightly different. The brain _____ the two images, giving information about _____ and _____. It seems to take about _____ for binocular vision to emerge. A classic experiment to test infants' depth perception is the _____, which has shown that visual cues for depth perception are developed within the first _____ months.

22. Newborns are _____ by loud sounds and are soothed by _____ sounds. For the first few weeks, there is still excess _____ and _____ in the middle ear, and hearing is believed to be _____. The _____ structures for transmitting and interpreting hearing are not fully developed. Infants are able to _____ sound and they prefer _____ voices.

23. A newborn will react negatively to _____ odors and as early as six days can distinguish the _____ of its mother from that of another woman. The sense of _____ is well developed even in preterm newborns.

24. Infants appear to have a built-in tendency to seek _____ links, and behavior and emotions become _____ over time as a result of the interaction of _____ and _____.

Cognitive Development

25. _____ is a set of interrelated processes by which we gain knowledge of our world, and _____ development refers to the growth and refinement of this intellectual process.

26. Piaget saw infants as beings who possess mental structures, called _____, which process and organize information and develop into more complex structures in a series of _____, the first of which is the _____ period. Infant schemes are modified and developed by a process called _____. Infants' early circular reactions involve the discovery of their own _____. Later circular reactions involve how they use their bodies or themselves to change the _____.

27. By 5 months, infants reach out and _____, _____ repeated events, match their _____ appropriately with various objects, and develop their understanding of the _____ world through pretending and imitation. By 9 months, most infants _____ objects. By 12 months, they _____ objects closely before putting them in their mouths. By 15 to 18 months, they try to use objects _____. Play becomes still more _____ by 24 months.

28. Within the first 2 months, infants do some sporadic imitation in the context of play with _____. An infant may imitate _____ expressions; but these early imitations _____ at 2 to 3 months, not to reappear for several months. By 6 or 7 months, infants imitate _____ and _____ fairly accurately, and by 9 months, they can imitate _____ gestures. Imitating something that happened hours or days before is called _____ imitation. Infants seem to be able to imitate novel actions _____ than Piaget predicted.

29. According to Piaget, _____ is a major accomplishment of the sensorimotor period. It involves the _____ that an object exists in time and space, whether or not it is in view. Infants do not fully develop this concept until they are about _____ old. At about 2 months of age, infants may watch a moving object _____ behind one side of a screen and then _____ their eyes to the other side to see if it reappears. Their visual _____ is excellent and well timed. Searching behavior proceeds through a predictable sequence of development beginning between _____. The _____ error, in which the infant searches for an object in its previous hiding place, has proved to be a _____ phenomenon.

30. Very young infants seem to have powerful _____ memory. A few studies indicate that infants have some long-term memory, at least for _____ events associated with an object that can enhance later recall.

31. _____ is the ability to visualize something not physically present. Between 6 and 12 months, children begin _____, by using actions to represent objects, events, or ideas. The first stage occurs by about _____ when most children pretend to eat, drink, or sleep. _____ is the ultimate system of symbolic representation.

32. For Piaget, the toddler is a _____ who tests and discovers the nature of physical objects and the social world. However, some theorists have criticized Piaget for paying too much attention to _____ development and too little attention to _____.

33. Eleanor Gibson believed that _____, the potential uses of objects depend on the individual's needs at the time as well as his or her past _____ and _____ awareness of the object.

34. Infants may be _____ wired to perceive some categories in the same way that older children and adults do. By 3 months, they can discriminate among the basic _____ and many shades and hues. They can discriminate between male and female _____ and _____ almost as well as adults can.

Language Development

35. By about _____ of age, most children say their first word; by _____, they put two or more words together; and by _____, they have mastered more than 100 words and have conversations. Language involves the use of _____ for communicating information, and has the three dimensions of _____ (the meaning of any written or spoken message), _____ (the particular symbol used to represent that content), and _____ (the social exchange between the speaker and the person spoken to). The details of the social exchange depend on the _____, the _____ between the speaker and the listener, and the _____ and _____ of the participants.

36. _____ language is the understanding of the spoken or written word, and _____ language refers to producing language through speaking or writing. They evolve _____. The production of language begins with undifferentiated _____ at birth. By about 6 weeks, infants begin making _____ sounds. By six months, infants purposely repeat and elongate sounds and pause in a precursor to speech called _____.

37. Early vocalizations involve only a few different _____. Sometime after 6 months, babbling takes on _____ and _____ like those of the parents' language. This highly developed babbling is _____. Such patterns of babbling appear to be the same for infants in all _____ groups and cultures. Although babbling is a means for babies to communicate and interact with other people, it is also a _____ activity. Recent research has found that babies are language _____, who can distinguish all the sounds of human language, while adults are language _____, who can only reproduce sounds in their native tongue.

38. Language perception is shaped by _____ at an earlier age than was originally thought. Although the babbling of groups of hearing babies and deaf babies is the _____ at first, only the babbling of the hearing infants move closer to the sounds of _____ and the babbling of deaf babies appears to _____ significantly after 6 months.

39. Very young children _____ words before they can _____ them. Throughout the first year, infants learn nonverbal aspects of communication in their _____ with caregivers.

40. Most children utter their first words around the end of the _____. There is wide individual variation in the _____ at which language learning progresses but the _____ of language follows a regular and predictable sequence.

41. Throughout the world, infants' first utterances most often are _____ and usually _____ of people and things in the immediate environment. Their early utterances are called _____ speech, one word utterances to convey more complex ideas. Children at this stage also use words that indicate _____ or _____. The individual words and category of words a child uses most may depend on the child's personal _____ style. Nelson identified children with a _____ style who tended to use nouns, and _____ children who learned more active verbs and pronouns. The _____ children had vocabularies that were dominated by naming words, whereas the _____ children had learned the naming words but also knew a higher percentage of words used in _____ interactions. Expressive children typically have _____ vocabularies and are more likely to use _____, which have no apparent meaning, to substitute for words they do not know.

42. Children tend to overextend, underextend, or overlap the _____ they use to determine what words refer to because they often do not share adults' knowledge of _____ functions and characteristics of objects.

43. Children's words and their meanings are closely linked to the _____ the children are forming. Piaget argued that the _____ is formed first and then the child finds a _____ to attach to it. _____ sometimes create their own private language, and _____ children create signs or gestures even when they are not taught sign language. Others researchers believe that _____ help shape _____. Both processes probably _____ each other as the child learns language.

44. Toward the middle of the second year, implicit rules of _____ appear. Children retain high-information words and omit the less significant ones in what Brown called _____ speech. The informative words, or _____, are nouns, verbs, and adjectives. The less important words, or _____, are articles, auxiliary verbs, and prepositions. At the two-word phase, _____ words are usually action words or possessives. They are few in number and occur frequently in combination with _____ words, which are usually nouns.

45. Children's first words are learned by hearing and _____. Conditioning through _____ aids in language acquisition, but does not explain the acquisition of _____. Noam Chomsky believes that human beings are born with cognitive structures for acquiring language called a language _____ device, which enables children to process linguistic information from their environment. The fourth major approach to language acquisition emphasizes the link between language learning and a child's developing _____ abilities.

POSTTEST

Now try to answer the following questions without referring back to the text. Check your answers with the Answer Key at the end of the chapter and then compare your score with your Pretest score. You should see an improvement.

1. All of the following reflexes usually disappear between two and four months of age EXCEPT
   a. pupillary.
   b. rooting.
   c. stepping.
   d. placing.

2. Who was a pioneer in the study of maturational markers?
   a. Fantz
   b. Gesell
   c. Gibson
   d. Watson

3. Which of the following is a fine motor skill?
   a. kicking a ball
   b. passing an object from hand to hand
   c. jumping and running
   d. pulling a wagon

4. Starvation or severe lack of food results in
   a. hemophilia.
   b. kwashiorkor.
   c. marasmus.
   d. SCID.

5. The translation of external stimulation into neural impulses is
   a. sensation.
   b. perception.
   c. habituation.
   d. discrimination.

6. For the first one or two months, infants prefer to look at patterns that are
   a. black and white.
   b. red and green.
   c. pink and blue.
   d. yellow and brown.

7. The growth and refinement of the process by which we gain knowledge of our world is called _____ development.
   a. cognitive
   b. sensory
   c. intellectual
   d. emotional

8. Piaget's first stage of cognitive development is the
   a. concrete operational stage.
   b. formal operational stage.
   c. preoperational stage.
   d. sensorimotor stage.

9. When a person changes his action patterns or schemes to fit a new object or piece of information, what has occurred?
   a. conservation
   b. accommodation
   c. assimilation
   d. intellectualization

10. Research has shown that infants as young as 2 months store _____ in memory.
    a. words
    b. visual patterns
    c. concepts
    d. verbal patterns

11. All of the following are dimensions of language EXCEPT
    a. contents.
    b. grammar.
    c. form.
    d. use.

12. The particular symbol used to represent the meaning of a message is called
    a. content.
    b. use.
    c. syntax.
    d. form.

13. The production of language begins with
    a. babbling.
    b. cooing.
    c. crying.
    d. holophrases.

14. The self-imitating precursor to speech produced by infants is called
    a. iteration.
    b. expressive jargon.
    c. babbling.
    d. cooing.

15. Infants tend to be language _____; whereas adults tend to be language _____.
    a. conservatives; liberals
    b. specialists; universalists
    c. nativists; environmentalists
    d. universalists; specialists

16. An infant's first words are usually
    a. verbs.
    b. pronouns.
    c. nouns.
    d. adjectives.

17. When a child who has learned that the family cat is called "kitty" begins to call rabbits, skunks and squirrels "kitty," the child is
    a. overextending.
    b. iterating.
    c. using expressive jargon.
    d. using holophrastic speech.

18. Which of the following contains the other three?
    a. adjectives
    b. contentives
    c. nouns
    d. verbs

19. The phase "Big house" is an example of which concept?
    a. negation
    b. attribution
    c. location
    d. identification

20. Who proposed the LAD?
    a. Gibson
    b. Brown
    c. Gesell
    d. Chomsky

Posttest Score _____

Pretest Score _____

Improvement _____

ESSAY QUESTIONS

Try to write out complete and well-structured answers for each of the following questions. In some cases, you might want to refer to material in the text for support material in formulating your answer. The purpose of these questions is to give you a chance to consolidate your knowledge of the material in this chapter. No answers are given for the essays in the Answer Key as many of them are open-ended and can have several different correct answers.

1. Distinguish between marasmus and kwashiorkor. Be sure to include not only symptoms and causes in your answer but also an indication of which is more dangerous to the child and likely to have the longest lasting effects.

2. Explain why infants are born with reflexes and why some reflexes disappear so quickly.

3. Relate what is known about SIDS and suggest what can be done to prevent this disorder.

4. Describe the various forms of infant locomotion.

5. Briefly describe the newborn's sensory capacities.

6. Describe a child in Piaget's sensorimotor stage of development. Give specific examples.

7. Define adaptation and give specific examples of assimilation and accommodation. Use examples from your own life, if possible.

8. Define object permanence and trace its development over the first two years of life. Include the debates concerning its development.

9. Describe the concept of affordances as set forth by Gibson.

10. Briefly describe the progression of language development from an infant's first cry to the speech of a two-year-old.

Answer Key

Key Names

1. e	3. b	5. h, a	7. g
2. i	4. d	6. c	8. f

Pretest

1. b	5. b	9. d	13. d	17. d
2. b	6. a	10. b	14. a	18. c
3. c	7. d	11. a	15. b	19. a
4. c	8. a	12. b	16. a	20. c

Programmed Review

1. recovery, adjustment, balance, underestimated, preferences, learn, attention
2. six, cycle, stimulated, activity, calm, sleep
3. survival, primitive, Moro
4. neurological, behavioral, Brazelton's, motor, range, regulation, autonomic
5. Habituation, method
6. orderly, predictable, environment, biological, maturation, socioeconomic, environment
7. doubled, focus, coo, smile, one-quarter, one-tenth, 4 or 5, cartilage, pliable, break, pull
8. sudden infant death syndrome (SIDS), healthy, medical, crib death, asleep, prenatal, back, side, winter, apnea
9. soles, guided, exploration, fine, objects, thumb, finger
10. muscles, body, sitting, support, stand, walking, crawl, creep, bearwalk, scoot, social
11. three, less, visual, exploration, manipulate, pincer, spoon, cup
12. blocks, scribble, imitate, tricycle, jump, balance, ball
13. iron deficiency anemia, 30%, stunting, maturation, learning, brain, attention, information
14. marasmus, muscles, fat, short, kwashiorkor, protein, iron, carbohydrates, protein, minerals
15. nutrients, ill, diet, alcohol, drugs, malnutrition, breastmilk, water, bacterial , 3 months, Weaning
16. sensation, perception
17. sensory, memory, respond
18. novelty, differences, preference, difference, surprise, expect, potential, electroencephalograph
19. visual, brightness, movements, track, 7 to 10, blurred, convergence, complex, edges, contours, curves, face
20. focus, six months, internal, regularly, distorted, mouth, expressions, movements, scanning, surveying
21. binocular, integrates, distance, depth, four months, visual cliff, 4 to 6
22. startled, low-pitched, fluid, tissue, muffled, brain, localize, human
23. strong, smell, touch
24. cognitive, integrated, experience, maturation
25. Cognition, cognitive
26. schemes, schemes, stages, sensorimotor, adaptation, bodies, environment
27. grasp, remember, actions, social, explore, examine, appropriately, realistic
28. caregivers, facial, disappear, gestures, actions, novel, deferred, earlier
29. object permanence, awareness, 18 months, disappear, shift, tracking, 5 and 8 months, A not B, universal
30. visual, dramatic
31. Symbolic representation, pretending, 11 or 12 months, Language
32. "little scientist," motor, perception
33. affordances, experience, cognitive
34. neurologically, colors, faces, voices

35. 1 year, 18 months, 2 years, symbols, content, form, use, situation, relationship, intentions, attitudes
36. Receptive, productive, simultaneously, cries, cooing
37. iteration, phonemes, inflections, patterns, expressive jargon, language, problem-solving, universalists, specialists
38. experience, same, language, lessen
39. understand, say, mutual dialogues
40. first year, rate, development
41. nouns, names, holophrastic, function, relationship, speech, referential, expressive, referential, expressive, social, smaller, dummy words
42. categories, appropriate
43. concepts, concept, name, twins, deaf, words, concepts, complement
44. syntax, telegraphic, contentives, functors, pivot, open
45. imitating, reinforcement, syntax, acquisition, cognitive

Posttest

1. a	6. a	11. b	16. c
2. b	7. a	12. d	17. a
3. b	8. d	13. c	18. b
4. c	9. b	14. a	19. b
5. a	10. b	15. d	20. d

6
Infants and Toddlers: Personality and Sociocultural Development

CHAPTER OUTLINE

Social and Emotional Development in Infancy
    First Relationships
    The Attachment Process
    Emotional Communication and Attachment
    Stranger Anxiety, Separation Anxiety, and Attachment

Patterns of Early Relationships
    Quality of Attachment
    Attachment and Infants with Special Needs

Fathers, Siblings, and the Family System
    Fathers
    Siblings
    Grandparents

Personality Development in the Second Year of Life
    Trust, Nurturance, and a Secure Base
    Social Referencing and Cultural Meaning
    Autonomy, Discipline, and Prosocial Behavior
    Development of the Self

Parental Employment
    The Social Ecology of Child Care
    Infant Day Care

KEY TERMS AND CONCEPTS

In order to increase your understanding of the chapter, look for each of the following terms as you read and write out the definition.

Attachment
Avoidant attachment
Child abuse
Child neglect
Day mothers
Dethroning
Discrepancy hypothesis
Disorganized/disoriented attachment
Failure-to-thrive syndrome
Imprinting
Insecure attachment
Interactive synchrony
Maternal separation model
Mutuality
Personality

Prosocial behavior
Quality of mothering model
Resistant attachment
Scaffolding
Secure attachment
Self-concept
Separation anxiety
Sibling rivalry
Social ecology
Social referencing
Strange situation test
Stranger anxiety
Temperament

KEY NAMES

After reading the chapter, try to match each of the following names with the person's contribution to the field of psychology. Then check your answers with the Answer Key at the end of this chapter.

_____ 1. Mary Ainsworth   a. contact comfort

_____ 2. Jay Belsky   b. early infant day care

_____ 3. John Bowlby   c. imprinting

_____ 4. Thomas and Stella Chess   d. preprogrammed attachment behaviors

_____ 5. Erik Erikson   e. six milestones in emotional development

_____ 6. Stanley and Nancy Greenspan   f. strange situation test

_____ 7. Harry Harlow   g. temperaments

_____ 8. Konrad Lorenz   h. trust and autonomy

Try to answer each of the following questions without looking in the text. Then check your answers with the Answer Key at the end of this chapter and record your score in the space provided.

1. The first and most influential relationship that an infant experiences is with the mother or caregiver. This bond becomes firmly established by what age?
   a. 1 to 2 months
   b. 3 to 4 months
   c. 5 to 6 months
   d. 8 to 9 months

2. Which of the following is among the social emotions that emerge during the second year of life?
   a. anger
   b. disgust
   c. guilt
   d. sadness

3. According to the Greenspans, what is the first milestone in the emotional development of the infant within the first relationship?
   a. Self-regulation and Interest in the World
   b. Falling in Love
   c. Developing Intentional Communication
   d. Creating Emotional Ideas

4. According to the Greenspans, in the milestone called "Emergence of an Organized Sense of Self," infants are able to do all of the following EXCEPT
   a. take an active role in the emotional partnership with their mothers and fathers.
   b. symbolize, pretend, and form images in their heads of people and things.
   c. begin to use words to communicate.
   d. have a well-developed sense of self.

5. Which of the following would Ainsworth call an orienting behavior?
   a. crying
   b. looking
   c. smiling
   d. vocalizing

6. Who thought babies were born with preprogrammed behavior that keeps their parents close by and responsive?
   a. Erikson
   b. Bowlby
   c. Greenspan
   d. Harlow

7. What did Lorenz call the following behavior that he observed in goslings immediately after hatching?
    a. attachment
    b. bonding
    c. imprinting
    d. independence

8. Which cognitive theory states that by 7 months of age children experience uncertainty and anxiety?
    a. discrepancy hypothesis
    b. stranger theory
    c. difference theory
    d. new object hypothesis

9. Who conducted research on contact comfort in infant monkeys?
    a. Harlow
    b. Lorenz
    c. Bowlby
    d. Ainsworth

10. According to Ainsworth, about _____ percent of middle-class babies are securely attached.
    a. 20 to 30
    b. 40 to 50
    c. 60 to 70
    d. 80 to 90

11. The pattern of mutuality found between caregiver and infant has also been called
    a. attachment.
    b. interactive synchrony.
    c. identity.
    d. affection.

12. Child neglect differs from child abuse in that
    a. child neglect is usually not intentional.
    b. children don't die from neglect.
    c. only mothers can neglect a child.
    d. neglect cannot cause failure-to-thrive.

13. Which pattern of sensitivity is most commonly found in abusive mothers?
    a. overstimulation
    b. understimulation
    c. no stimulation at all
    d. mixed

14. Failure-to-thrive may most accurately be called a(n)
    a. attachment disorder.
    b. nutritional disorder.
    c. disorder resulting from physical disabilities.
    d. birth defect.

15. When compared to sighted babies, blind babies
    a. develop a selective, responsive smile earlier.
    b. smile as often and as ecstatically.
    c. have fewer facial expressions.
    d. are unable to develop a set of hand signals.

16. Compared to mothers, fathers are
    a. more likely to hold infants for caregiving purposes.
    b. more likely to hold infants during play.
    c. less likely to participate in physical play.
    d. more likely to initiate conventional games such as pat-a-cake.

17. All of the following are accurate descriptions of sibling relationships EXCEPT
    a. younger siblings are often more attached to older siblings than the reverse.
    b. older siblings are important social models.
    c. the younger sibling experiences dethroning.
    d. in some cultures, older siblings are the principal caretakers of the younger child.

18. According to Erikson, the child in the first year of life should develop
    a. trust.
    b. autonomy.
    c. initiative.
    d. industry.

19. In comparison to girls, 2-year-old boys
    a. demand greater closeness to their mothers.
    b. are most likely to disengage themselves from their mothers.
    c. have more ambivalent feelings about being separate.
    d. tend to be more intelligent.

20. Which of the following descriptions of children in day care is correct?
    a. Poor children seem to do better when placed in day care.
    b. Girls from affluent families do better when cared for by their grandmothers.
    c. Boys from affluent families do better when cared for by a baby-sitter.
    d. Mothers and grandmothers seem to be the best caregivers for poor children.

Pretest Score _____

Try to fill in the blanks in the following chapter review without referring back to the chapter in the text. Then check your answers with the Answer Key at the end of this chapter and go back to the chapter in the text and reread any sections that gave you trouble.

1. Human infants are born into an environment that shapes their _____ (characteristic beliefs, attitudes, and ways of interacting with others). During the first two years, they become aware of their _____ and the ways they can interact with it, of the responsiveness or unresponsiveness of the _____ around them, and that they can do some things for themselves or get _____ when necessary. They become aware of family _____ and learn how _____ imposes a certain style of behavior.

2. Babies come into the world with a _____ or inborn behavioral style. Some are more _____ to light or sudden loud sounds than others. Some react more quickly and _____ to discomfort than others. Most infants can be classified as _____ (often in a good mood and predictable), _____ (often irritable and unpredictable), or _____ (moody and resistant to attention).

Social and Emotional Development in Infancy

3. The first and most influential relationship occurs between the infant and the _____, or primary caregiver. The relationship becomes firmly established by the time the child reaches _____ months of age. Since the mid-1960s, developmentalists have used the term _____ in referring to this first relationship, which is characterized by _____, intense mutual _____, and strong _____ ties.

4. The emotional states of newborns are limited to _____ and relaxed _____. A range of emotions quickly emerges, including sadness, anger, disgust, fear and _____. These are nurtured and given meaning in the context of _____. Later, primarily in the second year, _____ oriented emotions emerge.

5. Stanley and Nancy Greenspan described six stages in the emotional development of the infant within first _____. During "Self-regulation and Interest in the World," infants seek to feel _____ and _____, but at the same time, to use all their _____ and experience the _____. They become increasingly _____ responsive and do not _____ between primary caregivers and other people. During "Falling in Love," self-regulated infants become more _____ to the world around them, recognize familiar _____ and direct their attention increasingly toward _____ caregivers. In "Developing Intentional Communication," infants begin to engage in _____ with others, and mother and baby initiate their own playful sequences of _____.

6. In "Emergence of an Organized Sense of Self," the fourth milestone, infants can do more things for _____, and take a more active role in the _____ partnership with their mothers and fathers. They can _____ their needs more effectively and precisely and begin using _____ to communicate. At the end of this period, the infant has a sense of _____. In "Creating Emotional Ideas," toddlers are able to _____, pretend, and form mental images of people and things. They can learn about the social world through _____ and _____ play. They feel the ambivalent needs of _____ and _____, and they now experience _____ emotions. By the milestone of "Emotional Thinking: The Basis for Fantasy, Reality, and Self-esteem," the give-and-take of close relationships with significant people has settled into a kind of _____.

7. Ainsworth defines _____ behaviors as those that primarily promote nearness to a specific person. These include _____ behavior such as crying, _____ behavior such as looking, movements relating to another _____ such as following, and active attempts at _____ contact.

8. Bowlby proposed that attachment is initiated by _____ behaviors in both the infant and the caregiver and is maintained by _____ events. His theory combines _____ and _____ in the development and maintenance of attachment. The infant's attachment to the primary caregiver becomes internalized as a _____ model by the end of the first year. The infant uses this model to _____ and _____ the mother's behavior and _____ to it.

9. Lorenz found that orphaned goslings go through a critical period for _____. Researchers disagree about the similarities and differences between imprinting on birds and _____ behavior in humans. There is no clear evidence that a _____ exists for human bonding, but it is clearly necessary for human infants to establish some kind of relationship with one or more major caregivers within the first _____ if normal development is to occur.

10. Harlow found that separation from the _____ had a disastrous effect on young monkeys. He experimented with _____ monkey mothers, some cloth and some _____. Regardless of which surrogate supplied the food, all the young monkeys showed a distinct preference for the _____ form, clinging and vocalizing to it, especially when _____. He proposed that _____ was an important factor in early attachment. Even with cloth surrogates, however, orphaned monkeys failed to develop _____. As adults, they had difficulty engaging in normal _____ activity. Studies indicate that _____ contact among infant monkeys at least partially makes up for the deprivation of the infant-adult attachment bond.

11. One of the developmental landmarks of the attachment relationship is the appearance of both _____ and _____ anxiety, called by pediatricians _____ anxiety. Most developmentalists see these anxieties as a sign of the infant's _____ development. They can distinguish caregivers from strangers and become keenly aware when the primary caregiver is _____. When they detect a departure from the known or expected, they experience anxiety, known as the _____ hypothesis. The anxiety is based on the infant's new awareness that the caregiver's presence coincides with _____. Emotional signaling by the mother is called social _____ and gives children time to _____.

Patterns of Early Relationships

12. In the United States and much of Western Europe, child development experts have assumed that a _____ primary relationship is ideal for healthy infant development. The relationship is mutually _____, and characterized by _____ playing and interactive _____. In some cultures, infants have close _____ contact, but do not have frequent _____ interactions.

13. The _____ situation test is used to measure the infant's attachment to the primary caregiver. Ainsworth found that between 60 and 70 percent of middle-class babies display _____ attachment. They can separate themselves fairly _____ from their mothers and go _____. Ainsworth found that about a third of infants displayed _____ attachment and that this attachment took three forms. In _____ attachment, the child may become angry when the mother leaves and _____ her on her return. In _____ attachment, the child responds _____ to the mother by simultaneously seeking and rejecting affection. In _____ attachment, the child behaves in contradictory and confused ways.

14. Securely attached infants are more enthusiastic, persistent, and _____. By age 2, they are more effective in coping with _____. In elementary school, they _____ in their work longer, are more eager to _____ new skills, and exhibit more highly developed _____ skills.

15. In her studies of children in Uganda, Ainsworth found that children with the strongest attachment behavior had a highly _____ relationship with their mothers. In the United States, she reported that securely attached 1-year-olds had mothers who were more _____ to their cries, more _____, more _____, more competent in providing close _____ contact, and more likely than mothers of insecure children to _____ their rate of feeding and their play behavior with the baby's own pace.

16. Schaffer investigated the way in which mutuality, or interactive _____, between infant and caregiver is achieved. He observed that most infant behavior follows an _____ on-off pattern and that some caregivers respond to these patterns more _____ than others. Caregivers change the pace and nature of the _____ with a variety of techniques such as introducing a new _____, imitating and elaborating on the infant's _____ or _____, or making it easier for the child to _____ something of interest. The closer the similarity between maternal and infant behavior, the less _____ babies have to deal with and the more _____ they will be. Respecting the child's need for a pause is one of the earliest rules of _____ that a caregiver must learn.

17. Mixed patterns of sensitivity tend to be particularly true of _____ mothers, _____ mothers, some _____ mothers, and mothers whose _____ is very different from that of their child.

18. The term _____ has been used to describe the mother's or father's role in progressively structuring the parent-child interaction. Parents provide the _____ within which they and their infant interact. Mothers who respond promptly and consistently to infant crying in the first few months are most likely to have infants who cry _____ by the end of the first year. A quick response gives babies confidence in the effectiveness of their _____ and encourages them to develop other ways of _____ their mothers. Infants who have a relatively exclusive relationship with a parent tend to exhibit _____ intense stranger and separation anxieties. They also show these anxieties at an _____ age than infants whose relationship with the parent is not exclusive. Research indicates that in day care and with multiple caregivers, children often form _____ attachments.

19. Child abuse refers to physical or psychological injuries that are _____ inflicted by an adult. Child neglect is a failure to _____ to children. Neglect is a factor in _____ syndrome in which infants are small and _____. These infants weigh in the lower _____ for their age group and show no evidence of _____ or _____ that would explain their failure to grow.

20. When abuse begins in infancy, it betrays the _____ relationship on which the infant depends. Studies have shown that toddlers who experience physical maltreatment and insecure attachments have distortions and delays in the development of their sense of _____ and in their _____ and _____ development. Intervention that encourages _____ may include alternate caregivers, social support measures, and _____ visits.

21. Caregivers often feel that a blind infant is _____. It is essential for both that they establish a mutually intelligible _____ system that overcomes this disability. Blind infants fail to receive _____ that sighted babies use in formulating their own responses and do not develop a selective, responsive _____ as early as sighted children. They have fewer _____ expressions but they rapidly develop a large, expressive vocabulary of _____ signals for their caregivers.

22. In the first few months of life, the well-developed _____ sense of deaf infants generally makes up for the problems imposed by deafness. After the first six months, _____ between parents and infants begins to break down. The children's responses are not complete enough to meet parents' _____. Often the discovery of the child's deafness does not occur until the _____ year. One of the first indications of hearing impairment in 1-year-olds is seeming _____ as well as a _____ reaction when people approach.

23. When an infant is born with a severe disability, there is a high risk of parental _____, withdrawal, and _____. A severely disabled infant strains _____ ties and may trigger a variety of _____ in other children in the family.

Fathers, Siblings, and the Family System

24. Fathers are spending _____ time with their infants than they did in the past. Fathers are able to be as _____ to the infant's cues as mothers, and infants can become as _____ to their fathers as they are to their mothers. Fathers are more likely to hold infants during _____ and are more often _____ and _____. Play between fathers and infants occurs in _____, and fathers tend toward unusual, vigorous, and unpredictable games, which infants find highly _____. As infants grow older, father-infant interaction is likely to _____, and the father becomes an important _____ model. Numerous studies indicate that the father's emotional support of the mother during _____ and early _____ is important to the establishment of positive beginning relationships.

25. Younger siblings are often _____ attached to older siblings than the reverse. Often, older siblings are important _____ models and in some cultures, the older sibling is the principal _____ of the younger child. Two negative aspects of sibling relationships are sibling _____ and the _____ of the older sibling with the birth of the new infant.

26. Grandparents may be particularly important to the stability of _____ households, and in families where the mothers are in the _____ force. They frequently offer more _____ and support, or empathy and _____, and less _____. The stories they tell help to create a sense of family _____ and tradition.

Personality Development in the Second Year of Life

27. Erikson believed that the development of _____ marks the first stage of psychosocial development and it is conveyed to the infant through the mother's _____ behavior. In Italy, nurturance of the infant is a _____ affair and mothers and infants are rarely _____. In much of early-twentieth-century Europe, _____ was considered a dirty habit. Today some children are given a _____ on the assumption that they can give it up more easily than thumb sucking. Most children give them up as regular comfort devices by the end of _____ childhood.

28. An important area of parental influence is social _____, by which infants look to the parent for _____ signals. Parents also convey _____ meaning by including toddlers in social interactions, even when they are peripheral participants in the ongoing _____ life of the family and community. Sometimes toddlers are given direct _____ and help. Through _____ participation, adults bridge the gap caused by the child's limited knowledge of events.

29. Toward the end of the second year, toddlers experience increased emotional conflict between their greater need for _____ and their obvious _____ and limited _____. Toddlers may be torn between a desire to stay _____ to their mothers and a wish to be _____. Their new sense of _____ seems to frighten them.

30. To become sensitive to the needs of others, children need _____ that focuses on _____, not on the child, as the object of criticism. Children who have a strong attachment relationship are not spoiled by _____ or frightened by reasonable _____. Toilet training is one aspect of behavior affected by adult attitudes towards children's _____, the way children handle their own _____ and the children's need for _____.

31. The development of empathy, a _____ behavior, may relate to the toddler's developing sense of _____. Often, when toddlers see the distress of others, they are _____. In studies of cooperation in simple tasks, almost no _____-old infants cooperated with each other. At 18 months, cooperation is _____ and appears accidental, and at _____, nearly all cooperate.

32. Infants gradually begin to realize that they are _____ and _____ beings. From 3 to 8 months, they actively learn about their _____. At 7 or 8 months, infants become wary of _____, able to delay their _____, and more _____ in testing and exploring of their own responses and results. From 12 to 18 months, infants _____ themselves in pictures and in the mirror. From 18 to 30 months, they learn about their _____, and their _____ features and characteristics, and with this growing sense of self comes emotional reactions to others, sometimes in the form of _____ tantrums.

33. The self-conscious emotions depend on a fairly well-developed understanding of social rules and on a sense of _____. The infant must be able to determine how personal behavior compares to the _____ set by the culture. At around 21 months, an awareness of _____ behaviors begins to develop. Boys are likely to _____ themselves from their mothers, while girls seek _____ closeness to them and have more _____ feelings about being separate. By the end of the second year, children's language is filled with references to _____.

Parental Employment

34. The social _____ of child-care refers to the environment in which child care takes place. Parents in the United States receive little public _____. Employers in the United States must provide only _____ of family leave.

35. Both family day-care homes and well-run day-care centers are capable of fostering _____ development in infants and toddlers. In Sweden, children who began day care before age one were generally rated more competent on _____ tests, and more _____ competent than their home-reared peers. The way infants fare in day care is influenced by their _____, by the family's _____ status and by the quality of _____ the infant receives. Poor children seem to do better when cared for by their _____ or _____, while in more affluent families, _____ do better with baby sitters and _____ do better with their mothers.

36. According to the _____ model, the infant experiences daily, repeated separations from the mother as either maternal absence or maternal _____. In the _____ model, the key factor is how the maternal employment affects maternal _____. The employed mother is unable to be as _____ and _____.

POSTTEST

Now try to answer each of the following questions without referring to the text. Check your answers with the Answer Key and record your score in the space provided. Subtract your pretest score to get your improvement score.

1. The newborn is limited to which of the following emotions?
   a. sadness and pleasure
   b. distress and relaxed interest
   c. disgust and shame
   d. empathy and distress

2. According to the Greenspans, the second milestone in emotional development is
   a. falling in love.
   b. developing intentional communication.
   c. emergence of an organized sense of self.
   d. creating emotional ideas.

3. Which of the following is NOT a signaling behavior used by an infant?
   a. crying
   b. smiling
   c. looking
   d. vocalizing

4. Which of the following researchers investigated the impact of separation from the mother on infant monkeys?
   a. Ainsworth
   b. Bowlby
   c. Greenspan
   d. Harlow

5. All of the following are anxieties experienced by infants EXCEPT
   a. attachment.
   b. 7-months.
   c. separation.
   d. stranger.

6. The subtle emotional signals, usually from the parent, that influence the infant's behavior are called
   a. discrepancies.
   b. social referencing.
   c. emotional guidelines.
   d. scaffolding.

7. Which researcher developed the Strange Situation Test?
   a. Erikson
   b. Lorenz
   c. Ainsworth
   d. Bowlby

8. According to Ainsworth, about one-third of infants are
   a. insecurely attached.
   b. securely attached.
   c. avoidant.
   d. ambivalent.

9. The average mother responds quickly to her infant's distress about what percent of the time?
   a. 100
   b. 75
   c. 50
   d. 25

10. The progressive structuring by the parents of the parent-child interaction is called
    a. framework.
    b. infrastructuring.
    c. interaction.
    d. scaffolding.

11. One of the first indications that an infant is deaf is
    a. failure to look at a parent who enters the room.
    b. not paying attention to the television set.
    c. failure to speak.
    d. seeming disobedience.

12. Fathers are more likely to play what type of games with their children?
   a. board games
   b. pat-a-cake
   c. unpredictable
   d. pretend

13. Grandparents frequently offer more of all of the following EXCEPT
   a. approval.
   b. discipline.
   c. empathy.
   d. sympathy.

14. Prosocial behavior includes all of the following EXCEPT
   a. helping.
   b. sharing.
   c. cooperation.
   d. attachment.

15. Toddlers have a greater need for
   a. autonomy.
   b. initiative.
   c. trust.
   d. industry.

16. Toilet training is most closely related to the parents'
   a. discipline patterns.
   b. mental health.
   c. marriage stability.
   d. attachments.

17. At 7 to 8 months of age, children
   a. discover their own hands and feet.
   b. learn about their gender.
   c. become wary of strangers.
   d. realize they are separate and unique beings.

18. Children first recognize themselves in a mirror at what age?
   a. 7 to 8 months
   b. 12 to 18 months
   c. 18 to 30 months
   d. 2 years

19. The quality of mothering model focuses on
   a. the age of the mother.
   b. the problems of single-parent families.
   c. competing demands of work and family.
   d. maternal mental health.

20. According to the maternal separation model, the infant experiences insecurity when the mother goes to work because of
   a. the change in maternal behavior.
   b. a decrease in maternal responsiveness.
   c. a change in maternal sensitivity.
   d. the absence of the mother.

Posttest Score _____

Pretest Score _____

Improvement _____

ESSAY QUESTIONS

In order to develop your understanding of the material in this chapter, try to write a comprehensive answer for each of the following essay questions. Use the text for material to support your answer.

1. Describe the development of emotions from birth through 2 years of age, and specify which emotions are most common at each age.

2. Describe the six milestones in the emotional development of the infant within the first relationship.

3. Briefly describe the work of Lorenz and Harlow. In your opinion, what is their main contribution to the field of child development?

4. Discuss the importance of the appearance of stranger anxiety and separation anxiety.

5. Trace the development of an infant's self-knowledge throughout the first two years.

6. Describe secure attachment and both avoidant and ambivalent insecure attachment. Give an example of the behavior of a child in each of these situations.

7. Outline what processes are most effective in preventing child abuse and neglect.

8. Describe the special problems of blind and deaf infants and suggest things that the parents can do to help such children.

9. Compare and contrast the interactions that mothers and fathers have with their infants in the first two years of life.

10. Describe the child-care situation in the United States and suggest a program to improve that care.

ANSWER KEY

Key Names

1. f	3. d	5. h	7. a
2. b	4. g	6. e	8. c

Pretest

1. d	5. b	9. a	13. d	17. c
2. c	6. b	10. c	14. a	18. a
3. a	7. c	11. b	15. c	19. b
4. d	8. a	12. a	16. b	20. a

Programmed Review

1. personality, environment, world, help, relationships, gender
2. temperament, sensitive, dramatically, easy, difficult, slow-to-warm-up
3. mother, 8 or 9, attachment, interdependence, feelings, emotional
4. distress, interest, pleasure, relationships, socially
5. relationship, regulated, calm, senses, world, socially, discriminate, alert, figures, significant, dialogues, communication
6. themselves, emotional, signal, words, self, symbolize, make-believe, pretend, autonomy, dependency, social, partnership
7. attachment, signaling, orienting, physical
8. preprogrammed, pleasurable, heredity, environment, working, predict, interpret, respond
9. imprinting, attachment, critical period, 8 months
10. mother, surrogate, wire, cloth, frightened, contact comfort, normally, sexual, peer
11. separation, stranger, 7-months', cognitive, absent, discrepancy, safety, referencing, acclimate
12. single, responsive, game, dialogues, physical, face-to-face
13. strange, secure, easily, exploring, insecure, resistant, avoids, avoidant, ambivalently, disorganized/disoriented
14. cooperative, peers, persist, learn, social
15. responsive, responsive, affectionate, tender, bodily, synchronize
16. synchrony, alternating, skillfully, dialogue, object, sounds, actions, reach, discrepancy, attentive, conversation
17. abusive, depressed, adolescent, temperament
18. scaffolding, framework, less, communications, signaling, more, earlier, multiple
19. intentionally, respond, failure-to-thrive, emaciated, 3 percent, disease, abnormality
20. nurturant, self, language, cognitive, resiliency, home
21. unresponsive, communication, information, smile, facial, hand
22. visual, communication, expectations, second, disobedience, startled
23. rejection, depression, marital, disturbances
24. more, responsive, attached, play, physical, spontaneous, cycles, exciting, increase, role, pregnancy, infancy

25. more, social, caretaker, rivalry, dethroning
26. single-parent, labor, approval, sympathy, discipline, identity
27. trust, nurturing, social, alone, thumb-sucking, pacifier, early
28. referencing, emotional, cultural, social, instruction, guided
29. autonomy, dependence, skills, close, independent, separateness
30. feedback, behavior, attention, limits, explorations, body, autonomy
31. prosocial, self, confused, 12-month, infrequent, 24 months
32. separate, unique, bodies, strangers, actions, deliberate, recognize, gender, physical, temper
33. self, standards, gender-specific, disengage, greater, ambivalent, themselves
34. ecology, support, 12 weeks
35. healthy, cognitive, socially, gender, economic, care, mothers, grandmothers, girls, boys
36. maternal-separation, rejection, quality of mothering, behavior, sensitive, responsive

Posttest

1. b	5. a	9. b	13. b	17. c
2. a	6. b	10. d	14. d	18. b
3. c	7. c	11. d	15. a	19. c
4. d	8. a	12. c	16. a	20. b

7

Early Childhood: Physical, Cognitive, and Language Development

CHAPTER OUTLINE

Physical Development
    Body Size and Proportions
    Brain Development

Motor Skills Development
    Gross Motor Skills
    Fine Motor Skills
    Learning and Motor Skills

Cognitive Development
    An Overview of Preoperational Thinking
    Limitations on Preoperational Thinking
    Conservation
    Limitations of Piaget's Theory
    Beyond Piaget: Social Perspectives

Memory and Cognitive Development
    Memory Processes
    Recognition and Recall
    Rehearsal and Organization
    Event Scripts and Sequential Understanding

Language Development and Culture
    An Expanding Grammar
    More Words and Concepts
    The Influence of Parents' Language Use
    Children's Conversations
    Subdialects
    Bilingualism

Play and Learning
    Kinds of Play
    Play and Cognitive Development

KEY TERMS AND CONCEPTS

While reading the chapter in the text, find each one of the following terms and write out the definition for that term.

Animism	Myelination
Automaticity	Neurons
Brain growth spurt	Number abstraction abilities
Cerebral cortex	Numerical-reasoning principles
Collective monologues	Ossification
Conservation	Overregularize
Corpus callosum	Plasticity
Egocentric speech	Pragmatics
Egocentrism	Recall
Extrinsically motivated behavior	Recognition
Functional subordination	Reification
Intrinsically motivated behavior	Short term memory (STM)
Lateralization	Subdialects
Long term memory (LTM)	Symbolic representation
Mean length of utterance (MLU)	Synapses

KEY NAMES

Now try to match each of the following individuals with a major contribution to psychology and check your answers with the Answer Key at the end of this chapter.

_____ 1. Roger Brown   a. brain lateralization

_____ 2. Jean Piaget   b. competence motivation

_____ 3. Roger Sperry   c. mean length of utterance

_____ 4. Lev Vygotsky   d. preoperational thought

_____ 5. Robert White   e. zone of proximal development

Try to answer each of the following questions without referring back to the chapter in the text. Then check your answers with the Answer Key at the end of this chapter and record the number correct in the space provided.

1. At birth, the head comprises about _____ of the body length.
    a. one-quarter
    b. one-third
    c. one-half
    d. one-eighth

2. The process by which bones develop and harden is called
    a. maturation.
    b. epiphysis.
    c. ossification.
    d. development

3. Skeletal age is typically determined by measuring the bones of the
    a. hands.
    b. feet.
    c. ankles.
    d. wrist.

4. The specialized cells that make up the nervous system are
    a. ossified.
    b. myelin.
    c. glial cells.
    d. neurons.

5. Language development occurs very quickly in early childhood and is housed in the
    a. left hemisphere of the brain.
    b. right hemisphere of the brain.
    c. both hemispheres of the brain equally.
    d. either of the two hemispheres of the brain depending on heredity.

6. All of the following are accurate findings concerning the brain and handedness EXCEPT
    a. for the majority of right-handed people, language is localized in the left side of the brain.
    b. the brains of left-handed people may be less strongly lateralized.
    c. about 40 percent of the population are left-handed and have a mixed lateralization.
    d. many left-handed people appear to be ambidextrous.

7. Which of the following is a fine motor skill?
    a. running
    b. jumping
    c. throwing a ball
    d. using a fork

8. Children are able to vary the rhythm of their running by age
   a. two.
   b. three.
   c. four.
   d. five.

9. Motivation that comes from within the child and within the activity is
   a. extrinsic.
   b. intrinsic.
   c. external.
   d. internal.

10. According to Piaget, the preschool child is in the _____ stage.
    a. sensorimotor
    b. preoperational
    c. concrete operational
    d. formal operational

11. Which of the following contains the other three?
    a. preconceptual
    b. intuitive
    c. preoperational
    d. transitional

12. A child who thinks an inanimate object is alive is exhibiting
    a. animism.
    b. conservation.
    c. assimilation.
    d. egocentrism.

13. The use of actions, images, or words to represent objects and events is
    a. intrinsic motivation.
    b. conservation.
    c. symbolic representation.
    d. egocentrism.

14. The thinking of the preschool child may be described as any of the following EXCEPT
    a. concrete.
    b. irreversible.
    c. egocentric.
    d. abstract.

15. Focusing on only one aspect of a situation at a time is
    a. animism.
    b. irreversibility.
    c. conservation.
    d. centration.

16. A child is asked to compare two balls of clay. This child is being tested for conservation of
    a. volume.
    b. mass.
    c. number.
    d. liquid.

17. Which type of memory is also called working memory?
    a. sensory
    b. short-term
    c. long-term
    d. metamemory

18. All of the following first appear in the stage of two-word utterances EXCEPT
    a. telegraphic speech.
    b. pivot words.
    c. inflections.
    d. open words.

19. Bilingualism has been found to be
    a. harmful to children.
    b. inappropriate for American children.
    c. impossible to teach before adolescence.
    d. advantageous for children.

20. Catherine Garvey defined play as all of the following EXCEPT
    a. something that is engaged in to learn a skill.
    b. something that is chosen.
    c. something that is actively engaged in.
    d. something that relates to other areas of life.

Pretest score _____

PROGRAMMED REVIEW

This section is designed to help you develop a deeper understanding of the material throughout the entire chapter. Try to fill in as many answers as possible without referring back to the text. Check your answers with the Answer Key at the end of this chapter and then go back to the text and review any areas with which you had a problem.

Physical Development

1. Each child's physical growth is the result of _____, nutrition, and the opportunity to _____ and _____.

2. Sustained periods of malnutrition during early childhood limits children's _____ development because malnutrition produces _____ damage, delayed _____ growth, and delayed development of _____ skills.

3. From age 2 to 6 years, growth _____. Healthy children gain an average of _____ pounds a year and grow almost _____ inches.

4. Changes in body proportions also affect the location of the body's center of _____, which gradually _____ to the _____ area.

5. Bones develop and harden through the process of _____, which transforms soft tissue or _____ into bone. Skeletal age is determined by _____ maturation, and can be measured by X-rays of the bones of the _____.

6. By the time children are 5 years old, the brain is nearly _____ size. Neurons begin to form during the _____ period. The _____ cells, which insulate the neurons and improve the efficiency of transmission of nerve impulses, continue to grow rapidly throughout the _____ year. Maturation of the central nervous system also involves _____ -- the formation of insulating cells, that occurs in the motor reflexes and vision in early _____.

7. The cerebral cortex of the human brain is divided into two _____ -- the left and right. They have very different ways of processing information, a phenomena referred to as _____. Roger Sperry discovered many of these important properties of the cerebral cortex through surgery designed to reduce _____. The left side of the brain controls the _____ side of the body, and the right side of the brain controls the _____ side of the body.

8. For most people, right-side preference is associated with strong _____ dominance. For the majority of right-handed people, language is localized in the _____ hemisphere. For the remaining 10 percent of the population who are left-handed, language is often _____ by the two sides of the brain, suggesting that the brains of left-handed people may be less _____ and many left-handed people appear to be _____, able to use both hands with fairly good dexterity.

Motor Skills Development

9. _____ motor skills refer to running, hopping, and other such movements and _____ motor skills refer to capabilities such as writing. Some developmental sequences involve functional _____, in which actions that initially are performed for their own sake become part of a more complicated, purposeful skill.

10. Two-year-olds walk with a wide _____ and a swaying _____. Toddlers also tend to use _____ arms or legs when only one is needed. Three-year-olds are more likely to extend only the _____ hand to receive an item. By the age of 4, children are able to vary the _____ of their running. Many can also _____ rather awkwardly and execute a running _____ and a standing _____ jump. Five-year-olds can _____ smoothly, walk a _____ beam confidently, stand on one _____ for several seconds and imitate _____ steps. Many can throw a ball _____ and catch a _____ ball.

11. _____ motor skills involve the coordinated and dexterous use of hand, fingers, and thumb. Difficulty in mastering precise fine motor movements is linked to the _____ of the child's central nervous system. By the time children are 4 to 5 years old, they are able to dress and undress themselves without _____, and use _____ utensils very well. By age 6, children can tie their own _____.

12. Any new skill or learning generally requires a state of _____ on the part of the child. Children at the optimal point of readiness want to _____, enjoy the _____, and get excited over their own _____.

13. Practice is essential to _____ development. When children live in limited and restricted environments, the development of their motor skills _____. This development is also enhanced by paying _____. Children at age 2 or 3 learn new motor skills most efficiently by being _____ through the activity. Children between the ages of 3 and 5 focus their attention most effectively by active _____. When children are 6 or even 7, they can attend closely to _____ instructions.

14. Motivation that comes from within the child and within the activity is _____; whereas motivation that comes from earning praise, rewards, etc. is _____. The _____ children receive for their efforts helps to acquire and refine skills.

Cognitive Development

15. _____ described the course of cognitive development in terms of discrete _____ that children pass through on the way to an understanding of the world. Children build their own _____ through experimentation.

16. Piaget viewed children as little _____ working diligently to figure out how the world works. Children _____ their surroundings.

17. The _____ stage lasts from 2 to 7 years. The _____ period lasts from age 2 to about age 4 when the use of _____ and symbolic (pretend) _____ enable the child to think about something not immediately present. Children may think anything that moves is alive, a cognitive pattern called _____; and they display _____, the idea that people and things in thoughts or dreams are real. The tendency to see and understand things in terms of their own point of view is _____. The transitional child begins to separate mental from physical _____ and to understand _____ apart from social norms. Intuitive children are beginning to understand _____ points of view and _____ concepts.

18. The most dramatic cognitive difference between infants and 2-year-olds is in the use of symbolic _____ -- the use of actions, images, or words to represent events or experiences. Once children begin to use symbols, their thought processes become more _____. They become more aware of the _____ and form expectations for the _____, and they distinguish between _____ and the _____ they are addressing. This increased sensitivity to others helps the child make the transition into more _____ rather than egocentric thinking.

19. The thinking of preoperational children is _____ and they cannot deal with abstractions. Their thinking is _____ (events and relationships occur in only one direction), and _____ (centered on their own perspective). Their thought tends to be _____ on only one physical dimension of an object or situation at one time, a limitation best seen in class _____ problems. And, they have difficulty understanding that _____ exists along a continuum. Preoperational children do not have _____ skills such as volume or mass.

20. Preoperational children are more _____ in using numbers than Piaget believed. They possess number-_____ abilities, by which the child arrives at the number of an array of objects, and numerical-_____ principles, by which the child determines the correct way to operate on or transform an array.

21. According to social perspective theorists, the ways adults _____ how a problem is solved help children learn to think. All cultures initiate children into activities through what has been called guided _____. Katherine Nelson argues that a knowledge of _____ is the key to understanding the child's mind. The child's understanding of the world is embedded in _____ knowledge.

22. Vygotsky stated that children develop through participation in activities slightly _____ their competence with the assistance of adults or more skilled children. He believed _____ play to be an important means of moving children toward more advanced levels of social and _____ skills.

Memory and Cognitive Development

23. Information comes into the memory system and makes contact with the _____ register. The information is then either lost or transferred to _____ memory, often described as working memory, and finally to _____ memory, which is a permanent knowledge base. _____ memory is the first to develop. _____ encoded recollections appear after the ages of 4 to 6.

24. _____ refers to the ability to identify items previously experienced, whereas _____ refers to the ability to retrieve data about things currently not present. Preschool children's performance on _____ tasks is quite good but their _____ performance is poor. Preschool children do not spontaneously _____ or mentally _____ information that they want to remember. Children can remember information that is ordered _____.

Language Development and Culture

25. Brown identified _____ distinct increasingly complex stages of language development in terms of the mean length of _____, the average length of the sentence the child produces. The first stage is characterized by _____ utterances in which _____ speech, _____ words, and _____ words first emerge. In the second stage, utterances are slightly _____ and children begin to generalize the rules of _____ to words they already know. In the third stage, children learn to _____ simple sentences using _____ and _____ forms and asking yes-no _____. In the fourth and fifth stages, children begin to use _____ clauses and _____ within compound and complex sentences, and by age 4-1/2 have a good grasp of _____.

26. Psychologists call talking aloud to oneself _____ speech. Piaget suggested that the private speech of young children indicated their _____ and called it _____ speech. Vygotsky observed that private speech often mirrored adult _____ speech and served to help in the development of inner _____ and self-direction. In its earliest stages, private speech occurs _____ the action. At the second stage, it _____ the action, and finally it _____ an action.

27. Very young children's conversations are often _____ monologues and even school-age children have difficulty communicating to and _____ each other fully.

28. Children also learn _____, the social function of language. They learn that specific words, syntax, tone of voice, and mode of address depend on the _____ between speaker and listener. Children are quick to learn _____ of speech and to conform to a social _____. They are also quick to perceive degrees of _____ and the speech that fits.

29. Subcultural differences can produce _____, a variation of a language which most people can understand. True _____ differences occur when people of a language group cannot understand each other. The child who grows up amid two languages becomes _____. In Europe bilingualism is associated with being a _____ citizen of the world. In the United States, it is more often a sign of being a recent _____. Most researchers now believe that linguistically, culturally, and probably cognitively, it is an _____ for children to learn more than one language.

Play and Learning

30. Play has been called the "_____ of childhood." It promotes the growth of _____ capabilities and _____ skills and expands _____ skills. Garvey defined play as something that is engaged in simply for _____, has no _____ other than itself, is _____ by players, requires players to be _____ engaged in it, and _____ to other areas of life.

31. Sensory play teaches children about their bodies, and the qualities of things in the _____. Running and jumping are forms of play with _____. Rough-and-tumble play is a release for _____, a way to learn to handle _____, control _____, and to _____ behaviors inappropriate in a group. Children play with language by experimenting with its _____ and _____ and creating new _____. One of the major types of play consists of taking on roles or models and is called _____ play.

32. Two-year-olds will watch other children playing but usually not _____ them. Children 2 years old and younger may seem to be playing together but are almost always playing out _____ fantasies. Dramatic play reflects children's greater _____ maturity. Older children test their social knowledge in _____ play, which enables them to _____ themselves into other personalities, to experiment with different _____, and to experience a broader range of thought and _____.

33. When children are involved in pretend play, they usually display two levels -- the level of the _____ based meaning, and the level of the _____ meaning. When there are disagreements, children often "break _____" to resolve their disputes before continuing with their make-believe. Preschoolers are capable of various types of pretense, either about the _____ or _____ of an object, themselves, another person, an event, or action. As children become older, they rely less on _____ props. At first the child is both the agent and recipient of actions in _____ play. Children who have had a lot of practice with pretend play are also better at taking someone else's _____ or understanding someone else's _____.

POSTTEST

Now try to answer each of the following questions without referring back to the text and check your answers with the Answer Key at the end of this chapter. Record your score in the space provided and deduct your Pretest score. You should see a significant improvement.

1. Compared to the first two years, the growth rate for ages 2 to 6 years
   a. accelerates.
   b. slows.
   c. is the same.
   d. picks up speed.

2. All of the following are true about the body's center of gravity EXCEPT
   a. girls have a slightly higher center of gravity than do boys.
   b. the center of gravity is higher in children than in adults.
   c. being top heavy makes it more difficult to control the body.
   d. during the school years, the center of gravity descends to the pelvic area.

3. Myelination of neurons occurs during infancy for which areas?
   a. learning and hearing
   b. memory
   c. motor reflexes and vision
   d. self-control

4. Lateralization refers to the localization in functioning of the
   a. two hemispheres of the brain.
   b. two hands.
   c. hands and feet.
   d. two sides of the body.

5. Which of the following is NOT a gross motor skill?
   a. running
   b. hopping
   c. writing
   d. throwing

6. Which of the following are essential to motor development?
   a. lateralization and attention
   b. readiness and practice
   c. ossification and schooling
   d. maturation and coaching

7. Children can attend closely to verbal instructions by the age of
   a. 3 or 4.
   b. 4 or 5.
   c. 5 or 6.
   d. 6 or 7.

8. If given the opportunity to practice, most children can tie their own shoes by age
   a. 3.
   b. 4.
   c. 5.
   d. 6.

9. When children perform to earn praise or a reward, they are influenced by motivation, which is
   a. intrinsic.
   b. extrinsic.
   c. inherited.
   d. environmental.

10. Between 2 and 4 years of age, children are in Piaget's stage called
   a. sensorimotor.
   b. preconceptual.
   c. intuitive.
   d. transitional.

11. Objects and people in children's thoughts seem real to them. This is the process of
   a. reification.
   b. animism.
   c. conservation.
   d. assimilation.

12. The child's tendency to see things in terms of her own personal point of view is called
   a. animism.
   b. egocentrism.
   c. conservation.
   d. assimilation.

13. When a preschool child tells you that his brother does not have a brother, the child is displaying
   a. egocentrism.
   b. irreversibility.
   c. animism.
   d. centration.

14. The most dramatic cognitive difference between infants and two-year-olds is the use of
    a. animism.
    b. conservation.
    c. symbolic representation.
    d. assimilation and accommodation.

15. The level of skill at which children's ability develops with the assistance of adults or more skilled children is called the
    a. mastery point.
    b. zone of proximal development.
    c. mean length of utterance.
    d. linguistic relativity area.

16. The proper order of the stages of memory is
    a. sensory, short-term, long-term.
    b. short-term, long-term, sensory.
    c. long-term, sensory, short-term.
    d. sensory, long-term, short-term.

17. The ability to retrieve information without cue is
    a. recall.
    b. recognition.
    c. reversibility.
    d. relearning.

18. Last week, Marco told his mother that he "ran all the way home." Today, when he came home he said, "I runned all the way home." This is an example of
    a. discrimination.
    b. assimilation.
    c. accommodation.
    d. overregularization.

19. The social function of language is called
    a. semantics.
    b. syntax.
    c. pragmatics.
    d. grammar.

20. Experimentation with rhythm, cadences, and meaning are part of play with
    a. language.
    b. motion.
    c. drama.
    d. sensory pleasure.

Posttest Score _____

Pretest Score _____

Improvement _____

ESSAY QUESTIONS

These essay questions are designed to more thoroughly test your knowledge of the chapter. Try to write thorough, well-structured answers to each one. Use the textbook for any material you need to support your answer. I have not provided answers to these questions because you should be able to evaluate your own answers by this point in your work on this chapter.

1. Briefly trace the physical growth that occurs during the early childhood years.

2. Define lateralization, and describe how this process occurs in the brain and the impact it has on cognitive abilities.

3. Describe what you would tell a parent who asks you what gross and fine motor skills to expect as her child goes through early childhood.

4. Define and describe the relationship of intrinsic and extrinsic motivation and feedback in the development of competence.

5. Describe the limitations that occur in preoperational thinking.

6. Describe the three memory systems.

7. What are the advantages and disadvantages of bilingualism?

8. What are the pragmatics of speech? Do you think that the children you know or hear about have a good understanding of pragmatics? Explain your answer and give examples.

9. Discuss the importance of pretend in children's play in the early childhood years.

10. What is the role of private speech in children's development?

ANSWER KEY

Key Names

1. c	2. d	3. a	4. e	5. b

Pretest

1. a	5. a	9. b	13. c	17. b
2. c	6. c	10. b	14. d	18. c
3. d	7. d	11. c	15. d	19. d
4. d	8. c	12. a	16. b	20. a

Programmed Review

1. genetics, play, exercise
2. cognitive, brain, physical, motor
3. slows, 4-1/2, three
4. gravity, descends, pelvic
5. ossification, cartilage, bone, wrist
6. adults, embryonic, glial, second, myelination, infancy
7. hemispheres, lateralization, epileptic seizures, right, left
8. left hemisphere, left, shared, lateralized, ambidextrous
9. Gross, fine, subordination
10. stance, gait, both, preferred, rhythm, skip, jump, broad, skip, balance, foot, dance, overhead, large
11. Fine, immaturity, assistance, eating, shoelaces
12. readiness, learn, practice, success
13. motor, lags, attention, led, imitation, verbal
14. intrinsic, extrinsic, feedback
15. Piaget, stages, reality
16. scientists, explore
17. preoperational, preconceptual, symbols, play, animism, reification, egocentrism, reality, causation, multiple, relational
18. representation, complex, past, future, themselves, person, sociocentric
19. concrete, irreversible, egocentric, centered, inclusion, time, conservation
20. competent, abstraction, reasoning
21. demonstrate, participation, events, cultural
22. beyond, cognitive
23. sensory, short-term, long-term, Visual, Verbally
24. Recognition, recall, recognition, recall, organize, rehearse, temporally
25. five, utterance, two-word, telegraphic, pivot, open, longer, inflection, modify, negative, imperative, questions, subordinate, fragments, syntax
26. private, immaturity, egocentric, social, thought, after, accompanies, precedes
27. collective, comprehending
28. pragmatics, relationship, nuances, status, status
29. subdialects, dialects, bilingual, cultured, immigrant, advantage
30. work, sensory-perceptual, physical, intellectual, pleasure, purpose, chosen, actively, related
31. environment, motion, energy, feelings, impulses, avoid, rhythm, cadences, meanings, dramatic
32. approach, separate, social, dramatic, project, roles, feeling
33. reality, pretend, frame, identity, characteristics, concrete, solitary, perspective, feelings

Posttest

1. b	5. c	9. b	13. b	17. a
2. a	6. b	10. b	14. c	18. d
3. c	7. d	11. a	15. b	19. c
4. a	8. d	12. b	16. a	20. a

8

Early Childhood: Personality and Sociocultural Development

CHAPTER OUTLINE

Developmental Issues and Coping Patterns
    Fear and Anxiety
    Emotion Regulation and Self-regulation
    Developmental Conflicts

Aggression and Prosocial Behavior
    Aggression
    Prosocial Behavior

Peers, Play, and the Development of Social Skills
    Play and Social Skills
    Popularity and the Development of Social Skills
    The Role of Imaginary Companions

Understanding Self and Others
    Self-concept
    Self and Gender
    Gender and Socialization
    Social Concepts and Rules

Family Dynamics
    Parenting Styles
    Child Abuse
    Explanations of Child Abuse
    Discipline and Self-regulation
    Sibling Dynamics

KEY TERMS AND CONCEPTS

To become more familiar with the terminology of this chapter, look up the following terms in the text and write out the definitions of each.

Altruism
Androgynous personality
Anxiety
Assertiveness
Authoritarian parents
Authoritative parents
Autonomy
Compliance
Defense mechanisms
Emotion regulation
Fear
Frustration-aggression hypothesis
Gender
Gender constancy
Gender identity
Gender-role stereotypes

Gender roles
Gender schemes
Hostile aggression
Indifferent parents
Induction
Instrumental aggression
Imaginary companions
Permissive parents
Role playing
Self-regulation
Self-socialization
Sex
Sibling status
Social reciprocity
Systematic desensitization

KEY NAMES

After reading the chapter, try to match each of the following individuals with their contribution to the field of psychology.

_____ 1. Diana Baumrind

_____ 2. Judy Dunn

_____ 3. Erik Erikson

_____ 4. Sigmund Freud

_____ 5. Eleanor Maccoby

a. defense mechanisms

b. initiative vs. guilt

c. parenting styles

d. shared goals

e. sibling relationships

The following questions have been selected to test your knowledge of the chapter. Try to answer each question without referring back to the text. Then check your answers with the Answer Key at the end of this chapter and record the number correct in the space provided.

1. Which theory emphasizes the child's feelings, drives, and developmental conflicts?
    a. cognitive-developmental
    b. psychodynamic
    c. social learning
    d. sociological

2. Which theory emphasizes the child's own thoughts and concepts as organizer of his or her social behavior?
    a. cognitive-developmental
    b. psychodynamic
    c. social learning
    d. sociological

3. A younger child is LEAST likely to be afraid of
    a. strangers.
    b. unfamiliar objects.
    c. death.
    d. loud noises.

4. The process of incorporating the values, attitudes, and beliefs of others into oneself is the defense mechanism of
    a. reaction formation.
    b. projection.
    c. repression.
    d. identification.

5. When 4-year-old Juan hits his pillow instead of hitting his baby sister, he is using the defense mechanism of
    a. projection.
    b. reaction formation.
    c. displacement.
    d. identification.

6. According to psychodynamic theory, the unconscious act of erasing a frightening event or circumstance is the defense mechanism of
    a. repression.
    b. regression.
    c. projection.
    d. identification.

7. Ernie is a very timid child, but he hides his feelings and bullies other children instead. Ernie is using the defense mechanism of
    a. projection.
    b. reaction formation.
    c. regression.
    d. withdrawal.

8. Which of the following does not belong with the others?
    a. autonomy
    b. terrible twos
    c. "No"
    d. initiative

9. According to Erikson, preschoolers are in the stage of
    a. trust vs. mistrust.
    b. initiative vs. guilt.
    c. autonomy vs. shame and doubt.
    d. industry vs. inferiority.

10. When comparing aggression and assertion, it is most accurate to say
    a. both are equally likely to include actions intended to harm another.
    b. neither appear to be learned; they are both inherited traits.
    c. aggression includes intent to harm and assertion does not.
    d. they actually mean the same thing.

11. According to the frustration-aggression hypothesis,
    a. aggression is an inherited trait.
    b. frustration leads to depression and guilt.
    c. all forms of aggression are the result of physiological problems.
    d. frustration will result in some form of aggression.

12. Children playing next to each other, using similar toys, but not interacting, are engaged in which type of play?
    a. solitary
    b. onlooker
    c. parallel
    d. cooperative

13. A game such as baseball or monopoly would be classified as which type of play?
    a. onlooker
    b. parallel
    c. associative
    d. cooperative

14. Unselfish concern for the welfare of others is called
    a. altruism.
    b. social scripting.
    c. introjection.
    d. identification.

15. Gender based cultural standards or stereotypes are
    a. personal scripts.
    b. gender schemes.
    c. sex-role stereotypes.
    d. gender scripts.

16. Parents who are controlling and adhere rigidly to rules are classified as
    a. authoritative.
    b. authoritarian.
    c. indifferent.
    d. permissive.

17. Parents who put few if any restraints on their children in an attempt to show their children unconditional love are called
    a. authoritative.
    b. authoritarian.
    c. indifferent.
    d. permissive.

18. Children of permissive parents tend to be all of the following EXCEPT
    a. self-indulgent.
    b. impulsive.
    c. hostile.
    d. socially inept.

19. Which of the following children would be most likely to have the highest IQ?
    a. a first born child
    b. a middle born child
    c. a last born child
    d. an only child

20. Which explanation of child abuse focuses on the personality of the parents?
    a. psychiatric
    b. sociological
    c. situational
    d. cognitive

Pretest Score _____

For a more thorough review of the chapter, fill in the blanks of the programmed review without referring back to the text. Check your answers with the Answer Key at the end of the chapter and reread any sections in the text with which you had problems.

1. Although 2-year-olds have all the basic _____ of 6-year-olds, their expression of them is different. Expressions of dependency are direct and _____ at this age. In contrast, 6-year-olds are much more _____ and thoughtful; they are less quick to _____ and they _____ themselves better. Their coping patterns are more _____.

2. _____ perspectives emphasize the child's feelings, drives, and developmental conflicts. Freud emphasized that young children must learn to cope with powerful innate _____. Erikson has emphasized the growth of _____ and the need to balance it with dependence on parents during this period. _____ perspective emphasizes the link between _____ behavior and the environment. The child's behavior is shaped by external _____ and _____. _____ perspective emphasizes children's own thoughts and concepts as organizers of their social behavior.

Developmental Issues and Coping Patterns

3. Young children must deal with their need for _____, the strong drive to do things for themselves. One of the most important forces that children must learn to deal with is the _____ caused by fear and anxiety. _____ is a response to a specific stimulus or situation; whereas _____ is a more generalized emotional state. Many psychologists believe that anxiety inevitably accompanies _____, since the child attempts to avoid the pain of parental displeasure and discipline. Fear and anxiety may be increased or even created by the child's own _____, which may lead him to fear that his parents will _____ him. Or, anxiety may result from children's awareness of their own unacceptable _____.

4. In a classic study of children's fears, Jersild and Holmes found that younger children are most likely to be afraid of specific _____ or _____; whereas children aged 5 or 6 show fear of _____ or abstract things. The fears of the _____, of being _____, and of _____ things are now appearing at earlier ages.

5. When fears are mild, children can be gently and sympathetically encouraged to _____ and _____ them. With fears that are phobic, children may need systematic _____. The best way to help children cope with anxiety is to reduce the amount of unnecessary _____ in their lives. It is often helpful to simplify their lives for a few days by sticking to a daily _____, specifying clearly what is _____, and helping them to _____ special events. When children must cope with stress, parents and teachers should try to learn to recognize and interpret _____ reactions in children, provide a warm, secure base for children to regain _____, allow opportunities for children to discuss their _____, allow _____ behavior, and help children give _____ to the event or circumstance.

6. In response to more generalized feelings of anxiety, children learn strategies called _____ mechanisms, which are ways to disguise or reduce anxiety. A very common one is _____, in which the child simply pulls away from the situation either physically or mentally. _____ is the process of incorporating into oneself the values, attitudes, and beliefs or others. It helps reduce the anxiety that children feel about their own relative _____. When children attribute their own undesirable thoughts or actions to someone else, and in the process distort reality, they are using a defense called _____. And substitution of something or someone else for the real source of anger or fear is termed _____. The refusal to admit that a situation exists or that an event happened is called _____. An extreme form of this defense is _____, which involves the unconscious act of erasing a frightening event from conscious awareness. When a child returns to an earlier or more infantile form of behavior she is using the defense known as _____. With _____ children have thoughts or desires that make them anxious, and they react by behaving in a contradictory way. _____ is used when the child doesn't get something she wants.

7. A hundred years ago, children were afraid of _____ and _____. Fifty years ago, they worried about _____ and _____. Now their nightmares are populated with _____ and _____ robots.

8. Most parents expect their children to learn emotion _____, the process of dealing with their emotions in socially acceptable ways. Kopp refers to children's growing ability to control their behavior as self-_____, in which children adopt and _____ a composite of specific standards for behavior.

9. Children learn very early that open displays of negative feelings are _____ in public places. As children grow older, their parents' expectations for emotion regulation _____. Children who do not learn such lessons at home are at risk of being socially _____ outside the home. Children can come to _____ their angry feelings as a normal part of themselves, yet learn to control or redirect their _____ to such feelings. During the course of preschool socialization, spontaneous joy and affection become _____.

10. Two-year-olds are _____ creatures. In infancy this sensuality is _____, but the preschooler has a fascination with the _____ area. Children discover that self-_____ is pleasurable.

11. Out of the close connectedness 2-year-olds have with their caregivers emerges a new sense of _____, the conviction that they can do things themselves. The _____ between the opposing forces of autonomy and connectedness marks the early preschool period. Infants are usually fairly _____, but this changes at about the age of 2, when many children become quite uncooperative, a stage called the _____. They show their independence by saying _____. As they get older, they become more _____ and _____.

12. In an unfamiliar situation, 2-year-olds spend most of their time _____ close to their mothers. The older the children, the more they maintain _____ rather than _____ contact. In early childhood, children are discovering their own _____ and learning to control them. If their efforts at _____ are frustrated by criticism or punishment, they think they have failed and feel _____ and _____ about themselves.

117

13. Erikson suggests that the primary developmental conflict of the years from 3 to 6 is _____, which involves _____ and _____. Initiative refers to the _____ of young children as they ambitiously explore their surroundings. Guilt is inevitable when children go against their _____ wishes. The conflict between initiative and guilt is an extension of the toddler's struggle with _____.

14. An active, exploratory, self-confident approach to learning has been called learning _____. When children are made to feel anxious about their need for _____, they generally learn to deny, minimize, or disguise these needs. Children who are physically _____ or chronically _____ may have little opportunity to test their skills in mastering the environment.

Aggression and Prosocial Behavior

15. In the language of social psychology, _____ aggression is behavior intended to harm another or establish dominance. _____ aggression is harm as a byproduct of some behavior. _____ does not involve an intent to injure others. Physical aggression _____ at the beginning of early childhood. The frustration-aggression hypothesis states that all _____ is derived from _____, and that all _____ results in some direct or disguised form of _____. If children are punished for aggression, they will _____ these behaviors in the presence of the person who _____ them.

16. Observing aggressive _____ can strongly influence antisocial behavior. Imitation of models is more likely to occur when the observers sense a _____ between themselves and the model, or when the model is perceived as _____ or _____. Children are also more likely to imitate other children who have _____ personalities. Many varieties of potentially powerful models appear on _____. Before entering formal schooling, U.S. children are likely to have watched about _____ hours of television, a major _____ force in the United States. Studies have shown that exposure to televised violence produces significant _____ in the aggressiveness of viewers. Children also become _____ to the effects of violence and learn to _____ behaving violently when they believe they are right. Children develop _____ social beliefs and concepts by watching television. Television can also have a positive influence by teaching children many forms of _____ behavior.

17. _____ behavior is defined as actions intended to benefit others without the anticipation of an external reward. These actions fit under the definition of _____, the unselfish concern for the welfare of others. Prosocial behavior begins to develop in _____ childhood and may be found in children as young as _____. Young children who have a secure relationship with their _____ are more likely to attempt to comfort younger siblings.

18. In _____ playing, children act out roles as a way of seeing things from another's point of view. Parents who use _____ as discipline, give reasons for behaving in certain ways. U. S. children become less _____ as they grow older because they are raised to be _____.

Peers, Play, and Development of Social Skills

19. Children provide _____ support for each other in a variety of situations. They serve as _____, they _____ each other's behavior, and they encourage complex, imaginative _____. They continue to respond and react to each other in a fashion that supports and escalates the play, an interaction called social _____.

20. According to Parten, young children first engage in _____ play; then _____ play, in which the child's interaction consists merely of observing other children; _____ play, in which the child plays alongside, but does not interact with, another child; _____ play, in which children share materials and interact somewhat but do not coordinate their activities toward a goal; and _____ play, in which children engage in a single activity together with a common set of rules. Children often engage in _____ pretend play, which involves the construction and sharing of fantasies and imagination in accordance with specific rules. According to Vygotsky, it is through this play that children learn _____ and other _____ skills, as well as the ability to think about and _____ their own behavior.

21. Popular children are more _____ and display more _____ behavior during play with their peers. Unpopular children may either be more _____ or more _____, or they may simply be out of _____ with their peers' activities and social interactions.

22. Many young children create _____ companions who help them deal with _____, provide _____ during periods of loneliness, and provide _____. As many as _____ of preschoolers have imaginary friends and creation of such friends is associated with positive _____ characteristics. Those who have them are more _____, less _____, have more real _____, are more _____, and participate in more _____ activities. Imaginary companions also seem to help children learn _____ skills and practice _____.

Understanding Self and Others

23. By 21 months, the child is able to recognize herself in the _____ and by 2 years of age, language is full of assertions of _____. Children are increasing their understanding of self and others as _____ beings. Self-understanding is closely linked to the child's understanding of the _____ world.

24. During early childhood, children develop certain generalized _____ about themselves. Many of these ideas begin to emerge at a _____ level. They also develop _____ and begin measuring themselves against what they think they ought to be. Young children tend to define themselves in terms of _____ characteristics or _____. Older children are more likely to describe themselves in terms of their _____ and through their interpersonal _____. Young children commonly describe themselves through stories about their _____, and the tendency to portray themselves through _____ connections increases. They put together a cognitive theory or personal _____ about themselves that helps to integrate their behavior.

25. _____ is genetically determined and biological; _____ is culturally based and acquired. Gender _____ include what is appropriate for a male or a female to be or do.

119

26. Male babies are born slightly _____ and _____ than female babies. Newborn girls have slightly more mature _____ and are more responsive to _____. As toddlers, boys are more _____ and girls have an edge in _____ abilities. Gender-role _____ are fixed ideas about masculine and feminine behaviors.

27. The development of gender _____ (gender-based cultural standards or stereotypes) depends in part on the child's level of cognitive development and in part on aspects of the _____ that the child attends to. Children learn some aspects of gender roles by imitating _____ others and by being reinforced for gender _____ behavior. Children are _____ about what they imitate and internalize as they acquire gender _____, the sense of who they are as males and females. By about 2-1/2 most children can readily _____ people as boys or girls, or men or women. By age 5 to 7, children acquire gender _____, an understanding that their gender is _____ and permanent.

28. Many cognitive-developmental psychologists believe that children are intrinsically motivated to acquire values, interests, and behaviors consistent with their gender, a process called self _____. Exaggerated gender-specific behavior severely _____ the emotional and intellectual development of both women and men. A blend of traits in either a woman or a man is called _____ personality and is formed by specific child-rearing practices and parental attitudes that encourage desirable _____ gender behaviors.

29. Central to the development of social concepts and rules is _____ by which children learn to make the values and moral standards of their society part of their self-concept. Cognitive theorists point out that children's attempts to regulate their own behavior are influenced by their developing _____ and their developing _____ concepts. A clear understanding of friendship does not occur until _____ childhood. Children as young as 3 years are able to justify their behavior in terms of _____ rules or the _____ of an action.

Family Dynamics

30. Parental _____ refers to restrictiveness, and _____ refers to affection and approval. According to Baumrind, _____ parents combine a high degree of control with warmth, acceptance, and encouragement of the growing autonomy of their children. They set limits on behavior, but also provide _____. They are willing to _____ to their children's objections and to be _____ when it is appropriate. Their children are the most self-_____, self-_____, and socially _____, and develop higher _____.

31. Baumrind described _____ parents as controlling and adhering rigidly to rules. They tend to be low in warmth, issue _____ and expect them to be _____. Their children tend to be _____ and _____ and may become _____ and _____.

32. According to Baumrind, _____ parents are likely to put few if any restraints on the child's behavior. They are so intent in showing their children unconditional _____ that they fail to perform important parental functions. Their children tend to be _____ and _____ as well as self-_____, impulsive, and _____ inept.

33. _____ parents don't set _____ for their children either because they do not _____ or because their own lives are so _____ that they don't have enough energy left over to provide guidance. The children feel free to give rein to their most _____ impulses.

34. _____ parents conform to male and female roles in which the father may be _____ and the mother more _____ and _____.

35. Maccoby focused on the way parents and children _____. As children get older, parents need to _____ with them in order to make decisions. There must be an evolution to more _____-control and self-responsibility. Ideally parents and children come to agree on shared _____. Families that achieve this balance have a fairly high degree of _____, and their interactions are _____ and mutually _____.

36. In the United States, official reports of child abuse and neglect total about _____ a year. Physical abuse most often occurs at the hands of the child's _____. When someone other than a parent is responsible, _____ abusers outnumber _____ by four to one. The proportion of male _____ abusers is nearly 95%. Sexual abuse is more often inflicted on _____, physical abuse more often on _____. _____ children sustain more serious injuries than _____ ones. Physical abuse is always accompanied by _____ components. Children's _____ can be irreparably damaged and they may find it difficult to _____ anyone. Abused children also have trouble controlling their _____ and behavior and tend to be less _____ competent. A history of family conflict involving verbal and physical abuse may have a cumulative impact on children's reaction to _____.

37. The psychiatric explanation of child abuse focuses on the personality and family background of the _____. The _____ explanations focus on aspects of U.S. culture. In periods of high _____, male violence against wives and children increases. Abusive parents are often _____ from relatives, friends, and other support systems. The situational model looks at _____ factors with an emphasis on _____ among family members and the recognition that children are _____ participants in the process. Children with physical _____ or mental _____ or difficult _____ are at especially high risk.

38. Parenting guidelines include fostering an atmosphere of _____, caring and mutual _____ among family members; concentrating more on _____ desirable behaviors than on _____ undesirable ones; setting _____ expectations and demands, firmly _____ the demands, and being _____; avoiding the unnecessary use of _____, helping children gain a sense of _____ over themselves and their environment; and using _____ reasoning (induction) to help children understand social rules.

39. Siblings are the first and closest _____ who affect children's personality development. Although birth order seems to have few clear, consistent, and predictable effects on _____, many studies have found that _____ children have higher IQs and achieve more in school and in careers. Only children are also high _____, although their IQs tend to be slightly _____ on the average. Older siblings are powerful _____. The closer siblings are in _____ the more intense the relationship.

Now that you have gone through the programmed review, you should be able to answer these questions easily. Try to answer them without referring back to the text. Then record your score in the space provided and subtract the pretest score for your improvement score.

1. Which of the following theories emphasizes the link between cognition, behavior and the environment?
   a. cognitive developmental
   b. psychodynamic
   c. social learning
   d. evolutionary

2. A response to a specific stimulus is _____; whereas _____ is a more generalized state.
   a. fear; anxiety
   b. shame; guilt
   c. anxiety; fear
   d. guilt; shame

3. According to psychoanalytic theory, children learn to deal with feelings of anxiety by using strategies called
   a. anxiety reduction techniques.
   b. desensitizations.
   c. avoidances.
   d. defense mechanisms.

4. The most direct defense mechanism possible is
   a. denial.
   b. regression.
   c. reaction formation.
   d. withdrawal.

5. The tendency to attribute one's own undesirable thoughts or actions to someone else is called
   a. projection.
   b. reaction formation.
   c. denial.
   d. regression.

6. When Sally refuses to believe that her pet turtle has died, she is using the defense mechanism of
   a. regression.
   b. repression.
   c. denial.
   d. withdrawal.

7. When Bert's baby brother was born, Bert went back to sucking his thumb. This would be an example of
   a. repression.
   b. regression.
   c. withdrawal.
   d. rationalization.

8. Today's children are most likely to be afraid of
   a. extraterrestrials.
   b. wolves.
   c. goblins.
   d. bogeymen.

9. Dealing with emotions in socially acceptable ways is
   a. defense mechanisms.
   b. emotion regulation.
   c. self-regulation.
   d. compliance.

10. Behavior intended to harm another or establish dominance is
    a. instrumental aggression.
    b. assertiveness.
    c. hostile aggression.
    d. emotion regulation.

11. When a child's interaction consists merely of observing other children, the child is engaged in which type of play?
    a. solitary
    b. onlooker
    c. parallel
    d. cooperative

12. When children share materials and interact somewhat, but do not coordinate their activities toward a single theme or goal, they are engaged in which type of play?
    a. solitary
    b. onlooker
    c. associative
    d. cooperative

13. The sociological explanation of child abuse views all of the following as contributors to child abuse EXCEPT
    a. parental mental illness.
    b. cultural violence.
    c. poverty.
    d. social isolation.

14. As many as _____ percent of preschoolers have imaginary friends.
    a. 100
    b. 95
    c. 65
    d. 40

15. The concept that gender is stable and stays the same despite changes in superficial appearance is called gender
    a. identity.
    b. stability.
    c. constancy.
    d. integration.

16. Parents who combine a high degree of control with warmth, acceptance, and encouragement of the growing autonomy of their children are
    a. authoritative.
    b. authoritarian.
    c. permissive.
    d. indifferent.

17. Which parenting style combines no limits and little affection?
    a. authoritative
    b. authoritarian
    c. indifferent
    d. permissive

18. Children whose parents are authoritarian are likely to be
    a. independent and stable.
    b. aggressive and rebellious.
    c. hostile and destructive.
    d. self-controlled and indifferent.

19. Self-controlled, self-reliant, and socially competent children probably have parents who are
    a. authoritative.
    b. authoritarian.
    c. indifferent.
    d. permissive.

20. Who states that parents and children should have shared goals?
    a. Freud
    b. Baumrind
    c. Erikson
    d. Maccoby

Posttest Score _____

Pretest Score _____

Improvement _____

124

ESSAY QUESTIONS

In order to develop your mastery of this chapter, answer the following questions as completely as possible. Refer to the text for material to support your answers.

1. Compare and contrast the psychodynamic, social-learning, and cognitive developmental theories.

2. Describe how children's fears have changed over the last century and discuss how these fears change with the age of the child.

3. What would you advise a parent to do to help his or her child deal with stress?

4. Describe a typical child going through Erikson's stage of initiative versus guilt.

5. Describe the various theories of the causes of aggression and indicate which one you think is the most acceptable.

6. If you were advising a parent, which type of parenting style would you recommend? Why?

7. Describe the characteristics of popular children. Give at least two examples of popular children you have known.

8. Discuss the importance of imaginary friends in early childhood.

9. Trace the development of the self concept throughout the first five years of life.

10. Describe the types of child abuse and the various explanations of its cause.

ANSWER KEY

Key Names

1. c   2. e   3. b   4. a   5. d

Pretest

1. b	5. c	9. b	13. d	17. d
2. a	6. a	10. c	14. a	18. c
3. c	7. b	11. d	15. b	19. a
4. d	8. d	12. c	16. b	20. a

Programmed Review

1. emotions, physical, verbal, anger, control, refined
2. Psychodynamic, emotions, autonomy, Social-learning, cognition, rewards, punishment, Cognitive developmental
3. autonomy, stress, Fear, anxiety, socialization, imagination, reject, feelings
4. objects, situations, imaginary, dark, alone, unfamiliar
5. confront, overcome, desensitization, stress, routines, expected, anticipate, stress, confidence, feelings, immature, meaning
6. defense, withdrawal, Identification, helplessness, projection, displacement, denial, repression, regression, reaction formation, rationalization
7. wolves, bears, goblins, bogeymen, extraterrestrials, killer
8. regulation, regulation, internalize
9. unacceptable, increase, rejected, accept, reactions, subdue
10. sensual, oral, genital, stimulation
11. autonomy, ambivalence, cooperative, "terrible twos," "No," compliant, cooperative
12. physically, verbal, physical, bodies, autonomy, ashamed, doubtful
13. initiative versus guilt, mastery, competence, purposefulness, parents', autonomy
14. competence, autonomy, disabled, ill
15. hostile, Instrumental, Assertiveness, increases, aggression, frustration, aggression, avoid, punished
16. models, similarity, powerful, competent, dominant, television, 4,000, socializing, increase, desensitized, justify, unrealistic, prosocial
17. Prosocial, altruism, early childhood, 2, caregivers
18. role, induction, cooperative, competitive
19. emotional, models, reinforce, play, reciprocity
20. solitary, onlooker, parallel, associative, cooperative, social, cooperation, social, regulate
21. cooperative, prosocial, aggressive, withdrawn, sync
22. imaginary, fears, companionship, reassurance, 65%, personality, sociable, shy, friends, creative, family, social, conversations
23. mirror, possession, separate, social
24. attitudes, nonverbal, ideals, physical, possessions, activities, relationships, families, social, script
25. Sex, gender, roles
26. longer, heavier, skeletons, touch, aggressive, verbal, stereotypes
27. schemes, culture, significance, appropriate, selective, identity, label, constancy, consistent
28. socialization, limits, androgynous, cross
29. internalization, self-concept, social, middle, social, consequences
30. control, warmth, authoritative, explanations, listen, flexible, reliant, controlled, competent, self-esteem

31. authoritarian, commands, obeyed, withdrawn, fearful, rebellious, aggressive
32. permissive, love, rebellious, aggressive, indulgent, socially
33. Indifferent, limits, care, stressful, destructive
34. Traditional, authoritarian, nurturant, permissive
35. interact, negotiate, self, goals, intimacy, stable, rewarding
36. one million, parents, male, female, sexual, girls, boys, younger, older, psychological, self-esteem, trust, emotions, socially, anger
37. parents, sociological, unemployment, isolated, environmental, interaction, active, disabilities, disorders, temperaments
38. warmth, support, promoting, eliminating, realistic, enforce, consistent, power, control, verbal
38. peers, personality, oldest, achievers, models, age

Posttest

1. c	5. a	9. b	13. a	17. c
2. a	6. c	10. c	14. c	18. b
3. d	7. b	11. b	15. c	19. a
4. d	8. a	12. c	16. a	20. d

9

Middle Childhood: Physical and Cognitive Development

CHAPTER OUTLINE

Physical and Motor Development
    Physical Growth and Change
    Internal Changes
    Development of Motor Skills
    Health, Fitness, and Accidents

Cognitive Development
    Piaget and Concrete Operational Thinking
    Information Processing
    Language and Literacy

Intelligence and Achievement
    Intelligence Testing
    The Nature of Intelligence
    Limitations of Testing

Learning and Thinking in School
    New Demands and Expectations
    Developing Competent Learners and Critical Thinkers
    Success in School

Developmental Disorders
    Mental Retardation
    Learning Disorders
    Attention-deficit/Hyperactivity Disorder

KEY TERMS AND CONCEPTS

As you read through the chapter in the text, locate and write out the definition for each of the following terms. Be sure that you write out each definition.

Achievement motivation

Attention-deficit/hyperactivity disorder (ADHD)

Control processes

Criterion-referenced test

Deviation IQ

Dyscalculia

Dysgraphia

Dyslexia

Intelligence quotient

Learning disorders

Literacy

Mental retardation

Metacognition

Norm-referenced test

Physical education

KEY NAMES

Try to match each of the following names to his or her contribution to the field of psychology. Check your answers with the Answer Key at the end of this chapter.

_____ 1. Alfred Binet
a. achievement motivation

_____ 2. Howard Gardner
b. concrete operational thought

_____ 3. David McClelland
c. deviation IQ

_____ 4. Jean Piaget
d. mental age

_____ 5. Robert Sternberg
e. seven intelligences

_____ 6. Lewis Terman
f. Stanford-Binet

_____ 7. David Wechsler
g. triarchic concept of intelligence

To test your preliminary knowledge of the chapter, answer each of the following questions without referring back to the text. Check your answers with the Answer Key at the end of this chapter and record your score (the number right) in the space provided at the end of this section.

1. According to Erikson, the child in middle childhood is in the period of
    a. trust.
    b. initiative.
    c. industry.
    d. identity.

2. The "growing pains" experienced by children in middle childhood
    a. are usually most painful during the day.
    b. are usually episodes of stiffness and aching.
    c. indicate that there has been a serious injury.
    d. occur only in boys.

3. School-age children experience fewer illnesses than do younger children because of all of the following EXCEPT
    a. preschoolers are genetically programmed to be more susceptible to illness.
    b. school-age children have greater immunity because of previous exposure.
    c. school-age children practice somewhat better nutrition.
    d. school-age children have acquired some safety habits.

4. If one parent is obese, the child has a _____ percent chance of becoming obese.
    a. 20
    b. 40
    c. 60
    d. 80

5. Physical fitness requires that children engage in a sport or exercise that involves all of the following EXCEPT
    a. flexibility.
    b. muscle endurance.
    c. cardiovascular functioning.
    d. weight loss.

6. According to Piaget, the child in middle childhood is in the _____ stage.
    a. sensorimotor
    b. preoperational
    c. concrete operational
    d. formal operational

7. Training is most effective when children reach a(n)
   a. state of readiness.
   b. average level of intelligence at least.
   c. age of six years.
   d. critical period for learning.

8. Which term includes the other three?
   a. rehearsal
   b. scripts
   c. mental imagery
   d. control processes

9. The whole-language approach focuses on the
   a. distinct point at which children develop reading readiness.
   b. concept of emergent literacy.
   c. distinct point at which children develop writing readiness.
   d. idea that reading and writing are distinctly separate skills.

10. When a child is tested in order to determine the extent to which she has mastered specific skills and objectives, the test is most likely to be a(n)
    a. norm-referenced test.
    b. criterion-referenced test.
    c. intelligence test.
    d. achievement test.

11. Which of the following does not belong with the other?
    a. Binet
    b. Piaget
    c. Sternberg
    d. Wechsler

12. Using the formula for IQ, what would be the IQ of an 8-year-old child with a mental age of 10?
    a. 125
    b. 110
    c. 100
    d. 80

13. According to Sternberg, intelligence that involves the capacity to cope with new tasks or situations is
    a. triarchic.
    b. componential.
    c. experiential.
    d. contextual.

14. According to recent research, teachers in public schools spend _____ percent of the time in every half hour on academic work.
    a. 40 - 50
    b. 30 - 40
    c. 20 - 25
    d. 10 - 15

15. According to Costa, all of the following are skills children need to develop EXCEPT
    a. remembering.
    b. reasoning.
    c. relearning.
    d. relating.

16. Research indicates that girls tend to outperform boys in
    a. quantitative tasks.
    b. spatial tasks.
    c. verbal skills.
    d. physical skills.

17. On the PSAT, boys score higher than girls on
    a. grammar.
    b. spelling.
    c. perceptual speed.
    d. high school mathematics.

18. Parents of children who succeed in school
    a. have realistic beliefs about their child's abilities.
    b. are authoritarian.
    c. avoid talking too much to their children.
    d. are strict disciplinarians.

19. Moderate mental retardation falls in the IQ range of
    a. 10 to 25.
    b. 25 to 40.
    c. 40 to 55.
    d. 55 to 70.

20. Difficulty with writing is called
    a. dyslexia.
    b. dysgraphia.
    c. dyscalculia.
    d. dysfunction.

Pretest score _____

Try to fill in each of the blanks in this chapter review without referring back to the text. Check your answers with the Answer Key at the end of this chapter and then go back to the text and reread any sections that gave you trouble.

1. For most children, middle childhood--the period from _____ years--is a time for _____ and _____ skills. Erikson has referred to middle childhood as the period of _____.

Physical and Motor Development

2. During middle childhood, growth is _____ and _____ until the adolescent growth _____ begins. Girls are slightly _____ and _____ than boys until age 9, when girls' growth _____ because of hormonal changes that occur earlier in girls than in boys.

3. Bones grow longer, and this growth may be associated with growing _____, episodes of stiffness and aching caused by skeletal growth that are particularly common at _____. At this time of development, stringent _____ training may cause injuries. There is also a loss of "baby" _____, and when the first permanent teeth emerge, they often appear too _____ for the mouth.

4. Fat deposits gradually _____ until 6 to 8 years of age, with a more marked decrease in _____. The strength of girls and boys is _____ throughout middle childhood .

5. Between 6 and 8 years, the frontal lobe of the brain _____ slightly because of continuous branching of neurons. In addition, _____ of the brain's hemispheres becomes more pronounced. The corpus callosum also becomes more _____ in both structure and function.

6. Children's newly acquired physical abilities are reflected in their interest in _____ and daredevil _____. Gender differences in motor skills before the onset of puberty are more a function of _____ and _____ expectations than of real physical differences. Most of the fine motor skills required for _____ develop during a child's sixth and seventh years.

7. Most 6- to 12-year-olds experience _____ illnesses, partly because of greater _____ due to previous exposure. Also, most school-age children have better _____, health, and _____ habits. During this period, _____, or myopia, is often diagnosed and as a result, _____ of white, middle-class sixth graders have been fitted with glasses. It has been suggested that minor illnesses play a positive role in children's _____ development because they develop a realistic _____ of the role of "being sick."

8. A seriously _____ child weighs the same as or more than 95% of children of the same age. The child of one obese parent has a _____ chance of becoming obese; the proportion leaps to _____ if both parents are obese. If the child is adopted, the weight of her _____ parents has the greatest influence on her adult weight. One environmental factor contributing to this problem is _____ viewing. Children should not be placed on drastic _____ programs even if they are seriously overweight because they need a balanced, nutritious diet. Peers may _____ overweight children, resulting in a negative _____.

9. Physical _____ is the optimal function of the heart, lungs, muscles, and blood vessels. It requires that children engage in a sport or exercise that involves _____, muscle _____, muscle _____, and _____ efficiency.

10. Physical _____ is defined as a program of carefully planned and conducted motor activities that prepare students for skillful, fit, and knowledgeable performance. A national health objective calls for physical education classes to engage students in _____ physical exercise, preferably _____ activities such as jogging and swimming for at least _____ of class time.

11. From infancy on, children's need to perform their newfound skills often conflicts with their need for _____ against the dangers associated with these skills. Children's risk of harming themselves often exceeds their ability to foresee the _____ of their actions. About half of all deaths in middle childhood results from _____ and _____.

Cognitive Development

12. In Piaget's theory, the period between ages 5 and 7 marks the _____ from preoperational to concrete operational thought. Thought becomes less _____ and _____ and more _____. Children can evaluate _____ relationships, especially if they have the concrete object right in front of them. School-age children can now use logical _____. They know that differences between similar objects can be _____. And they can _____ about the world.

13. Children learn concrete operational thought largely on their _____. As they _____ explore their physical environment, they acquire a more sophisticated form of thinking.

14. Training is most effective when children have reached a state of _____. Many of the basic concepts presented by Piaget have been applied to _____, especially in the areas of science and math, including the use of _____ objects for teaching 5- to 7-year-olds. Addition and subtraction involve an understanding of _____.

15. Children are _____ learners, they _____ their own theories about how the world operates, and they are motivated to _____ these theories when pieces of information do not fit. Educational psychologists warn against structuring education in ways that encourage children to seek _____ from teachers rather than to solve problems for their own sake. They emphasize that children's interest in learning depends on the _____ rewards they find in the encounter with the subject matter itself, and that children gain confidence from _____ problems or _____ principles. They point out that too often, teachers instruct young children by _____ them instead of _____ them. Children need to learn by actively _____ ideas and relationships, and by solving problems in _____ contexts.

16. Information-processing theorists see the human mind as analogous to a _____. Between 5 and 7, most children begin making conscious efforts to _____ information. They look at material to be remembered and begin to _____ it over and over to themselves. Later, they may _____ the material into categories. Elementary schoolchildren learn different strategies to help them remember, which are sometimes called _____ processes: _____, organization, _____ elaboration, mental _____, retrieval, and _____.

17. _____ refers to the intellectual processes that enable children to monitor their own thinking, memory, knowledge, goals, and actions. The ability to monitor one's own thinking and memory begins at about age _____ and emerges more fully between ages _____.

`18. The recognition that oral and written language learning are interconnected has led to the _____ approach to literacy. Theorists focus on the concept of _____ literacy, the skills associated with oral and written language acquisition that begin to develop in _____.

19. Children learn to read and write in the context of relevant _____ situations. Children acquire literacy while _____ with their parents, siblings, teachers, and peers. Teachers help children _____ the knowledge and skills they need to become expert readers and writers, but peer interactions give children the opportunity to _____ ideas and problems spontaneously.

Intelligence and Achievement

20. _____ referenced tests measure the extent to which a child has mastered specific skills or objectives. _____-referenced tests compare one child's score with the scores of a large number of other children.

21. The first comprehensive intelligence test was designed in the early twentieth century by _____. In 1916, his test was revised by _____ at Stanford University and introduced to the Untied States as the _____. To measure intelligence, Binet used test items involving _____ solving, word _____, and general _____. The test score he used was a _____ age. Later psychologists expressed the relationship between mental and chronological age as the _____. IQ is now assessed by a _____ IQ.

22. On the bell-shaped curve, about _____ of the general population scores between an IQ of 85 and 115 and _____ percent of the population falls between an IQ of 70 and 130, leaving about _____ percent as mentally retarded and _____ percent as gifted.

23. _____ generated a great deal of controversy when he stated his belief that 80% of what is measured on IQ tests is _____ and only 20% is determined by a child's _____. The consensus currently is that both factors are _____ important in determining how well a child will do on an IQ test.

24. Gardner identified _____ distinct intelligences. Sternberg developed a _____ concept of intelligence, which includes _____ intelligence involving adaptation to the environment, _____ intelligence involving the capacity to cope with new tasks or situations as well as with old ones, and _____ intelligence, which corresponds to the abilities measured by IQ tests.

25. Some minority groups believe that tests are unfair to those who have different _____ backgrounds. And research also suggests that minority children may be victims of a _____ prophecy. They have acquired low _____ about their academic performances on tests designed by the white community, and these low expectations further lower their _____, and thus their test scores.

Learning and Thinking in School

26. Regardless of the school a child enters, there is always a _____ between what is acceptable at home and what is expected in the classroom. How well a child has coped with dependency, autonomy, authority, _____ and _____ will influence his adjustment to school. Relations with classmates involve finding the right balance between _____ and _____, and relations with teachers involve a compromise between _____ and _____.

27. With knowledge becoming obsolete literally overnight, children need to become _____ learners. Costa and colleagues believe that children need to develop six kinds of thought, including _____ or recalling a fact, idea, or concept; _____, which is following a model or procedure; _____, or relating a specific instance to a general principle or concept; _____, which is extending knowledge to a new context for an original solution; _____, or connecting newly acquired knowledge with past or personal experience; and _____, or exploring the thought itself and how it occurred.

28. McClelland concluded that _____ motivation is an acquired, culturally based drive. Maccoby and Jacklin concluded that girls tend to outperform boys in _____ skills and boys tend to do better in _____ and _____ skills. Different _____ expectations for boys and girls profoundly influence behavior. Recent research has found that gender differences have _____ in recent years, but the gender gap remains constant in the higher levels of performance of high school _____. Negative experiences in the _____ and at _____, combined with widely accepted _____ of males and females, do more to produce sex differences than actual _____ physiology.

29. Parents of successful children have _____ beliefs about their children's current abilities but high _____ for the future. These parents help their children develop _____ by encouraging age-appropriate tasks. Parent-child relationships are _____ and _____ and parents have _____ and _____ strategies that are authoritative. Parents _____ to their children, _____ to them, _____ to them, and have regular _____ with them.

Developmental Disorders

30. The DSM-IV states that to be diagnosed as mentally retarded a child must be significantly _____ in intellectual functioning, impaired in _____ behaviors, and the onset must be before age _____.

31. An IQ of 55 to 70 designates _____ retardation, 40 to 55 designates _____ retardation, 25 to 40 designates _____ retardation, and below 25 designates _____ retardation.

32. _____ mental retardation is caused by neurological defects and physical disabilities. _____ retardation arises from social and environmental factors.

33. There are three main categories of learning disorders: _____ (difficulty in learning how to read), _____ (difficulty with writing), and _____ (difficulty with math).

34. Dyslexic children may be delayed in learning to _____, or their speech may be at a lower _____ level than that of their age mates. It is clear that _____ plays a role in the disorder. It runs in the same families that exhibit _____. Treatment involves intensive _____ work in reading and language, including carefully sequenced _____ instruction.

35. There are many suggested causes for ADD including malnutrition, _____ poisoning, organic _____ damage, heredity, _____ abnormalities, prenatal exposure to _____, and _____ during fetal development or childbirth. Studies of identical and fraternal twins suggest a strong _____ link. Some children respond to the drug _____, a stimulant in the amphetamine family. The drug appears to lower children's threshold of _____ to events around them. An alternative form of treatment is _____ management.

POSTTEST

Now answer the following questions, again without referring back to the text. Check your answers with the Answer Key at the end of this chapter and record your score in the space provided at the end of this section. Then record your pretest score, subtract and find your improvement score.

1. Girls are slightly shorter and lighter than boys until their growth accelerates at approximately what age?
   a. 5
   b. 7
   c. 9
   d. 11

2. Which of the following is LEAST responsible for gender differences in motor skills before the onset of puberty?
   a. physical differences
   b. opportunity
   c. cultural factors
   d. practice

3. A child who weighs as much as or more than _____ of children of the same age is considered seriously overweight.
   a. 35 percent
   b. 55 percent
   c. 75 percent
   d. 95 percent

4. Which of the following causes the most deaths in children?
   a. congenital abnormalities
   b. AIDS
   c. cancer
   d. accidents

5. Which of the following would be the best physical activity for schools to use in physical education classes?
   a. parallel bars
   b. weight-lifting
   c. jogging
   d. hurdles

6. In the concrete operational stage of cognitive development, thought becomes
   a. more intuitive.
   b. less egocentric.
   c. less logical.
   d. more irreversible.

7. Which of the following is an application of Piaget's concepts in a school setting?
   a. Children are asked to listen and take notes.
   b. Teachers lecture instead of demonstrating.
   c. Blue ribbons and trophies are awarded on a daily basis.
   d. Children are asked to discover relationships.

8. The strategies that children learn to help them remember things are generally called
   a. control processes.
   b. remembering strategies.
   c. metamemory keys.
   d. cognitive tools.

9. Intellectual processes that enable children to monitor their own thinking, memory, and knowledge are
   a. control processes.
   b. guidance instruments.
   c. thinking styles.
   d. metacognition.

10. Who developed the first comprehensive intelligence test?
    a. Wechsler
    b. Terman
    c. Sternberg
    d. Binet

11. Today's intelligence tests yield which measure of a child's intelligence?
    a. mental age
    b. deviation IQ
    c. ratio IQ
    d. chronological age

12. According to Jensen, how much of IQ is inherited?
    a. 20 percent
    b. 40 percent
    c. 60 percent
    d. 80 percent

13. Gardner identified how many categories of intelligence?
    a. 3
    b. 5
    c. 7
    d. 9

14. According to Sternberg, _____ intelligence involves adaptation to the environment.
    a. contextual
    b. experiential
    c. componential
    d. inherited

15. Children who do well in school are most likely to have parents who use which parenting style?
    a. authoritative
    b. authoritarian
    c. permissive
    d. indulgent

16. Severe mental retardation includes IQs between
    a. 10 and 25.
    b. 25 and 40.
    c. 40 and 55.
    d. 55 and 70.

17. Most mild to moderate retardation is
    a. genetic.
    b. organic.
    c. custodial/vegetative.
    d. psychosocial.

18. Up to _____ percent of children with learning disorders are boys.
    a. 80
    b. 70
    c. 60
    d. 50

19. A child who has difficulty in math would be diagnosed as having
    a. dyslexia.
    b. dysgraphia.
    c. dyscalculia.
    d. hyperactivity.

20. All of the following might be given to a hyperactive child EXCEPT
    a. Ritalin.
    b. a sedative.
    c. an amphetamine.
    d. a stimulant

Posttest score _____

Pretest score _____

Improvement _____

ESSAY QUESTIONS

To reinforce your knowledge of this chapter, answer each of the following questions as thoroughly as you can, referring back to the text for material to support your answer. Think carefully about each question.

1. Compare the health of preschool children with those in middle childhood and explain the difference. Why do some theorists believe that the experience of childhood illnesses plays a positive role in psychological development?

2. A parent approaches you for advice about dealing with his or her overweight grade-school aged child. What advice would you give?

3. Briefly compare the cognitive development of the preoperational and the concrete operational child.

4. How have Piaget's concepts been applied to education? Give specific examples that you have experienced.

5. Describe the memory control processes used by children in middle childhood. Do adults use these processes too?

6. What are the adjustments a child must make when entering school for the first time? What factors in the child's home environment will help in making those adjustments?

7. Costa and colleagues state that children need to develop six kinds of thought. List and describe them.

8. Explain the sex differences that exist during the middle childhood years and discuss the possible causes of such differences where they exist.

9. Describe the approaches to intelligence suggested by Gardner and Sternberg. Which of these would be the most difficult to test? Why?

10. Describe the parental variables that lead to school success.

ANSWER KEY

Key Names

1. d	3. a	5. g	7. c
2. e	4. b	6. f	

Pretest

1. c	5. d	9. b	13. c	17. d
2. b	6. c	10. b	14. d	18. a
3. a	7. a	11. b	15. c	19. c
4. b	8. d	12. a	16. c	20. b

Programmed Review

1. 6 to 12, learning, refining, industry
2. slower, steadier, spurt, shorter, lighter, accelerates
3. pains, night, physical, teeth, big
4. decrease, boys, comparable
5. increases, lateralization, mature
6. sports, stunts, opportunity, cultural, writing
7. few, immunity, nutrition, safety, nearsightedness, 25 percent, psychological, understanding
8. overweight, 40 percent, 80 percent, biological, television, weight-loss, reject, self-image
9. fitness, flexibility, endurance, strength, cardiovascular
10. education, active, lifelong, 50 percent
11. protection, consequences, injuries, accidents
12. transition, intuitive, egocentric, logical, cause-and-effect, inference, measured, theorize
13. own, actively
14. readiness, education, concrete, reversibility
15. active, construct, change, praise, intrinsic, mastering, discover, telling, showing, exploring, realistic
16. computer, memorize, repeat, organize, control, rehearsal, semantic, imagery, scripts
17. Metacognition, 6, 7 and 10
18. whole-language, emergent, infancy
19. social, interacting, learn, discuss
20. Criterion, Norm

141

21. Binet, Terman, Stanford-Binet, problem, definitions, knowledge, mental, IQ, deviation
22. two-thirds, 96, 2, 2
23. Jensen, inherited, environment, equally
24. seven, triarchic, contextual, experiential, componential
25. subcultural, self-fulfilling, expectations, self-confidence
26. gap, aggression, conscience, cooperation, competition, autonomy, obedience
27. lifelong, remembering, repeating, reasoning, reorganizing, relating, reflecting
28. achievement, verbal, quantitative, spatial, social, declined, mathematics, classroom, home, stereotypes, brain
29. realistic, expectations, self-confidence, warm, affectionate, discipline, control, talk, read, listen, conversations
30. subaverage, adaptive, 18
31. mild, moderate, severe, profound
32. biological, psychosocial
33. dyslexia, dysgraphia, dyscalculia
34. speak, developmental, heredity, left-handedness, remedial, tutorial
35. lead, brain, intrauterine, drugs, anoxia, genetic, Ritalin, sensitivity, educational

Posttest

1. c	5. c	9. d	13. c	17. d
2. a	6. b	10. d	14. a	18. a
3. d	7. d	11. b	15. a	19. c
4. d	8. a	12. d	16. b	20. b

10
Middle Childhood: Personality and Sociocultural Development

CHAPTER OUTLINE

Personality Development in an Expanding Social World
    Three Perspectives on Middle Childhood
    Self-concept

Social Knowledge and Reasoning
    Development of Social Cognition
    Piaget on Moral Reasoning and Judgment
    Kohlberg's Six-Stage Theory
    Gilligan's Alternative View
    Eisenberg's View

Continuing Family Influences
    Parent-child Interactions and Relationships
    The Changing Nature of the Family
    Children of Divorce

Peer Relationships and Social Competence
    Concepts of Friendship
    Functions of Friendship
    Peer Groups
    In-groups, Out-groups, and Prejudice

KEY TERMS AND CONCEPTS

In order to better understand the material in this chapter, look up each of the following terms in the text and write out its definition.

Coregulation   Prejudice
Discrimination   Reconstituted family
Moral absolutism   Resilient children
Moral dilemmas   Self-esteem
Moral identity   Self-regulated behavior
Moral realism   Social cognition
Moral relativism   Social inference
Morality   Social regulations
Peer group   Social responsibility

KEY NAMES

After reading the chapter in the text, try to match each of the following individuals with his or her contribution to the field of psychology. Check your answers with the Answer Key provided at the end of this chapter.

_____1. Carol Gilligan   a. coregulation

_____2. Erik Erikson   b. friendships

_____3. Sigmund Freud   c. industry versus inferiority

_____4. Lawrence Kohlberg   d. justice and care perspectives

_____5. Eleanor Maccoby   e. latency

_____6. Jean Piaget   f. moral realism and relativism

_____7. Robert Selman   g. resilient children

_____8. Emmy Werner   h. three levels of moral reasoning

Try to answer each of the following questions without referring back to the text. Check your answers with the Answer Key at the end of this chapter and record your Pretest score in the space provided at the end of this section.

1. Freud described middle childhood as a period of
   a. latency.
   b. industry versus inferiority.
   c. concrete operations.
   d. the genital stage.

2. Which of the following theorists viewed morality from a cognitive perspective?
   a. Erikson
   b. Freud
   c. Kohlberg
   d. Skinner

3. Seeing oneself in a favorable or unfavorable light is
   a. self-concept.
   b. self-esteem.
   c. self-actualization.
   d. self-absorption.

4. Thought, knowledge, and understanding that involve the social world is
   a. socialization.
   b. sociology.
   c. social cognition.
   d. social regulation.

5. Customs and conventions are social
   a. responsibilities.
   b. regulations.
   c. inferences.
   d. concepts.

6. Which of the following includes the other three?
   a. social cognition
   b. social inference
   c. social regulations
   d. social responsibility

7. Social learning theorists believe that children learn morality through
   a. conditioning and observational learning.
   b. thinking and reasoning.
   c. strict discipline.
   d. anxiety caused by guilt and shame.

8. According to Piaget, children in the stage of moral realism judge actions by the
   a. intentions of the actor.
   b. intentions of the recipient of the action.
   c. consequences of the action.
   d. amount of guilt an individual feels.

9. In Kohlberg's first stage of moral development, an individual behaves morally
   a. to avoid punishment.
   b. to obtain reward.
   c. to maintain authority.
   d. because of individual principles.

10. According to Gilligan, men's moral decisions are based on
    a. induction.
    b. coregulation.
    c. caring.
    d. justice.

11. Kohlberg's theory has been criticized on the basis of moral
    a. absolutism.
    b. realism.
    c. relativism.
    d. justice.

12. About _____ of all births today are to unmarried mothers.
    a. one-eighth
    b. one-quarter
    c. one-third
    d. one-half

13. Werner found that "resilient" children had been temperamentally _____ babies.
    a. easy
    b. difficult
    c. slow-to-warm-up
    d. powerful

14. Nearly _____ of all marriages in the United States now end in divorce.
    a. one-quarter
    b. one-third
    c. one-half
    d. two-thirds

15. The way children respond to divorce depends on all of the following EXCEPT
    a. the amount of hostility accompanying the divorce.
    b. the amount of actual change in the child's life.
    c. the nature of the parent-child relationship.
    d. the income of both the custodial and noncustodial parent.

16. According to Selman, the first stage of friendship is based on
    a. reciprocity.
    b. physical or geographic considerations.
    c. genuine give-and-take.
    d. a stable continuing relationship.

17. According to Selman, friends are seen as people who help each other and the concept of trust appears in friendship stage
    a. 1.
    b. 2.
    c. 3.
    d. 4.

18. Popular children
    a. rarely have athletic ability.
    b. are usually average in academic performance.
    c. are usually from small families.
    d. are in sync with their peers.

19. Acting on the basis of prejudice is
    a. stereotyping.
    b. negativism.
    c. ethnicity.
    d. discrimination.

20. Ethnic awareness begins to develop in
    a. early childhood.
    b. middle childhood.
    c. later childhood.
    d. adolescence.

Pretest score _____

To test your knowledge of this chapter, try to fill in each of the blanks in the following chapter review without referring back to the text. Check your answers with the Answer Key at the end of this chapter and then reread any sections of the chapter that gave you problems.

Personality Development in an Expanding Social World

1. Freud described middle childhood as a period of _____, when children could turn their emotional energies toward _____ relationships, _____ efforts, and learning the _____ prescribed tasks in the school or the community.

2. Erikson believed that the central focus of middle childhood is the crisis of _____, in which much of the child's time and energy is directed toward acquiring new _____ and _____. When children are able to _____ in school, they integrate a sense of industry into their self-image.

3. During middle childhood, children form increasingly _____ pictures of themselves, but their self-concept is not always _____. Children also refine their _____ stereotypes, and develop greater _____ in interacting with others.

4. _____ is an evaluation of oneself. During the school years, it is significantly correlated with _____ achievement, but the correlation is far from _____.

5. Development of self-esteem is a _____ process. In moderation, _____ can be quite effective; however, too much praise can prevent children from developing an accurate sense of their _____ and _____.

Social Knowledge and Reasoning

6. Social _____ is thought, knowledge, and understanding pertaining to the self in social interactions with others. A primary component of social cognition is social _____, guesses and assumptions about what another person is feeling, thinking, or intending. By age 6, children can usually infer that another person's thoughts may _____ from their own. By age 8, they realize that people can _____ about their thoughts. By age 10, they can infer what another person is _____. A second component of social cognition is the child's understanding of social _____, and the third aspect is the understanding of social _____, such as customs and conventions.

7. Social-learning theorists believe that children learn morality by _____ and _____ learning. Psychodynamic theorists believe that morality develops as a defense against _____, guilt, and _____. Cognitive-developmental theorists believe that morality develops in progressive _____ stages.

8. Piaget defined morality as an individual's respect for the _____ of the social order and his sense of _____. At the moral _____ stage, children think all rules should be obeyed because they are real and indestructible and judge the morality of an act by its _____. In the moral _____ stage, children realize rules are created and agreed on _____ by individuals, that rules can be changed, and that morality depends on _____.

9. Kohlberg defined three broad _____ of moral reasoning, each subdivided into _____ stages. Some researchers have attacked Kohlberg's theory on the grounds of moral _____. They point out that Kohlberg's scale measures moral _____, not moral behavior.

10. Gilligan claims that Kohlberg based his theory entirely on interviews with _____ subjects. Boys are trained to strive for _____ and value _____ thinking. Girls are taught to be _____ and caring and to value _____. Men often focus on _____, while women see moral issues in terms of concern for the _____ for others.

11. Eisenberg feels that Kohlberg's mistake was in making the stages too _____ and _____. She finds that _____ between ages 10 and 12 give more caring and empathetic responses than _____ of these ages, probably because girls _____ earlier.

Continuing Family Influences

12. In middle childhood, children express less direct _____ toward their parents and parents are less concerned with promoting _____ and more concerned with children's _____ habits and _____. Contemporary research emphasizes that a major goal of parenting is to increase children's _____ behavior. When a parent relies on verbal reasoning and suggestions, the child tends to _____ rather than react with _____.

13. Parents who remind their children of the effect of their actions on others tend to have children who are more _____ and who manifest internalized _____ standards. Children who comply with adults' demands when adults are present, but not when they are absent, are more likely to have parents who used _____ techniques. Parents are more successful in fostering self-regulated behavior if they gradually increase the child's involvement in family _____. Eleanor Maccoby concluded that children are best adjusted when their parents foster _____, build _____ and share _____.

14. _____ parenthood has become commonplace, and about _____ of all births are now to unmarried mothers. Once children enter school, the majority of American _____ enter the paid workforce.

15. One factor that determines a child's ability to cope constructively with stress is the sheer _____ of stressful situations in a child's life. A second factor is the child's _____ or understanding of the event.

16. Researchers have found that children living in "war zone" inner-city environments often exhibit similar behavioral patterns to _____. Parents are likely to _____ the extent of their children's psychological distress.

17. Over the past 30 years, Werner has studied a group of what she calls _____ children. She found that they had been temperamentally _____ and lovable babies who had developed a secure _____ to a parent or grandparent in the first year of life. Later, these children had the ability to find someone else to give them the emotional _____ they needed.

18. About _____ of U. S. families with two parents have incomes below the poverty line, but nearly_____ of all families headed by single women live in poverty. Not having a father lowers a family's _____ status as well as its _____ status. Housing is likely to be _____, and frequent _____ are common. Meals may be skimpy and _____ poor. _____ care may be lacking. The women who head these homes are often _____ stressed as a result of their struggle for survival.

19. Researchers found that when mothers in single-parent families work at jobs they like, their children have greater _____ and there is a greater sense of _____ organization and togetherness. Working single mothers had a particularly strong impact on their _____, who placed greater emphasis on _____ and _____. Maternal _____ and work _____ have an indirect negative effect on children's well-being.

20. A single parent should accept responsibilities and _____, and maintain a _____ attitude; must prioritize the _____ role; use consistent, nonpunitive _____; emphasize open _____; foster _____ within a supportive family unit; recognize the need for _____; and emphasize _____ and _____.

21. About _____ of all marriages end in divorce, and each year over one _____ children experience the breakup of their families. The breakup of a family means that both parents will no longer be equally _____, and that children have been a part of a family under _____ and stress for a long time. The children may fear that the other parent will also _____ them. They feel that they are to _____ for the divorce.

22. The most important factors in determining how children respond to divorce are the amount of _____ accompanying the divorce, the amount of actual _____ in the child's life, and the nature of the parent-child _____. Whereas in the past, the world was _____, unpredictability is now the _____. Consequently, children often test the _____ to see if the world still works the same way. These children are more likely to repeat a _____ or be _____ from school.

23. When the custodial parent remarries, there is no longer any chance of _____ the parents. Many children have the additional problem of learning to live with _____.

Peer Relationships and Social Competence

24. Selman studied the _____ of children aged 7 to 12. At the first stage (6 and younger), a friend is someone who lives _____, goes to the same _____, or has desirable _____. At the second stage from age 7 to 9, the awareness of another person's _____ begins to form. At the third stage from 9 to 12, the concept of _____ appears. At the fourth stage, occurring only rarely among the 11- and 12-year-olds, children are capable of looking at a relationship from another's _____.

25. Friendships help children learn _____ concepts and social skills and develop _____. Friendship provides structure for _____; reinforces and solidifies group _____, attitudes, and _____; and serves as a backdrop for individual and group _____.

26. Friendship _____ shift during childhood. The _____ pattern of Selman's first stage changes during middle childhood, when children begin to form closer _____ and have best _____. In later childhood and adolescence, _____ friendships become common. Although research indicates that virtually all children have at least one _____ friendship, many children lack _____ friendships characterized by give-and-take.

27. Children who are _____ by their peers are at risk for maladjustment later in life. Even a single _____ friend helps a child cope with the negative effects of being disliked and isolated from peers.

28. A peer group's members must _____ with each other. A peer group is relatively _____, and its members share _____. In early middle childhood, peer groups are relatively _____ and are usually created by the _____. They have very few operating _____ and a rapid turnover in _____. The group takes on a _____ significance for members when children reach 10 to 12 years. _____ becomes extremely important to the child. Peer pressures become more _____ and groups develop a more _____ structure. At this time the _____ of the sexes becomes noticeable.

29. Popular children are _____ than average and do well in school. _____ ability is particularly important in settings like camps or playgrounds. The overly _____ child is shunned, and the timid, anxious child is at risk of becoming a chronic _____.

30. One of the main reasons children bestow nicknames on each other is to separate _____ from _____. Children who have no nicknames are considered too _____ to bother with.

31. Highly conforming children have feelings of _____ and low _____ strength. They tend to be more _____ or anxious than other children and are exceptionally _____ to social cues for behavior. They also tend to _____ what they do and say very closely. They are especially concerned with how they _____ to others, and constantly compare themselves to their _____.

32. When peer pressure involves antisocial acts, _____ are more likely than _____ to yield to it. Children who are unsupervised after school also tend to conform to _____ peer pressure.

33. Prejudice is a _____ attitude toward people because of their membership in a group. It implies an _____ of people who possess certain desired characteristics, and an _____ of those who are different and therefore undesirable.

34. Discrimination means acting on the basis of _____. Ethnic _____ begins to develop during early childhood.

35. Understanding group differences and what it means to be a member of a group requires social _____, which in turn depends on _____ development. As children grow older, they become more skilled at seeing people as _____, but this is offset by the strong tendency of older school-age children to _____ to group standards and _____ those who are different from them in any way. During middle childhood, children absorb the cultural _____ of those around them.

POSTTEST

Now try to answer each of the following questions without referring back to the text. Check your answers with the Answer Key at the end of this chapter and record your Posttest score in the space provided. Then enter your Pretest score and subtract to find your improvement score.

1. Which theorist has a psychosocial approach?
   a. Lawrence Kohlberg
   b. Jean Piaget
   c. Erik Erikson
   d. Sigmund Freud

2. During middle childhood, the self-concept
   a. develops into a complete adult form.
   b. is not always accurate.
   c. provides a realistic view of what the child really is.
   d. has not even begun to develop.

3. During the school years, self-esteem is significantly correlated with
   a. discipline.
   b. athletic ability.
   c. academic achievement.
   d. self-actualization.

4. During middle childhood, parents and teachers should remember that
   a. praise is essential for every effort the child makes.
   b. without praise for every effort, the child will not develop adequately.
   c. praise should be withheld completely until the child matures.
   d. in moderation, praise can be quite helpful.

5. Guesses and assumptions about what another person is feeling, thinking, or intending are called social
   a. inference.
   b. relationships.
   c. regulation.
   d. understanding.

6. According to Piaget, a child who believes that there are no absolute right or wrong answers and judges actions by the intentions of the actor is in which stage of moral development?
   a. moral realism
   b. postconventional
   c. moral relativism
   d. preconventional

7. Who developed a three level, six stage theory of moral development?
   a. Piaget
   b. Kohlberg
   c. Gilligan
   d. Eisenberg

8. Who stated that in moral judgments, males have a justice perspective and females have a care perspective?
   a. Kohlberg
   b. Freud
   c. Gilligan
   d. Piaget

9. Contemporary research emphasizes that a major goal of parenting is to increase children's
   a. self-confidence.
   b. self-regulated behavior.
   c. feelings of self worth.
   d. feelings that they are at the center of the universe.

10. According to Maccoby, the best parents use all of the following EXCEPT
    a. cooperation.
    b. shared responsibility.
    c. coregulation.
    d. authoritarian parenting.

11. Recent research indicates that children living in inner city "war zones" show the symptoms of
    a. phobic disorders.
    b. posttraumatic stress disorder.
    c. autism.
    d. panic disorder.

12. About _____ percent of American families with two parents have incomes below the poverty line, but _____ of all families headed by women live in poverty.
    a. 13; half
    b. 20; one third
    c. 30; one-quarter
    d. 40; one tenth

13. In 1996, _____ percent of mothers of school age children worked outside the home.
    a. 26
    b. 33
    c. 51
    d. 76

14. Young children are likely to blame _____ for their parents' divorce.
    a. themselves
    b. both their parents
    c. their mother
    d. their father

15. A couple with at least one partner who is a parent and has remarried is a _____ family.
    a. single-parent
    b. nuclear
    c. reconstituted
    d. extended

16. According to Selman, between ages 7 and 9,
    a. friendship is based on geographical considerations.
    b. an awareness of another person's feelings begins to form.
    c. genuine give and take occurs.
    d. friendship becomes a stable relationship based on trust.

17. Group friendships are common in
    a. early and middle childhood.
    b. middle and late childhood.
    c. later childhood and adolescence.
    d. early adulthood.

18. Highly conforming children tend to
    a. be insensitive.
    b. feel superior.
    c. be independent.
    d. self-monitor.

19. A negative attitude toward people because of their membership in a group is called
    a. discrimination.
    b. stereotyping.
    c. bias.
    d. prejudice.

20. People who are different and undesirable are the
    a. in-group.
    b. out-group.
    c. minority group.
    d. inferior group.

Posttest score _____

Pretest score _____

Improvement _____

ESSAY QUESTIONS

To further develop your understanding of the material in this chapter, answer each of the following essay questions as completely as possible, using the text for material to support your answer.

1. Compare and contrast the explanation of middle childhood as proposed by the psychodynamic, cognitive developmental, and social learning perspectives.

2. Researchers have recently raised the concern that when children are told that the most important thing in the world is how highly they think of themselves, they are being sent a clear message that they are at the center of the universe. How does this statement apply to the children you see today?

3. Describe the moral development theories of Piaget, Kohlberg, Gilligan, and Eisenberg.

4. Summarize the research on resilient children.

5. Describe the functions of friendships in childhood.

6. What are the seven guidelines for a parent to make a single-parent family work?

7. What three factors are most important in influencing the way a child will respond after divorce?

8. How are prejudice and discrimination related to in-groups and out-groups?

9. Explain the components of social cognition.

10. Discuss the importance of nicknames in middle childhood.

ANSWER KEY

Key Names

1. d	3. e	5. a	7. b
2. c	4. h	6. f	8. g

Pretest

1. a	5. b	9. a	13. a	17. c
2. c	6. a	10. d	14. c	18. d
3. b	7. a	11. a	15. d	19. d
4. c	8. c	12. c	16. b	20. a

Programmed Review

1. latency, peer, creative, culturally
2. industry versus inferiority, knowledge, skills, succeed
3. stable, accurate, gender, flexibility
4. Self-esteem, academic, perfect
5. reciprocal, praise, weaknesses, strengths
6. cognition, inference, differ, think, thinking, responsibility, regulations
7. conditioning, observational, anxiety, shame, age-related
8. rules, justice, realism, consequences, relativism, cooperatively, intentions
9. levels, two, absolutism, attitudes
10. male, independence, abstract, nurturing, relationships, rights, needs
11. rigid, absolute, girls, boys, mature
12. anger, autonomy, work, achievement, self-regulated, negotiate, defiance
13. popular, moral, power-assertive, decisions, coregulation, cooperation, responsibility
14. Single, one-third, mothers
15. number, perception
16. posttraumatic stress disorder, underestimate
17. resilient, easy, attachment, support
18. 13 percent, half, social, economic, crowded, moves, nutritionally, Medical, psychologically
19. self-esteem, family, daughters, independence, achievement, unemployment, interruption
20. challenges, positive, parental, discipline, communication, individuality, self-nurturance, rituals, traditions
21. half, million, available, tension, abandon, blame
22. hostility, change, relationship, predictable, rule, rules, grade, expelled
23. reuniting, stepsiblings
24. friendships, nearby, school, toys, feelings, trust, perspective
25. social, self-esteem, activity, norms, values, competition
26. patterns, egocentric, relationship, friends, group, unilateral, reciprocal
27. rejected, close

28. interact, stable, values, informal, children, rules, membership, greater, Conformity, effective, formal, separation
29. brighter, Athletic, aggressive, victim
30. us, them, insignificant
`31. inferiority, ego, dependent, sensitive, self-monitor, appear, peers
32. boys, girls, antisocial
33. negative, in-group, out-group
34. prejudice, awareness
35. cognition, cognitive, multidimensional, conform, reject, attitudes

Posttest

1. c	5. a	9. b	13. d	17. c
2. b	6. c	10. d	14. a	18. d
3. c	7. b	11. b	15. c	19. d
4. d	8. c	12. a	16. b	20. b

11

Adolescence: Physical and Cognitive Development

CHAPTER OUTLINE

Adolescence Today

Physical Development and Adjustment
    Physical Growth and Change
    Puberty
    Body Image and Adjustment

Sexual Attitudes and Behavior
    The Sexual "Revolution"
    Masturbation
    Gender Differences in Sexual Expression
    Factors Influencing Early Sexual Relationships
    Sexual Abuse of Adolescents
    Teenage Parents

Cognitive Changes in Adolescence
    Abstract Thinking
    Information-processing
    Scope and Content of Thought

KEY TERMS AND CONCEPTS

To help you understand the material in this chapter, look up each of the following terms in the chapter and write out the definition.

Adolescent growth spurt

Androgens

Anorexia nervosa

Anovulatory

Bulimia nervosa

Endocrine glands

Estrogen

Foundling fantasy

Growth hormone

Hormones

Hypothalamus

Imaginary audience

Marginal group

Menarche

Personal fable

Pituitary gland

Progesterone

Puberty

Rites of passage

Same sex orientation

Sebaceous glands

Testosterone

Trophic hormone

KEY NAMES

After reading the chapter in the text, try to match each of the following individuals with his or her contribution to the field of psychology. Then check your answers with the Answer Key provided at the end of this chapter.

_____1. David Elkind

a. formal operational thought

_____2. Lawrence Kohlberg

b. imaginary audience and personal fable

_____3. Jean Piaget

c. moral education

Try to answer each of the following questions without referring to the text. Then check your answers with the Answer Key at the end of this chapter and record your score in the space provided.

1. Symbolic events, name changes, or challenges which occur at puberty are often called
   a. rites of passage.
   b. adolescent growth trends.
   c. school stunts.
   d. growth periods.

2. Sebaceous glands produce
   a. hormones.
   b. proteins.
   c. oils.
   d. neurotransmitters.

3. The attainment of sexual maturity in males and females is called
   a. ageism.
   b. menarche.
   c. the growth spurt.
   d. puberty.

4. The female hormones are
   a. testosterone and androgen.
   b. estrogen and progesterone.
   c. testosterone and estrogen.
   d. androgen and progesterone.

5. The part of the brain that initiates growth and reproduction during adolescence is the
   a. hippocampus.
   b. hypothalamus.
   c. pons.
   d. amygdala.

6. In males, the first indication of puberty is
   a. growth of the testes and scrotum.
   b. facial hair.
   c. body hair.
   d. change of voice.

7. Menarche generally occurs when a girl
   a. reaches her eleventh birthday.
   b. becomes active in athletics.
   c. falls in love.
   d. stores some body fat.

8. Compared to girls, adolescent boys worry more about
   a. being too fat.
   b. their complexion.
   c. height and muscles.
   d. body hair.

9. Which of the following would be at the greatest advantage?
   a. early-maturing boys
   b. early-maturing girls
   c. late-maturing boys
   d. late-maturing girls

10. Anorexics are usually all of the following EXCEPT
    a. under the age of 25.
    b. women.
    c. not menstruating.
    d. easily treated and cured.

11. Which of the following includes the other three?
    a. AIDS
    b. syphilis
    c. STD
    d. gonorrhea

12. Which of the following is a factor that leads to early sexual activity?
    a. high academic performance
    b. restrictive parenting
    c. two-parent families
    d. late puberty

13. The most common form of sexual abuse occurs between
    a. a boy and his stepmother.
    b. a girl and her stepfather.
    c. a boy and a stranger.
    d. a girl and a teacher.

14. According to Piaget, the adolescent is in which stage of cognitive development?
    a. sensorimotor
    b. preoperational
    c. concrete operational
    d. formal operational

15. Information processing theorists emphasize the adolescent's improvement in
    a. metacognition.
    b. moral development.
    c. formal operational thought.
    d. egocentrism.

16. What percent of teenage pregnancies are carried to term?
    a. 10
    b. 30
    c. 50
    d. 70

17. Which of the following does not belong?
    a. adolescent egocentrism
    b. imaginary audience
    c. meta components
    d. personal fable

18. According to Elkind, the foundling fantasy is part of
    a. the imaginary audience.
    b. sensorimotor thought.
    c. the search for identity.
    d. adolescent egocentrism.

19. According to Kohlberg, the first level of moral development is
    a. conventional.
    b. preoperational.
    c. postconventional.
    d. preconventional.

20. According to Kohlberg, moral development
    a. is genetically programmed.
    b. is a part of the unconscious mind.
    c. can be taught.
    d. is completely linked to the biological development of the nervous system.

Pretest score _____

In order to test your knowledge of the chapter, fill in the blanks in the following chapter review without referring back to the text. Then check your answers with the Answer Key at the end of this chapter and reread any parts of the chapter that gave you problems.

1. Despite the mixed opinions about its boundaries, there is agreement that adolescence as a prolonged _____ period from childhood to adulthood is a modern phenomenon. In less complex societies, the young person goes through a symbolic ceremony referred to as a _____.

Adolescence Today

2. The developmental niche in which today's adolescents live is influenced by age _____, prolonged economic _____, the state of the _____, and the mass _____. Adolescents' separation from younger children deprives them of opportunities to _____ and _____ those who are less knowledgeable than themselves. Their separation from the adult world means that they miss the opportunity to serve an _____. Adolescents and young adults fight in _____, participate in _____, put their energies into movements for social _____, support radical _____ and _____ movements with their idealism, and lose their jobs during _____ downturns. Individuals of any age learn best when they can act on their _____, perceive the _____ of their actions, and have some power to cause _____. Adolescents are particularly vulnerable to the passive role of consumer of the _____.

Physical Development and Adjustment

3. The biological hallmarks of adolescence are a marked increase in the rate of _____, rapid development of the _____ organs, and the appearance of such secondary sex characteristics as body _____, increases in body _____ and _____, and enlargement and maturation of _____.

4. The physical changes of adolescence are controlled by _____ which are biochemical substances secreted in very small amounts by the endocrine glands. They trigger the adolescent _____ spurt.

5. During adolescence, there is an increase in size and activity of _____, or oil-producing glands, in the skin, which causes the teenager's face to break out in _____. A new kind of sweat gland also develops in the skin, resulting in a stronger body _____.

6. Males begin to produce more of the hormones called _____, of which the most important is _____. Females begin to produce more of the hormones _____ and _____. The balance of hormones is maintained by the _____ and the _____ gland, which produces _____ hormones and secondary _____ hormones to stimulate and regulate sex glands.

7. Puberty is marked in females by the first menstrual period or _____ and by the first emission of _____ in males.

8. In males the first indication of puberty is the accelerating growth of the _____ and _____, followed one year later with the growth of the _____. The first emission of _____ may take place between ages 11 and 16. The actual voice change takes place relatively _____ in the sequence. In girls, the _____ are usually the first signal that puberty has begun, with simultaneous development of the _____ and _____. Menarche occurs _____ and only after the girl has reached adult _____ and has stored some body _____. The first menstrual periods are usually irregular and _____.

9. Adolescents belong to what sociologists call a _____ group, between cultures or on the fringe of the dominant culture, and they are extremely intolerant of _____. Concern for body image for boys involves physical _____ and for girls being too _____ or too _____. The late maturing boy is at a disadvantage in most _____, has lower _____ status among his peers and is perceived as being less _____ by adults. Early maturing boys tend to gain social and athletic _____. Early maturity is a _____ blessing for girls. The early maturing girl has fewer opportunities to discuss with her friends the _____ and _____ changes she is undergoing, but she frequently feels more _____, is more _____ with older boys, and goes out on _____ more frequently.

10. Victims of anorexia nervosa literally _____ themselves to death. Most are _____ under the age of _____ and may be victims of our culture's obsession with _____. As yet, there is no _____ and no generally accepted method of _____. The goal of therapy is to help anorexics to separate their feelings about _____ from their feelings about _____ and to develop a sense of _____ and _____.

11. The bulimic has an uncontrollable need to _____ and consumes huge quantities of _____ in a very short time. To compensate for overeating, bulimics _____ or take _____. Most bulimics are _____ and in late _____. They tend to be more _____ to treatment than anorexics. The fact that _____ drugs often help treat this disorder suggests to some researchers that a _____ abnormality may be involved.

Sexual Attitudes and Behaviors

12. Prior to the mid-1960s, most young people felt that premarital sex was _____. Although older adolescent boys were under some pressure to acquire sexual _____, girls were under pressure to remain _____ until marriage. Sexual attitudes changed considerably, in part because of the development and widespread distribution of _____. By the late 1970s, the sexual _____ was in full swing, however, many of the large number of adolescents who were having sexual intercourse did not use _____. The sexual revolution began to _____ in the 1980s and young people started being more cautious about _____ activity and _____ became fashionable again.

13. In adolescence, girls spend more time fantasizing about _____ as an outlet for their sexual impulses. Boys are more likely to _____.

14. The expression of sexuality for both sexes always depends on the society's prevailing _____. Although society as a whole has become somewhat more _____ with regard to sexual behavior, teenagers continue to be highly _____ sexually. About 60% of boys and girls have had intercourse by age _____.

15. Those who attain higher levels of _____ more frequently come from the middle and upper middle classes which have more _____ views about sex. Sexually experienced male adolescents tend to have relatively _____ self-esteem, while sexually experienced females tend to have _____ self-esteem. Both overly _____ and overly _____ parenting are associated with earlier sexual activity in adolescents. Adolescents who are sexually active are more likely to report poor _____ with their parents. In general, teenagers from _____ families have less sexual experience than those from _____ families. Adolescents may become sexually active earlier today because of the decline in the average age at which _____ occurs.

16. The impact of sexual abuse on children depends on the _____ of the abusive act, the _____ and vulnerability of the victim, whether the offender is a _____ or a _____ member, whether there was a _____ incident or an ongoing _____ of abuse, and the _____ of adults in whom the child confides. The most common form of sexual abuse occurs between a young adolescent _____ and an adult _____ relative or family _____. The abuse often _____ over a period of time, and becomes a _____ between abuser and the victim.

17. Adolescent girls who are involved in sexual abuse often feel _____ and _____, yet are _____ to avoid the abuse. They may feel _____ or alienated from peers and _____ of adults. Some have _____ problems, others have _____ complaints, and others become sexually _____. Some turn their anger in on themselves becoming _____ and contemplating _____. As adults, they have difficulty establishing normal _____ relationships. Sexual abuse also involves young boys, mainly in _____ encounters. Abusers are usually not _____ members, and the abuse generally takes place _____ the home.

18. The proportion of babies born to adolescents in the United States has _____, as has the proportion of babies born _____ of marriage. About 3 out of 10 sexually active adolescents do not use _____, the most common reasons being _____ of the facts of reproduction, unwillingness to accept _____ for sexual activity, or a generally _____ attitude about life. Both sexes tend to view the male as the sexual _____, and the female as the one who sets _____.

19. Teenage mothers may drop out of _____, work at _____ jobs, and experience greater job _____. They are more likely to become dependent on _____ support. Teenage fathers tend to leave _____, take _____, low-paying jobs, and have more _____ problems later on. Children of teenage parents are at a _____ compared to children of older parents.

Cognitive Changes in Adolescence

20. Piaget characterized the abstract thinking of the adolescent in terms of _____ thinking. It involves thinking about _____ as well as comparing _____ with things that might or might not be, the ability to formulate, test, and evaluate _____, and an increasing ability to _____ and think ahead.

21. The first order of thinking is discovering and examining _____ between objects. The second order involves thinking about one's _____, looking for links between _____, and maneuvering between _____ and _____. Adolescents and adults who attain this level do not always use it _____. A certain level of _____ is necessary as well.

22. Information-processing theorists emphasize the adolescent's improvement in _____. Cognitive development during adolescence involves a more efficient use of _____ retention and transfer of _____, more complex _____ for problem solving, more effective ways of acquiring and storing information _____, and the development of higher-order _____ functions.

23. Adolescents contrast their _____ parent with the real parent they see on a daily basis. Family _____ tends to increase during early adolescence, and parents and teenagers _____ new relationships with each other.

24. Adolescent egocentrism includes the idea that one is being constantly watched, a concept that Elkind calls the _____, as well as the _____, a feeling that one is so special as to be exempt from the ordinary laws of nature. The _____ is the belief that one's parents are too ordinary to be one's real parents.

25. By the time they reach their teens, most adolescents have arrived at the _____ level of morality. Kohlberg and others have set up experimental moral _____ classes for children and have shown that moral judgment can be _____.

POSTTEST

Now answer each of the following questions without referring back to the text. Check your answers with the Answer Key at the end of this chapter, record your score in the space provided, enter your Pretest score and subtract to find your improvement score.

1. All of the following have been among the most frequently cited factors that contribute to the developmental niche of adolescents in the late twentieth-century EXCEPT
   a. age segregation.
   b. world affairs.
   c. mass media.
   d. economic independence.

2. Hormones are produced by the
   a. endocrine system.
   b. nervous system.
   c. respiratory system.
   d. cardiovascular system.

3. Which of the following does not belong?
   a. female
   b. estrogen
   c. progesterone
   d. male

4. The first menstruation is called
   a. testosterone.
   b. puberty.
   c. estrogen.
   d. menarche.

5. The secretion of testosterone influences all of the following EXCEPT
   a. growth of penis.
   b. broadening of shoulders.
   c. broadening of hips.
   d. hair growth on face.

6. Girls experience the growth spurt of puberty about _____ boys.
   a. two years before
   b. one year before
   c. one year after
   d. two years after

7. During the first few menstrual cycles,
   a. girls will feel no premenstrual discomfort.
   b. cycles are regular.
   c. ovulation occurs more often than normal.
   d. girls are anovulatory.

8. Adolescent girls are most likely to worry about
   a. not being tall enough.
   b. being too fat.
   c. not having enough power or strength.
   d. having too much muscle development.

9. The major sources of concern for 10th graders include all of the following EXCEPT
   a. complexion.
   b. hair.
   c. height.
   d. weight.

10. Which of the following is an accurate statement about menarche?
    a. It has a gradual onset.
    b. Most girls view it as a routine occurrence.
    c. Girls are usually not well-informed about it.
    d. It is tied to a feeling of coming of age.

11. Ill-timed maturation is a problem in adolescence especially for
    a. early-maturing boys.
    b. early-maturing girls.
    c. late-maturing boys.
    d. late-maturing girls.

12. The early-maturing girl
    a. has more opportunities to discuss her development with her friends.
    b. is less popular than other girls her age.
    c. feels unattractive and out of place.
    d. goes out on dates more frequently than her peers.

13. Which of the following does not belong with the other three?
    a. binge eating
    b. anorexia nervosa
    c. bulimia
    d. binge and purge

14. Most bulimics are _____ in _____ adolescence.
    a. females; late
    b. males; late
    c. females; early
    d. males; early

15. The double standard as applied to sexual behavior of males and females
    a. is exactly the same as it was a decade ago.
    b. has increased greatly in the past ten years.
    c. is rejected by the majority of adolescents.
    d. has reversed the positions of males and females.

16. What percent of sexually active adolescents do not use contraceptives?
    a. 60
    b. 50
    c. 30
    d. 10

17. The self-esteem of sexually active adolescents is
    a. high in both males and females.
    b. low in both males and females.
    c. high in males and low in females.
    d. low in males and high in females.

18. Second-order thinking involves all of the following EXCEPT
    a. discovering and examining relationships.
    b. thinking about one's thoughts.
    c. looking for links between relationships.
    d. maneuvering between reality and possibility.

19. Mary Ellen claims that she does not need to use contraceptives of any kind because she and her boyfriend are really in love, and if they do have sex in a spontaneous moment of passion, she knows that she won't get pregnant. Mary Ellen is showing evidence of the
    a. foundling fantasy.
    b. personal fable.
    c. imaginary audience.
    d. use of formal operational thinking.

20. According to Kohlberg,
    a. moral judgment can be taught.
    b. morality is genetically programmed.
    c. moral thinking cannot be taught.
    d. adolescents rarely are above the preconventional level of moral development.

Posttest score _____

Pretest score _____

Improvement _____

ESSAY QUESTIONS

For an even better understanding of the material in this chapter, answer each of the following essay questions as completely as you can, using the text for material to support your answer.

1. Define rites of passage. What, if any, rights of passage have you experienced? Which rites of passage do you think are important for an individual's development?

2. How has the developmental period of adolescence changed over the past century? Evaluate these changes and suggest the direction you think changes in adolescence should take from now on.

3. Describe the physical changes of puberty and how they differ between males and females.

4. Describe the affects of early and late maturation on adolescent boys and girls.

5. Describe anorexia nervosa and bulimia and discuss the suggested causes and possible treatments for both.

6. Describe the evolution of sexual attitudes from the 1950s to the present.

7. What is the impact of the media on the gender role development of adolescents today?

169

8. Describe the typical level of moral development of adolescents.

9. If you were to give a speech aimed at preventing adolescent pregnancy, what would you tell a group of adolescents?

10. How does adolescent egocentrism affect adolescent behavior? What behaviors would you expect to see created by the personal fable, imaginary audience, and foundling fantasy?

ANSWER KEY

Key Names

1. b   2. c   3. a

Pretest

1. a	5. b	9. a	13. b	17. c
2. c	6. a	10. d	14. d	18. d
3. d	7. d	11. c	15. a	19. d
4. b	8. c	12. b	16. c	20. c

Programmed Review

1. transitional, rite of passage
2. segregation, dependence, world, media, guide, tutor, apprenticeship, wars, riots, reform, political, religious, economic, environment, consequences, change, mass media
3. growth, reproductive, hair, fat, muscle, genitalia
4. hormones, growth
5. sebaceous, acne, odor
6. androgens, testosterone, estrogen, progesterone, hypothalamus, pituitary, growth, trophic
7. menarche, semen
8. testes, scrotum, penis, semen, late, breast buds, uterus, vagina, late, height, fat, anovulatory
9. marginal, deviation, strength, fat, tall, sports, social, competent, advantage, mixed, physical, emotional, attractive, popular, dates
10. starve, women, 25, thinness, cure, treatment, food, themselves, self-worth, autonomy
11. binge, carbohydrates, purge, laxatives, female, adolescence, responsive, antidepressant, biochemical
12. immoral, experience, chaste, birth control pills, revolution, birth control, decline, sexual, monogamy
13. romance, masturbate
14. norms, conservative, active, 18
15. education, conservative, high, low, restrictive, permissive, communication, two-parent, single-parent, puberty

16. nature, age, stranger, family, single, pattern, reactions, girl, male, friend, continues, secret
17. guilty, shamed, powerless, isolated, distrustful, academic, physical, promiscuous, depressed, suicide, sexual, same sex, family, outside
18. declined, outside, contraceptives, ignorance, responsibility, passive, initiator, limits
`19. school, lower-paying, dissatisfaction, government, school, low-skilled, marital, disadvantage
20. formal operational, possibilities, reality, hypotheses, plan
21. relationships, thoughts, relationships, reality, possibility, consistently, intelligence
22. metacognition, memory, information, strategies, symbolically, executive
23. ideal, bickering, negotiate
24. imaginary audience, personal fable, foundling fantasy
25. conventional, education, taught

Posttest

1. d	5. c	9. b	13. b	17. c
2. a	6. a	10. d	14. a	18. a
3. d	7. d	11. c	15. c	19. b
4. d	8. b	12. d	16. c	20. a

12
Adolescence: Personality and Sociocultural Development

CHAPTER OUTLINE

Developmental Tasks in Adolescence
    Independence and Interdependence
    Identity Formation

Family Dynamics
    Intergenerational Communication
    Changes in Family Composition
    Leaving Home

Relationships During Adolescence
    Social Comparison
    Peer Relationships
    Negotiating the Borders: Peers and Parents

When Adolescence Goes Awry
    Risk Taking
    Drug Abuse
    Delinquency

Stress, Depression, and Adolescent Coping
    Depression and Other Disorders
    Protective Factors and Coping Behaviors

For a better understanding of the material in this chapter, look up each of the following terms in the chapter and write out the definition.

Clique
Crowd
Delinquents
Diffusion status
Foreclosure status
Identity achievement
Identity crisis

Identity formation
Interdependence
Moratorium status
Self-definition
Social comparison
Social reference gruops
Sturm und drang

KEY NAMES

After reading the chapter in the text, try to match each of the following individuals with his or her major contribution to the field of psychology. Check your answers with the Answer Key at the end of this chapter. You will notice that some of these names have appeared in earlier chapters.

_____1. Diana Baumrind

_____2. David Elkind

_____3. Erik Erikson

_____4. Anna Freud

_____5. James Marcia

_____6. Bruce Roscoe

a. functions of dating

b. identity formation

c. identity statuses

d. parenting styles

e. personal fable

f. storm and stress

Try to answer each of the following questions without referring back to the text. Check your answers with the Answer Key at the end of this chapter and record your answers in the space provided.

1. The term "storm and stress" was adopted to describe adolescence by
   a. Anna Freud.
   b. Erik Erikson.
   c. B. F. Skinner.
   d. David Elkind.

2. A social group or collection of people with whom an individual shares attitudes, ideals, or philosophies is called a(n)
   a. significant other.
   b. ideal group.
   c. social reference group.
   d. social group.

3. According to Erikson, the adolescent must form a(n)
   a. sense of industry.
   b. intimate relationship.
   c. knowledge of the world.
   d. inner sense of identity.

4. According to Marcia, adolescents who have made a commitment without going through a decision-making process are in
   a. moratorium.
   b. foreclosure.
   c. identity achievement.
   d. diffusion.

5. According to both Marcia and Erikson, the adolescent who is in the midst of an ongoing identity crisis is in
   a. emotional turmoil.
   b. moratorium.
   c. foreclosure.
   d. diffusion.

6. Anxiety is a dominant emotion for adolescents in
   a. moratorium.
   b. foreclosure.
   c. identity achievement.
   d. diffusion.

7. Which outcome is seen frequently in teenagers who have experienced rejection or neglect from detached or uncaring parents?
    a. identity achievement
    b. moratorium
    c. foreclosure
    d. diffusion

8. Compared to mothers, fathers are more likely to
    a. encourage intellectual development.
    b. emphasize household responsibilities.
    c. discipline children in and out of the home.
    d. follow up on homework.

9. Which of the following parenting styles is most likely to yield normal and healthy adolescent behavior?
    a. authoritarian
    b. authoritative
    c. permissive
    d. traditional

10. Adolescents raised in authoritarian homes may
    a. become dependent and anxious.
    b. develop strong self-control.
    c. develop inadequate self-control.
    d. develop a sense of inferiority.

11. The process of evaluating our personal abilities and behaviors against the characteristics of others is called social
    a. evaluation.
    b. discrimination.
    c. comparison.
    d. referencing.

12. The adolescent crowd is
    a. made up of many smaller friendship groups.
    b. a group of about 3 to 9 individuals.
    c. highly cohesive.
    d. about 15 to 30 members and consists of several cliques.

13. About _____ percent of adolescents do not join any groups.
    a. 10
    b. 20
    c. 30
    d. 40

14. Many researchers believe that adolescents who take risks underestimate the likelihood of bad outcomes. This is most consistent with the
    a. foundling fantasy.
    b. personal fable.
    c. imaginary audience.
    d. identity crisis.

15. Which of the following is a risk factor from the social environment?
    a. poverty
    b. low self-esteem
    c. poor school work
    d. problem drinking

16. Research in trends in smoking since the 1970s has indicated that
    a. all adolescents are smoking less now than ever before.
    b. adolescents are smoking more than ever before.
    c. adolescent boys are smoking more than adolescent girls.
    d. adolescent girls are smoking more than adolescent boys.

17. All of the following are true of the typical alcohol abusing adolescent EXCEPT
    a. he is male.
    b. he has low academic grades.
    c. he does not use drugs other than alcohol.
    d. he has a family history of alcoholism.

18. Most crack users are
    a. young adolescents.
    b. older adolescents.
    c. prepubescent children.
    d. young adults.

19. Depression when under stress is most likely to be found in adolescents from
    a. Cuban-American groups.
    b. White-American groups.
    c. Mexican-American groups.
    d. African-American groups.

20. All of the following are factors that place adolescents at risk for depression and stress EXCEPT
    a. decreased capacity to reflect on the developing self and the future.
    b. negative body image.
    c. family dysfunction.
    d. parental mental health problems.

Pretest score _____

176

PROGRAMMED REVIEW

To test your knowledge of this chapter, try to fill in each of the blanks in this chapter review without referring back to the text. Then check your answers with the Answer Key at the end of this chapter and reread any sections in the text that gave you difficulty.

1. Prolonged adolescence gives the young person repeated opportunities to _____ with different adult styles without making irrevocable commitments. The need to appear _____ and sophisticated when one is, in fact, still financially _____ creates conflicts.

Developmental Tasks of Adolescence

2. Most theorists agree that adolescents must confront two major tasks: the achievement of _____ and _____ from parents, and formation of an _____. Adolescence has traditionally been seen as a period of _____, a term adopted by _____ to describe the dramatic upheaval of emotions during adolescence.

3. Most of the research indicates that the degree of conflict in adolescent relations with the rest of the family has been _____. The vast majority of teenagers in all countries get along well with their _____ and have positive attitudes towards their _____.

4. Becoming an adult is a _____ transformation. It requires being simultaneously _____ and _____ (defined as _____ dependence).

5. Erikson saw the task of _____ formation as the major task of adolescence. Adolescents derive many of their ideas of suitable roles and values from social _____ groups. They are sometimes drawn to the values and attitudes of one person, referred to as a _____.

6. According to Erikson, identity formation is often a lengthy and complex process of _____. It provides _____ between the individual's past, present, and future. It forms a _____ for organizing and integrating behaviors in diverse areas of one's life. It _____ the person's own inclinations and talents with earlier roles and also provides a basis for _____ comparisons.

7. Marcia defined four different identity _____ according to whether or not the individual has gone through a decision-making period called an _____ and whether or not the individual has made a _____ to a selected set of choices. Adolescents who are in _____ status have made a commitment without going through a decision-making period. The choice was determined by _____ and _____ rather than themselves. Young people who lack a sense of direction and have little motivation to find one are in _____ status. Adolescents or young adults in _____ status are in the midst of an ongoing identity crisis. Identity _____ is the status attained by people who have passed through the crisis and made their commitments.

8. Anxiety is the dominant emotion for young people in _____ status because of their unresolved decisions. They are often tied to their _____ in an ambivalent relationship; they struggle for _____, yet they fear and resent parental _____. Many _____ students are in this status. Adolescents in _____ status experience a minimum of anxiety and hold more _____ values. Young men in this status tend to have lower _____ and are more easily _____ by others. _____ status is seen frequently in teenagers who have experienced rejection or neglect from detached or uncaring parents. These adolescents may become _____. Those who have attained identity _____ have the most balanced feelings toward their parents and family. Their quest for independence is less _____ charged. The proportion of people in this status increases with _____.

9. Researchers have found that for family and career choices, girls of senior high school age were most likely to be in _____ status, while boys were most likely to be in _____ status. For _____ beliefs, research indicates that there are no significant differences between the genders, but with respect to _____ beliefs, there seems to be a significant sex difference between older adolescents. Males are more often in identity _____, and females are more often in _____ status.

Family Dynamics

10. Most adolescent conflicts generally center on family _____, curfew _____, dating, grades, personal _____, and _____ habits. Generally, _____ adolescence is more conflict laden than _____ adolescence.

11. Fathers tend to encourage _____ development and are frequently involved in _____ family problems. Mothers and adolescents interact in the area of _____ responsibilities, _____, _____ in and out of the home, and _____ activities. This may cause a greater _____ and conflict between mothers and their children, but also tends to create greater _____.

12. The _____ parenting style is most likely to result in normal or healthy adolescent behavior. Adolescents raised under the influence of _____ parents may be dependent and anxious in the presence of authority figures or defiant and resentful.

13. Teenagers in dual-income families tend to help _____ around the house than those in traditional families where the mother stays at home. The demands on adolescents are divided along _____ lines. When the adolescent is about to leave home, it helps during the separation process if families have moderate but not extreme levels of _____ and _____. Open _____ helps to preserve the family cohesion. Fathers who place strong emphasis on _____ give their adolescents the room they need to form their own identity and begin to take responsibility for their own actions.

Relationships during Adolescence

14. Social _____ is a major element in a teenager's ability to make new friends and maintain old ones, and its development is based on the adolescent's ability to make social _____.

15. During early adolescence, teenagers spend time and energy defining _____. They focus on their _____ and the personality characteristics that make them _____. This process involves a wide circle of _____ but few close _____. Many of their relationships lack _____. During late adolescence, teenagers seek friends with whom they share similar _____. Most adolescents report that they have one or two _____ as well as several _____. These friendships tend to be _____ and usually last for at least a _____. One of the chief reasons teenagers cite for terminating a friendship is _____.

16. The larger peer group of 15 to 30 members is the _____, the smaller, more cohesive group of 3 to 9 members is the _____. According to Dunphy, small _____ cliques merge or relate to other groups, expand to include _____ groups, and finally re-emerge as groups that include both _____.

17. About _____ percent of adolescents do not join peer groups. Solitude allows an experience of _____ or healing. _____ aloneness is an opportunity for creativity, relief from pressures, or psychological _____. Involuntary aloneness can bring on feelings of _____ and _____.

18. Close relationships with opposite-sex friends are reported at an earlier age by _____ than by _____. During early adolescence, most interactions with the opposite sex take place in _____ settings. _____ is a popular pastime throughout adolescence, and it becomes increasingly _____ as adolescence progresses. This type of interaction is often the first step in learning how to _____ to the opposite sex.

19. According to Roscoe and colleagues, dating serves the following functions during adolescence: an opportunity for _____ and _____ with friends, an opportunity to increase one's _____, selection of a _____, an opportunity to experiment with or to obtain _____ satisfaction, _____ and _____ with a person of the opposite sex.

20. Young adolescents look for dates who are _____ attractive, _____ well, and are _____ by others. Older adolescents are more concerned about _____ characteristics and the person's _____ for the future. Females consider _____ to be more important than _____, while males consider _____ the most important.

When Adolescence Goes Awry

21. Many researchers believe that adolescents who take risks _____ the likelihood of bad outcomes; they see themselves as _____. This explanation is consistent with Elkind's concepts of the personal _____. When adolescents develop _____, a sense of _____, and a sense of _____ to a stable family and social order, they are less likely to feel the need to engage in high-risk behaviors.

22. Of all the legal and illegal drugs that are widely available in this country, _____ and _____ have the highest potential for abuse. Since the 1970s, more adolescent _____ than _____ report daily smoking. A powerful factor in teenage alcohol use is the view that alcohol consumption is a symbol of _____ and social _____. A pattern of heavy drinking is highest for those in the seven years after _____, for _____, for _____ youth, and for those who live in _____.

23. The use of marijuana by adolescents and young adults is now on the _____, but the use of cocaine is _____. The use of hallucinogens has _____ off, and the use of inhalants has recently _____.

24. Persons under the age of 16 or 18 who commit criminal acts are called _____. Statistically delinquency rates are highest in poor _____ areas. Delinquency is more likely to occur among _____ groups recently assimilated into urban life, and young males from _____ homes headed by a mother.

25. Sociological statistics and theories help link delinquency to _____ factors. Psychological theories maintain that individuals who are delinquent have been unable or unwilling to _____ to society or develop adequate _____ or outlets for anger or frustration. Delinquency satisfies certain special needs for _____, provides acceptance within the _____ group and a sense of _____.

Stress, Depression, and Adolescent Coping

26. Studies of psychiatric disorders during adolescence have found a fairly low incidence of moderate to severe _____, but symptoms may be _____ in those affected. Troubled teenage boys are likely to engage in _____ behaviors, whereas girls are more likely to turn their symptoms _____ and become _____.

27. _____ is the third leading cause of adolescent death, and it tends to be _____ because of religious taboos against it and concern for family. The generally accepted risk factors include a previous _____ attempt, strong feelings of _____ and helplessness, drug and alcohol _____, life events that are _____, increased accessibility and use of _____, and _____ problems.

28. Factors that place adolescents at risk for depression and stress are negative _____ image, increased capacity to reflect on _____ and the future, family _____ or parental _____ health problems, marital _____ and _____ hardship, low peer _____, and poor _____ achievement.

29. Many girls emerge from early adolescence with a poor _____, relatively low _____ from life, and much less _____ in themselves and their abilities than boys.

30. Adolescents are helped to cope with the transitions by good relationships with _____, and by middle adolescence, with _____, a particular area of _____ or expertise, and a role that includes _____ for others. Positive coping strategies like careful _____ and _____, setting _____, or finding a close _____ or _____ can help relieve moderate stress.

180

POSTTEST

Now answer each of the following questions without referring back to the text. Then check your answers with the Answer Key at the end of this chapter and record your Posttest score in the space provided. Enter your Pretest score and subtract to find your improvement score.

1. Reciprocal dependence is also called
   a. independence.
   b. interdependence.
   c. intradependence.
   d. codependence.

2. A close friend, relative, teacher, or famous person whose opinions are highly valued is called a
   a. reference source.
   b. role model.
   c. significant other.
   d. guide.

3. According to Marcia, all of the following are identity statuses EXCEPT
   a. commitment.
   b. achievement.
   c. foreclosure.
   d. moratorium.

4. Young people who avoid the issue of identity are in which status?
   a. achievement
   b. moratorium
   c. foreclosure
   d. diffusion

5. People who have passed through the crisis and have made their commitments are in which identity status?
   a. achievement
   b. moratorium
   c. foreclosure
   d. diffusion

6. Mothers and adolescents primarily interact in all of the following areas EXCEPT
   a. household responsibilities.
   b. schoolwork done at home.
   c. leisure-time activities.
   d. problem-solving activities.

7. Which of the following parenting styles is most likely to produce adolescents who are either dependent or anxious in the presence of authority figures or defiant and resentful?
   a. authoritative
   b. permissive
   c. authoritarian
   d. laissez-faire

8. When adolescents leave home, it helps if the family has
   a. high levels of cohesion and adaptability.
   b. moderate levels of cohesion and adaptability.
   c. low levels of cohesion and high levels of adaptability.
   d. moderate levels of cohesion and low levels of adaptability.

9. Most adolescents report that they have one or two
   a. best friends.
   b. good friends.
   c. sexual partners.
   d. boyfriends or girlfriends.

10. One of the chief reasons that teenagers cite for terminating a friendship is
    a. lack of similar interests.
    b. arguments over members of the opposite sex.
    c. disloyalty.
    d. incompatibility.

11. Close relationships with opposite-sex friends are reported
    a. at about the same age for girls and boys alike.
    b. at an earlier age by girls than by boys.
    c. at an earlier age by boys than by girls.
    d. before the age of 13 for most adolescents.

12. According to Roscoe and colleagues, dating serves all of the following functions EXCEPT
    a. recreation.
    b. socialization.
    c. sex.
    d. identification.

13. For young adolescents, it is important for dates to
    a. have compatible plans for the future.
    b. be potential mates.
    c. be liked by others.
    d. be good companions.

14. A group of from 3 to 9 members that is very cohesive is called a(n)
    a. clique.
    b. crowd.
    c. association.
    d. club.

15. Which of the following is a personality risk factor?
    a. high in intelligence
    b. poverty
    c. low self-esteem
    d. problem drinking

16. Which of the following is an hallucinogenic drug?
    a. cocaine
    b. heroin
    c. amphetamines
    d. LSD

17. Moderate smoking shortens a person's life by
    a. 30 years.
    b. 20 years.
    c. 15 years.
    d. 7 years.

18. The pattern of occasional heavy drinking is highest for
    a. people in middle adulthood.
    b. females.
    c. noncollege youth.
    d. those who live in rural areas.

19. Which of the following is an accurate statement about delinquency?
    a. The age at cut-off varies by state.
    b. It involves only nonviolent crimes.
    c. Females are equally as delinquent as males.
    d. It is caused by genetic factors.

20. From first to third, what is the correct order of the causes of adolescent death?
    a. suicide, homicide, accidents
    b. accidents, homicide, suicide
    c. homicide, suicide, accidents
    d. suicide, accidents, homicide

Posttest score _____

Pretest score _____

Improvement _____

ESSAY QUESTIONS

To increase your knowledge of the material in this chapter, answer each of the following essay questions, using the text for material to support your answer.

1. Discuss the theory of "storm and stress" in adolescence. Based on your own experiences, do you think that adolescence is a period of storm and stress? Explain your answer.

2. Describe the research findings on adolescent alcohol and tobacco use.

3. Describe Erikson's concept of identity formation in adolescence and Marcia's expansion of this theory.

4. Discuss the affects of the authoritative and authoritarian parenting styles on adolescent behavior.

5. How is the American family changing and what impact has this change had on adolescent development?

6. Based on the research presented in this chapter, do you think it is best for adolescents to leave home right after high school or stay at home at least until they are finished with college or well established in a job?

7. What is the extent of peer influence in adolescence?

8. Describe the seven functions of dating suggested by Roscoe and colleagues.

9. What are the risk factors associated with suicide and what can be done to prevent adolescents from attempting suicide?

10. What are the three sets of counterbalancing factors that help adolescents cope with the transition of this period?

ANSWER KEY

Key Names

1. d	3. b	5. c
2. e	4. f	6. a

Pretest

1. a	5. b	9. b	13. b	17. c
2. c	6. a	10. a	14. b	18. d
3. d	7. d	11. c	15. a	19. b
4. b	8. a	12. d	16. d	20. a

Programmed Review

1. experiment, independent, dependent
2. autonomy, independence, identity, storm and stress, Anna Freud
3. exaggerated, parents, families
4. gradual, independent, interdependent, reciprocal
5. identity, reference, significant other
6. self-definition, continuity, framework, reconciles, social
7. statuses, identity crisis, commitment, foreclosure, parents, teachers, diffusion, moratorium, achievement
8. moratorium, parents, freedom, disapproval, college, foreclosure, authoritarian, self-esteem, persuaded, Diffusion, drop-outs, achievement, emotionally, age
9. foreclosure, diffusion, religious, political, achievement, foreclosure
10. chores, hours, appearance, eating, earlier, later
11. intellectual, solving, household, homework, discipline, leisure, strain, closeness
12. authoritative, authoritarian
13. less, gender, cohesion, adaptability, communication, separateness
14. competence, comparisons
15. themselves, appearance, popular, acquaintances, friends, intimacy, characteristics, best friends, good friends, stable, year, disloyalty
16. crowd, clique, same-sex, opposite-sex, sexes
17. 20, renewal, Voluntary, renewal, isolation, depression
18. girls, boys, group, Hanging-out, coeducational, relate
19. recreation, socialization, status, mate, sexual, companionship, intimacy
20. physically, dress, liked, personality, plans, intimacy, sex, sex
21. underestimate, invulnerable, fable, self-esteem, competence, belonging
22. nicotine, alcohol, girls, boys, adulthood, maturity, high school, males, noncollege, cities
23. rise, minimal, leveled, declined
24. delinquents, urban, ethnic, single-parent
25. social, adjust, self-control, self-esteem, peer, autonomy
26. depression, life-threatening, antisocial, inward, depressed
27. Suicide, underreported, suicide, hopelessness, abuse, stressful, firearms, psychiatric
28. body, oneself, dysfunction, mental, discord, economic, popularity, school
29. self-image, expectations, confidence
30. parents, peers, competence, responsibility, planning, organization, priorities, friend, confidante

Posttest

1. b	5. a	9. a	13. c	17. d
2. c	6. d	10. c	14. a	18. c
3. a	7. c	11. b	15. c	19. a
4. d	8. b	12. d	16. d	20. b

13
Young Adulthood: Physical and Cognitive Development

CHAPTER OUTLINE

Perspectives on Adult Development
    Age Clocks and Social Norms
    Contextual Paradigms or Approaches

General Physical Development
    Strength and Stamina
    Fitness and Health

Sex and Sexuality
    Fertility
    Sexual Responsiveness
    Same-sex Orientation and Sexual Activity
    Sexually Transmitted Diseases and Social Change

Cognitive Continuity and Change
    Cognitive Growth or Decline?
    "Stages" of Thought in Young Adulthood
    Flexibility in Intelligence

Seasons and Tasks of Adult Development
    Havighurst's Developmental Tasks
    Erikson's Developmental Tasks
    Levinson's Seasons of a Man's Life
    Levinson's Seasons of a Woman's Life
    Gould's Transformations

KEY TERMS AND CONCEPTS

To enhance your understanding of this chapter, look up each of the following words or phrases in the text and write out the definition.

Age clock	Intimacy vs. Isolation
Biological age	Lesbian
Bisexual	Life structure
Chronological age	Normative
Contextual paradigms	Psychological age
Dialectical thinking	Sexual orientation
Gay	Social age
Homophobia	Systems of meaning
Idiosyncratic	

KEY NAMES

After reading the chapter, try to match each of the following individuals with his or her contribution to the field of psychology.

_____1. Erik Erikson   a. commitment and responsibility

_____2. Roger Gould   b. developmental tasks

_____3. Robert Havighurst   c. dialectical thinking

_____4. Robert Kegan   d. intimacy versus isolation

_____5. Gisela Labouvie-Vief   e. seasons of life

_____6. Daniel Levinson   f. stages of adult thinking

_____7. William Perry   g. systems of meaning

_____8. Klaus Riegel   h. transformations

_____9. K. Warner Schaie   i. young adult intellectual development

**Try to answer each of the following questions without referring back to the text.
Then check your answers with the Answer Key at the end of this chapter and record
your Pretest Score in the space provided.**

1. Events that are expected at specific times or are shared with most people in a cohort are called
    a. normative.
    b. non-normative.
    c. idiosyncratic.
    d. normal.

2. A person's _____ clock lets him know whether he is progressing too quickly or too slowly in
    terms of social events.
    a. internal
    b. external
    c. age
    d. social

3. A person's age with respect to life expectancy is _____ age.
    a. social
    b. psychological
    c. evolutionary
    d. biological

4. Striated or voluntary muscles reach their maximum physical strength in
    a. childhood.
    b. early adolescence.
    c. late adolescence.
    d. young adulthood.

5. The leading preventable cause of death among males between 25 and 44 is
    a. accidents.
    b. HIV infection.
    c. cardiovascular disease.
    d. homicide.

6. As many as _____ of Americans have sex at least twice a week.
    a. one-quarter
    b. one-half
    c. one-third
    d. three-fourths

7. Research indicates that less than _____ percent of women report always having an orgasm during sex.
   a. 5
   b. 10
   c. 20
   d. 30

8. Which of the following is likely to lead to urinary tract infections or inflammation?
   a. chlamydia
   b. syphilis
   c. herpes
   d. gonorrhea

9. Which of the following skills increases throughout middle adulthood?
   a. reasoning and judgment
   b. rote memory
   c. speed-related performance
   d. manipulation of matrices

10. According to Klaus Riegel, the understanding of contradictions is
    a. formal operational thought.
    b. dialectical thinking.
    c. commitment and responsibility.
    d. the acquisition stage of thinking.

11. According to Schaie, young adults are in which stage of adult thinking?
    a. acquisition
    b. social responsibility
    c. executive
    d. achieving

12. The final stage in Schaie's stages of adult thinking is
    a. executive.
    b. achieving.
    c. reintegrating.
    d. acquisition.

13. Whose theory emphasized systems of meaning?
    a. Piaget
    b. Schaie
    c. Kegan
    d. Erikson

14. According to Erikson, in addition to forming an identity, the young adult must deal with the crisis of
    a. industry versus inferiority.
    b. initiative versus guilt.
    c. generativity versus self-absorption.
    d. intimacy versus isolation.

15. According to Havighurst, adjusting to aging parents is a developmental task of
    a. adolescence.
    b. early adulthood.
    c. middle adulthood.
    d. later maturity.

16. Which of the following contains the other three?
    a. novice phase
    b. early adult transition
    c. entry life structure
    d. age 30 transition

17. Who did research on the seasons of a person's life?
    a. Erikson
    b. Valliant
    c. Kegan
    d. Levinson

18. Women differ from men in their experience of the seasons of life in that they
    a. have no dream.
    b. always find a mentor.
    c. have trouble finding a special mate.
    d. develop early career choices.

19. Which of the following does NOT belong?
    a. special woman
    b. split dream
    c. gender splitting
    d. basic identity

20. Who described the progression from dualistic to relativistic thinking?
    a. Riegel
    b. Schaie
    c. Perry
    d. Gould

Pretest score _____

To test your knowledge of this material, fill in each of the blanks in the chapter review without referring back to the text. Check your answers with the Answer Key at the end of this chapter and reread any parts of the chapter that gave you trouble.

1. _____ events and transitions are expected at specific times or are shared with most people in an age cohort. In contrast, _____ events and transitions happen at any time. Because these events are not anticipated or broadly shared with others, they create considerable _____ and the need for a major _____ of a person's life.

Perspectives on Adult Development

2. Age _____ serve as a form of internal timing; they let us know when certain events in our life should occur. Neugarten and Neugarten suggest that there has been a _____ of traditional life periods, with the result that age clocks are more _____ now than they were in previous decades.

3. _____ age, a person's position with respect to life expectancy, varies from individual to individual. A person's _____ age is judged by what status that person has when compared with the cultural norms. _____ age refers to how a person adapts to environmental demands. All the age factors combine to determine _____, but the primary ingredients are the psychological characteristics of physical and social _____ and _____, independent _____ making, and some degree of _____, wisdom, reliability, integrity, and _____.

4. A _____ is a hypothetical model or framework and _____ paradigms seek to organize the effects of different kinds of forces on development.

General Physical Development

5. Organ _____, reaction _____, strength, motor _____, and _____ coordination are at their maximum between ages 25 and 30; after age 30 they _____ gradually. The major functional drop-off in most of the body's biological systems occurs after age _____. Declines in physical skills and capacities are most notable in _____ situations or at times when physical demands are _____.

6. Many _____ reach their peak of skill and training during early adulthood. This is related to the fact that between the ages of 23 and 27, the striated, or voluntary _____ achieve their maximum physical strength. In addition, peak _____ strength is achieved between the ages of 20 and 30, and peak _____ strength is achieved at about age 20. Better _____ and _____ throughout the adult years more than compensates for advanced age.

7. Despite overall declines in death rates for all age levels, _____ causes of death remain high during young adulthood. The leading preventable cause of death among people aged 25 to 44 is _____.

8. Many physically disabled people may become _____ by their limitations during this future-oriented period. In order to adapt to a physical disability, it is important to understand the disability and its _____. The second aspect of adaptation involves _____ with the attitudes and values of others and their social expectations. The physically disabled are often _____ and must deal with _____. Finally, one must cope with an array of hopes, fears, dreams, frustrations, lost _____, and guilt and anger. Some individuals adopt a definition of themselves as physically _____ rather than physically disabled. This attitude is particularly common among disabled _____. The ADA was passed in 1990 and makes it illegal to _____ against individuals with disabilities in employment, public accommodations, transportation and telecommunications, and requires companies to make reasonable _____ for the needs of their disabled employees.

Sex and sexuality

9. There are three basic patterns of sexual relations: one-third of Americans have sex at least twice a _____, one-third have sex several times a _____, and one-third a few times a _____ or not at all. The vast majority of Americans are _____. The group having the most sex, and who are most likely to have orgasms during sex, are _____ couples.

10. During the young adult years, a woman's supply of _____ remains relatively stable. Females are _____ with their life supply of approximately 400,000 ova, but men continually produce _____ following puberty.

11. It appears that college students became more _____ in their rates of sexual intercourse during the 1980s. This may be attributable to an increased fear of _____, and may also reflect the growing _____ of young women.

12. The dominant pattern of sexual intimacy between men and women in the 1990s appears to be one of increased _____ and mutual _____, yet there is a marked difference in the patterns of male and female _____.

13. Sexual _____ refers to which sex a person is physically attracted to as well as which sexual _____ he or she might wish to become emotionally involved with. It is a distinct part of most people's _____ and sense of _____. For a small but significant minority who discover in themselves a _____ orientation altogether or in part, sexual identity formation is often extremely difficult. In the United States, _____ (better called sexual _____) remains pervasive. By young adulthood, some same-sex oriented individuals _____ the larger society's prejudiced view of them.

14. Chlamydia is a leading cause of _____ tract infections in men and is also responsible for about half of the reported cases of _____ infection. In women, it can cause inflammation of the _____ and _____ tubes. Gonorrhea can cause _____. For herpes, there is no _____. Syphilis can cause severe health problems including _____ and even _____ if left untreated. Pregnant women with untreated syphilis can infect their developing _____.

Cognitive Continuity and Change

15. Older adults have a broader _____ base. In a longitudinal design, individuals usually show some _____ on intelligence test performance through their 20s and 30s, leveling off at around age _____. _____-related performances, _____ memory, and the manipulation of _____ are skills that peak in the late teens and early adulthood. Skills that are _____ frequently are maintained better and cognitive abilities such as _____ and _____ continue to develop throughout life.

16. Perry says that students move through a progression of stages from a basic _____ to tolerance for many competing points of view (conceptual _____) to self-chosen _____ and _____.

17. Klaus Riegel emphasizes the understanding of _____ as an important achievement of adult cognitive development. He calls this _____ thinking.

18. For Labouvie-Vief, the course of cognitive development should involve both the evolution of _____ and the evolution of self-_____ from childhood well into adulthood. She describes a longer process of _____ in which adults become truly _____ and are able to handle the _____ and _____ of their life experience.

19. Schaie suggests that during childhood and adolescence we acquire increasingly complex structures for _____ the world. The powerful tools of formal operational thinking are the key achievement of this period which he calls _____. In young adulthood, we use our intellectual abilities to pursue our careers and choose a lifestyle in the _____ period. Individuals who successfully do this acquire a certain degree of personal _____ and move on to the period involving _____ responsibility. In middle age, we use our cognitive abilities to solve _____ for others in an _____ function. In the later years, the central task is one of _____ many of the elements experienced earlier in life.

20. Kegan emphasizes that human beings continue to develop systems of _____ well into adulthood. Our own particular systems of meaning become _____.

Seasons and Tasks of Adult Development

21. Havighurst described a series of developmental _____. In young adulthood, the tasks mostly involve starting a _____ and establishing a _____. In middle age, they center on _____ what was established earlier. In later years, _____ are made.

22. Erikson's _____ theory states that the crisis of _____ is the issue most characteristic of young adulthood. Intimacy involves establishing a mutually _____, close _____ with another person. It represents the union of two _____, but without the loss of each individual's _____ qualities. Isolation is the inability or failure to achieve _____.

23. Levinson believes that the person constructs a _____ structure composed of the person's social and environmental _____. He found that maturation and adjustment depended greatly on the individual's growth in a _____ phase from ages 17 to 33. Within this stage were three distinct periods called early adult _____, entering the adult _____, and the _____ transition. To achieve complete entry into adulthood, the person must define a _____ of adult accomplishment, find a _____, develop a _____, and establish _____.

24. Men tend to have a _____ vision of their futures focused on their career, while women tend to have _____ dreams. Although relations with mentors are considered important to the career and life development of young adults, women enter into this relationship less _____ than men. Women may also have trouble finding a special _____ to support their dream. A male mate rarely sustains the female's dream if it starts to _____ his preeminence. Women settle on a _____ much later than men and generally do not cease being beginners in the world of work until well into _____.

25. Gould views growth as the process of casting off childish _____ and false _____ in favor of self-reliance and self-acceptance. From ages 16 to 22, the major false assumption is "I'll always belong to my _____ and believe in their _____." From 22 to 28, young adults make an assumption that reflects their continuing doubts about _____. From 28 to 34, the major false assumption is "Life is _____ and controllable." From 35 to 45, there is full _____ in the adult world.

POSTTEST

Now try to answer each of the following questions without referring back to the text and check your answers with the Answer Key at the end of this chapter. Record your Posttest score in the space provided, then enter your Pretest score and subtract to find your improvement score.

1. Which of the following is most likely to be an idiosyncratic event?
   a. high school graduation
   b. a heart attack
   c. puberty
   d. retirement

2. Which age is judged by the position an individual has when compared with cultural norms?
   a. biological
   b. psychological
   c. social
   d. cognitive

3. The _____ age refers to how a person adapts to environmental demands.
   a. psychological
   b. biological
   c. social
   d. intellectual

4. Major league baseball players generally peak around age
   a. 18 to 20.
   b. 20 to 25.
   c. 25 to 28.
   d. 27 to 30.

5. Lung, heart, and kidney diseases, among others, start to appear in
   a. adolescence.
   b. young adulthood.
   c. middle adulthood.
   d. late adulthood.

6. After age 38, fertility declines because
   a. men stop making sperm.
   b. women lose interest in sex.
   c. people are often too tired for sex.
   d. there is a rapid decline in ova.

7. Which of the following STDs can cause sterility?
   a. chlamydia
   b. gonorrhea
   c. herpes
   d. AIDS

8. All of the following skills peak in the teens and early twenties EXCEPT
   a. speed-related performance.
   b. rote memory.
   c. judgment and reasoning.
   d. manipulation of matrices.

9. According to Perry, the progression of thought in college students is
   a. basic dualism, conceptual relativism, chosen ideas and convictions.
   b. chosen ideas and convictions, basic dualism, conceptual relativism.
   c. basic dualism, chosen ideas and convictions, conceptual relativism.
   d. conceptual relativism, chosen ideas and convictions, basic dualism.

10. Piaget placed the young adult in which stage?
    a. concrete operations
    b. conceptual relativism
    c. formal operations
    d. dialectical thinking

11. According to Schaie, social responsibility first appears in
    a. childhood.
    b. adolescence.
    c. young adulthood.
    d. middle adulthood.

12. Kegan based his theory on the work of
    a. Erikson.
    b. Levinson.
    c. Loevinger.
    d. Havighurst.

13. Who suggested developmental tasks for young adulthood which include selecting a mate and rearing children?
    a. Freud
    b. Levinson
    c. Havighurst
    d. Erikson

14. Which of the following is a task for older adulthood?
    a. Selecting a mate.
    b. Developing adult leisure-time activities.
    c. Relating to one's spouse as a person.
    d. Meeting social and civic obligations.

15. According to Levinson, the overall pattern that underlines a person's life is the
    a. structure of living.
    b. life pattern.
    c. system of meaning.
    d. life structure.

16. According to Levinson, a young man must master all of the following developmental tasks EXCEPT
    a. finding a mentor.
    b. developing a career.
    c. finishing schooling.
    d. establishing intimacy.

17. Women are more likely than men to experience
    a. split dreams.
    b. mentoring.
    c. a special woman.
    d. formal thinking.

18. According to Gould, the belief that life is simple and controllable is characteristic of people aged
    a. 16 to 22.
    b. 22 to 28.
    c. 28 to 34.
    d. 35 to 45.

19. Roger Gould's focus was
    a. psychoanalytic.
    b. social.
    c. psychiatric.
    d. cognitive.

20. Which theorist emphasized commitment and responsibility as the hallmark of adult maturity?
    a. Erikson
    b. Labouvie-Vief
    c. Perry
    d. Levinson

Posttest score _____

Pretest score _____

Improvement _____

ESSAY QUESTIONS

To add to your understanding of the chapter material, answer each of the following essay questions as completely as possible, using material from the text to support your answer.

1. Describe normative and idiosyncratic influences and give examples of each from your own experiences. Explain which you think had the greatest impact on your life.

2. How are Erikson's and Havighurst's theories related?

3. As a person enters early adulthood, he or she experiences physical changes. Describe the major physical changes a person should expect to experience in this stage of development.

4. What is dialectical thinking and how does it compare to formal operational thought?

5. Discuss the research on sexuality in young adulthood.

6. Compare and contrast same-sex and heterosexual relationships.

7. Describe what Perry suggests are stages of "college thought."

8. Describe Gould's transformations.

9. Contrast Levinson's "seasons of a man's life" with the stages a woman goes through.

10. Which theory of adult development makes the most sense to you? Explain your answer.

ANSWER KEY

Key Names

1. d	3. b	5. a	7. i	9. f
2. h	4. g	6. e	8. c	

Pretest

1. a	5. a	9. a	13. c	17. d
2. c	6. c	10. b	14. d	18. c
3. d	7. d	11. d	15. c	19. d
4. d	8. a	12. c	16. a	20. c

Programmed Review

1. Normative, idiosyncratic, stress, reorganization
2. clocks, blurring, flexible
3. Biological, social, Psychological, maturity, independence, autonomy, decision, stability, compassion
4. paradigm, contextual
5. functioning, time, skills, sensorimotor, decline, 40, emergency, extreme
6. athletes, muscles, leg, hand, nutrition, training
7. preventable, accidents
8. overwhelmed, limitations, coping, stereotyped, prejudices, opportunities, challenged, athletes, discriminate, accommodations
9. week, month, year, monogamous, married
10. ova, born, sperm
11. conservative, sexually transmitted disease, self-assurance

12. communication, satisfaction, satisfaction
13. orientation, partners, identity, self-concept, same-sex, homophobia, prejudice, internalize
14. urinary, testicular, cervix, fallopian, sterility, cure, sterility, death, fetus
15. knowledge, increase, 45, Speed, rote, matrices, exercised, judgment, reasoning
16. dualism, relativism, ideas, convictions
17. contradictions, dialectical
18. logic, regulation, evolution, autonomous, contradictions, ambiguities
19. understanding, acquisition, achieving, independence, social, problems, executive, reintegrating
20. meaning, idiosyncratic
21. tasks, family, career, maintaining, adjustments
22. psychosocial, intimacy versus isolation, satisfying, relationship, identities, unique, mutuality
23. life, relationships, novice, transition, world, age-30, dream, mentor, career, intimacy
24. unified, split, frequently, man, threaten, career, middle adulthood
25. illusions, assumptions, parents, world, self-sufficiency, simple, involvement

Posttest

1. b	5. b	9. a	13. c	17. a
2. c	6. d	10. c	14. d	18. c
3. a	7. b	11. d	15. d	19. d
4. d	8. c	12. c	16. c	20. b

14

Young Adulthood: Personality and Sociocultural Development

CHAPTER OUTLINE

Continuity and Change

Self, Family, and Work
    The Personal Self: Self-actualization and Self-regard
    Self as Family Member
    Self as Worker

Forming Intimate Relationships
    Adult Friendships
    Sternberg's Triangular Theory of Love
    Couple Formation and Development

Parenthood and Adult Development
    The Family Life Cycle
    The Transition to Parenthood
    Coping with Children's Developmental Stages
    Coping with Single Parenthood

The Occupational Cycle
    Stages of Vocational Life
    Occupational Choice and Preparation
    Gaining a Place in the Workforce

Work and Gender
    A Changing Statistical Picture
    Changes in Work Patterns
    The Many Meanings of Work
    Myths and Stereotypes That Affect Women's Employment
    Dynamics of the Dual-Earner Couple

KEY TERMS AND CONCEPTS

To help increase your understanding of this chapter, look up each of the following terms in the chapter and write out the definition.

Conditions of worth
Decision/commitment
Dual-earner couple
Extrinsic factors of work
Family leave
Humanistic psychologists

Intimacy
Intrinsic factors of work
Occupational cycle
Passion
Reality shock
Self-actualization
Unconditional positive regard

KEY NAMES

After reading the chapter, match each of the following individuals to his or her contribution to the field of psychology and then check your answers with the Answer Key at the end of this chapter.

_____1. Urie Bronfenbrenner

_____2. Richard Centers

_____3 Erik Erikson

_____4. Sigmund Freud

_____5. Ellen Galinsky

_____6. Robert Havighurst

_____7. Lois Hoffman

_____8. Abraham Maslow

_____9. Bernard Murstein

_____10. Carl Rogers

_____11. Robert Sternberg

a. attitudinal independence

b. conditions of worth

c. ecological systems model

d. identity

e. instrumental theory of mate selection

f. psychoanalytic theory

g. self-actualization

h. stages of vocational life

i. stages of parenthood

j. stimulus-value-role theory

k. triangular theory of love

After reading the chapter, try to answer each of the following questions without referring to the text. Check your answers with the Answer Key at the end of this chapter and record your score in the space provided.

1. What is the lowest need on Maslow's hierarchy of needs?
   a. physiological
   b. safety
   c. belongingness and love
   d. esteem

2. Who proposed that we should view ourselves and others with unconditional positive regard?
   a. Maslow
   b. Bronfenbrenner
   c. Erikson
   d. Rogers

3. All of the following are extrinsic factors of work EXCEPT
   a. salary.
   b. convenient hours.
   c. the abilities of the individual.
   d. the status of the job.

4. Who developed the triangular theory of love?
   a. Freud
   b. Sternberg
   c. Erikson
   d. Centers

5. According to Sternberg, intimacy and passion without commitment is called
   a. romantic love.
   b. infatuation.
   c. companionate love.
   d. empty love.

6. Who proposed the stimulus-value-role theory?
   a. Centers
   b. Freud
   c. Murstein
   d. Erikson

7. According to Murstein, the final stage of marital choice involves
   a. complementary needs.
   b. determining whether the couple can function in compatible roles.
   c. negotiating boundaries.
   d. a focus on need gratification.

8. In the United States, _____ percent of men and women marry at some time in their lives.
    a. 30
    b. 50
    c. 70
    d. 90

9. The second milestone in the family life cycle is
    a. the transition to parenthood.
    b. leaving the family of origin.
    c. establishing the family of procreation.
    d. marriage.

10. According to Galinsky, the first stage of parenthood is
    a. the image-making stage.
    b. the authority stage.
    c. the interpretive stage.
    d. the departure stage.

11. When children become teenagers, parents pass into which of Galinsky's suggested stages of parenthood?
    a. departure
    b. image-making
    c. interdependence
    d. interpretive

12. Which of the following is NOT one of the three most important reasons for the increase in single parent families headed by women?
    a. a substantial increase in separation from spouses
    b. an increase in the divorce rate
    c. a growing number of never-married mothers
    d. an increase in widowhood

13. In looking at custodial parents, which of the following is true about single fathers as compared to single mothers?
    a. They are less committed to the care of their children.
    b. They are in a better financial state.
    c. They worry less about the time and attention they give their children.
    d. They maintain more moderate levels of emotional involvement with their children.

14. Which of the following is a humanistic psychologist?
    a. Freud
    b. Havighurst
    c. Rogers
    d. Levinson

15. African-Americans and women are
    a. underrepresented in lower paying jobs.
    b. over-represented in highly paid professions.
    c. underrepresented in service occupations.
    d. over-represented in lower status jobs.

16. According to Havighurst, the first vocational life stage involves
    a. identification with a worker.
    b. acquiring the basic habits of industry.
    c. acquiring an identity as a worker.
    d. contemplating a productive and responsible life.

17. Workers are at the high-point of their careers in which of Havighurst's vocational life stages?
    a. maintaining a productive society
    b. acquiring an identity as a worker
    c. contemplating a productive and responsible life
    d. identification with a worker

18. Mentors perform all of the following roles EXCEPT
    a. teaching and training.
    b. serving as role models.
    c. providing financial support.
    d. easing transition to independent work status.

19. Informal job training involves all of the following EXCEPT
    a. acquisition of role expectations.
    b. learning attitudes.
    c. absorbing norms.
    d. attending college.

20. Researchers have found that working women, compared to nonworking women,
    a. experience more physical health problems.
    b. have higher self-esteem.
    c. experience more psychological problems.
    d. feel less connected to others.

Pretest score _____

To test your knowledge of this chapter, fill in the blanks in the following chapter review without referring to the text. Then check your answers with the Answer Key at the end of this chapter and reread any sections in the chapter with which you had trouble.

1. Erikson referred to the achievement of _____ and _____ as the milestones of successful
    adulthood.

Continuity and Change

2. We become socialized to new roles within the contexts of _____, independent _____, sustained _____ with another person, marriage, and family. Stable personality is typically not achieved until the latter part of _____ adulthood or in early _____ adulthood.

Self, Family, and Work

3. In Bronfenbrenner's _____ systems model, development is a dynamic, multidirectional process involving the individual's immediate _____, the social _____, and the values, laws, and customs of the _____ in which the individual lives.

4. Maslow's theory stresses each person's goal for _____, the full development and utilization of talents and abilities, which can only be expressed after _____ needs are met. He arranged human needs in a _____ with the most basic _____ needs at the bottom, followed by the needs for _____, to _____ and feel loved, to feel self-_____, and finally to reach self-actualization.

5. Rogers, another _____ psychologist, was concerned with an individual's conditions of _____ which can lead to low _____, a sense of _____, and recurrent _____ and _____. He proposed that we should view ourselves and others with unconditional positive _____.

6. Erikson emphasized _____. There are three basic identity styles in adults in each age range: those who are predominantly _____ and unrealistically prefer to see themselves as _____; those who are predominantly _____ and too _____; and those who are _____ and realistically _____ positive and negative experiences into their identities.

7. Young unmarried adults are often in _____ from the family they grew up in to the family they create. Hoffman identified four aspects of this process including _____ independence, in which the young adult becomes less socially and psychologically dependent on the parents for support and affection; _____ independence, in which attitudes, values, and belief systems are developed that differ from those of parents; _____ independence, which is the ability to support oneself financially; and _____ independence, involving separating from parents without feelings of guilt or betrayal.

8. Characteristics of a job and the abilities of the individual are _____ factors of work, and the rewards of salary and status are examples of _____ factors of work. Workers who talk more about the intrinsic factors of work tend to report more job _____ and higher _____ and personal _____ in their jobs, and their _____ is defined largely by their work or career. Friendship seems to be an important _____ factor of jobs.

Forming Close Relationships

9. Sternberg's _____ theory of love demonstrates the complexity of achieving love relationships. Love has three components including _____, the feeling of closeness that occurs in love relationships, _____, which is physical attraction and sexual arousal, and _____, which in the short-term is reflected in the decision that a person loves someone and in the long-term by maintaining that _____.

10. Freud's psychoanalytic theory states that the attraction that children feel to the _____ of the opposite sex is transferred to their potential _____. The _____ theory of mate selection, developed by Centers, focuses on needs gratification, and the _____ theory of Murstein states that mate selection is motivated by each partner's attempt to get the best possible deal. During the stimulus stage, initial judgments are formed on the other's _____, personality and intelligence. The second stage is a time when _____ reveal whether interests, attitudes, beliefs, and needs are compatible, and during the final stage, the couple determines if they can function in compatible _____ in a marriage or other type of relationship. According to the family _____ perspective, the task of _____ negotiations is crucial to couple formation.

11. In the United States, over _____ of men and women will marry at some point in their lives. _____, or living together, is characterized by an overt acknowledgment that the couple is not married. It has been estimated that about _____ of all cohabitating couples marry. The couple living together must deal with the issues of _____, _____, and _____.

12. Periodically, large groups of people have remained _____. Many choose this way of life as a means of enjoying _____ relationships when they are successful and avoiding the problems of a bad _____.

Parenthood and Adult Development

13. Families go through a predictable family _____ cycle marked by specific events. The first milestone is reached when the individual leaves his of her family of _____. The second milestone is usually _____, and the third is the _____ of the first child and the beginning of _____. Other milestones include enrollment in _____ of the first child, the _____ of the last child, the _____ of the last child, and the _____ of the spouse.

14. The transition to parenthood is marked by changes in _____ and inner _____, shifts in _____ and _____ within the marriage, shifts in the _____ roles and relationships, changing roles and relationships _____ the family, and new _____ roles and relationships.

15. Women characteristically adjust their lifestyles to give priority to their _____ and family roles. Men more often intensify their _____ efforts. Some men are _____ of their partner's ability to reproduce and of the close emotional _____ established between mother and infant. Couples need to find _____ for each other because there appears to be less _____ and sharing of _____, and increased _____ after the birth of a child.

16. Social _____, especially from the husband, seems to be crucial for a new mother. Happiness in marriage during _____ is an important factor in determining how both husband and wife adjust. In fact, the father's _____ is especially affected by the mother's evaluation of both the marriage and her pregnancy. Parental _____ is also important to good adjustment, as are the baby's _____.

17. Each critical period for the child produces or reactivates a critical period for the _____. Galinsky described six stages of _____ beginning with the _____ stage, which takes place from conception to birth, and followed by the _____ stage from birth to 2 years, the _____ stage from the second to fifth year, the _____ stage in the middle childhood years, the _____ stage during the teenage years, and the _____ stage when children leave home. During each stage, parents must resolve their own _____ at a new and more advanced level of integration.

18. Single parents are becoming increasingly _____ in the United States. One-third of homes were maintained by a single _____ in 1995. This increase in single parents was due to the rising _____ rate, and to the increase in _____ mothers and women with children who are _____ from their spouses.

19. Single mothers consistently _____ less than single fathers, and single-mother homes are more numerous and more often poor among people who identify as _____. The majority of black children will spend at least half of their childhood in _____. However, African-Americans and Hispanic-Americans are more likely to live in _____ households, and these extended families may help provide additional _____, psychological, and _____ resources for the single mother.

20. Single fathers are usually better off _____. Many of them take on extensive _____ roles after their divorces, and most maintain high levels of _____ involvement with their children, are heavily invested in and committed to their _____, and worry about _____ them or not spending enough _____ with them.

21. Families with _____ parents are relatively new and less research has been conducted. So far there appears to be an overall picture of _____ adjustment.

The Occupational Cycle

22. An adult's working life follows what is called an _____ cycle beginning with the thoughts and experiences that lead to a _____ of occupation, continuing through the pursuit of the chosen _____, and ending with _____ from the workforce.

23. Havighurst deals with the _____ of attitudes and work skills. During "_____ with a worker", children identify with working parents and the idea of working enters their self-concepts. In "acquiring the basic habits of _____," students learn to organize their time and efforts to accomplish tasks. In "acquiring an _____ as a worker," people choose their occupations and begin to prepare for them. In "becoming a _____ person," adults perfect the skills required by their chosen jobs and begin to move ahead in their careers. In "maintaining a _____ society," workers are at the high point of their careers, and in "_____ a productive and responsible life," workers are retired.

24. People who identify as black and women tend to be over-represented in the lower _____ and lower _____ jobs and under-represented in the highly _____ professions. This is possibly because of the _____ that ultimately led to their occupation, and to _____.

25. Formal occupational preparation includes structured _____ in schools as well as _____ training. Informal occupational preparation is the process of adopting the attitudes, norms, and role _____ appropriate for a particular job.

26. When young adults start working, they may experience reality _____. When the training ends and the job begins, novices quickly learn that some of their expectations were _____. The shock of reality may result in a period of _____ and _____ until the young workers adjust to the new situation.

27. Levinson emphasizes the role of _____. They perform _____ and _____ roles, sponsor the young worker's _____, serve as _____ for social as well as work-related behavior, and ease the transition to _____ adult work status.

28. For those who follow a classic occupational cycle, the mid-career period is a time of _____. For Levinson's men, the late 30s was a time of establishing a _____ in society, forgetting about attractive _____ careers, and striving for _____. It also involved attempting to create some _____ at work and in life, and for some, it involved increasing _____ and _____, drawing away from the _____, and becoming _____.

29. The classic occupational cycle is no longer the _____ pattern. Only a _____ of workers now stay with the same company throughout their careers.

Work and Gender

30. One of the most notable developments in employment has been the great increase in the percentage of _____ in the U. S. workforce. Currently, less than _____ of married women stay home full-time with their children.

31. Women follow a greater _____ of patterns of career development and most still _____ work at least temporarily to care for _____. These interruptions may contribute to the _____ gap between men and women.

32. Women participate in the working world primarily for _____ necessity. They tend to find work _____ and _____, consider their work an opportunity for _____, like the benefits of _____, increased _____ security, and the possibility of _____.

33. Working women tend to be both _____ and _____ healthier than nonworking women and they have higher _____.

`34. It has been found that many women are similar to men in their attitudes about _____ taking, _____, and _____.

35. The dual-earner couple has been defined as one in which the husband works _____ and the wife works _____ or more hours a week. The gains in _____ provide for a higher standard of living. For college-educated dual-earner couples, the most important benefit is the wife's _____. Husbands in such families report more marital _____ and over a third of couples studied reported role _____ resulting from job _____, work _____, scheduling _____ between family and work, and family _____.

36. Women who work are still primarily responsible for _____ and _____. In the United States, both males and females are entitled to a minimum of 12 weeks of _____ leave.

37-43. Place a "yes" or "no" in each of the spaces following the seven types of love in the table below to indicate whether or not the factor is present in that type of love.

Kind of Love	Intimacy	Passion	Decision/Commitment
37. Liking	_____	_____	_____
38. Infatuated love	_____	_____	_____
39. Empty love	_____	_____	_____
40. Romantic love	_____	_____	_____
41. Companionate love	_____	_____	_____
42. Fatuous love	_____	_____	_____
43. Consummate love	_____	_____	_____

Now try to answer each of the following questions without referring to the text. Check your answers with the Answer Key at the end of this chapter and record your Posttest score in the space provided. Enter your Pretest score and subtract to find your improvement score.

1. Which of the following individuals proposed the ecological systems model of development?
   a. Bronfenbrenner
   b. Erikson
   c. Levinson
   d. Havighurst

2. Who developed a hierarchy of needs?
   a. Erikson
   b. Maslow
   c. Rogers
   d. Sternberg

3. Which of the following is NOT one of the forms of independence described by Hoffman as part of the process of transition from the family one grows up in to the family one creates?
   a. emotional
   b. attitudinal
   c. conflictual
   d. intellectual

4. The characteristics of a job and the particular abilities possessed by workers are the _____ factors of work.
   a. extrinsic
   b. motivational
   c. intrinsic
   d. explicit

5. According to Sternberg, the feeling of closeness that occurs in love relationships is
   a. commitment.
   b. intimacy.
   c. passion.
   d. compassion.

6. In Sternberg's triarchic theory of love, companionate love consists of
   a. passion and commitment.
   b. passion and intimacy.
   c. only intimacy.
   d. intimacy and commitment.

7. According to Freud, we choose the person we will marry based on
   a. transferring our feelings for our parent of the opposite sex.
   b. the reinforcements received from the person.
   c. social pressures.
   d. innate biological pressures.

8. The instrumental theory of mate selection was proposed by
   a. Freud.
   b. Murstein.
   c. Centers.
   d. Erikson

9. It has been estimated that _____ of cohabitators eventually marry.
   a. one-quarter
   b. one-third
   c. one-half
   d. two-thirds

10. Which of the following is the first "milestone" in the family life cycle?
    a. leaving the family of origin
    b. leaving the family of procreation
    c. beginning the transition to parenthood
    d. the birth of the first child

11. From the birth of a child to his or her second birthday, parents are in which stage?
    a. image making
    b. authority
    c. nurturing
    d. interpretive

12. The middle childhood years are in which parenting stage?
    a. interdependence
    b. nurturing
    c. authority
    d. interpretive

13. African-American homes are more likely to be all of the following EXCEPT
    a. single parent.
    b. at the poverty level.
    c. headed by men.
    d. intergenerational.

14. What is at the top of Maslow's hierarchy of needs?
    a. physiological needs
    b. self-actualization
    c. esteem needs
    d. belongingness

15. Which of the following is true of dual-earner couples?
    a. There are fewer stresses and role conflicts.
    b. Husbands report more marital satisfaction.
    c. Domestic tasks are shared equally.
    d. The amount of work men do around the house decreases **as** income increases.

16. According to Havighurst, between 10 and 15 years of age, young people are
    a. acquiring the basic habits of industry.
    b. acquiring an identity as a worker.
    c. becoming a productive person.
    d. contemplating a productive and responsible life.

17. In a dual-earner couple, the man works full time and the wife works at least _____ hours a week.
    a. 5
    b. 10
    c. 15
    d. 20

18. What percent of black families are headed by women?
    a. 11
    b. 33
    c. 58
    d. 72

19. For those who follow a classic occupational cycle, the mid-career period is the time of
    a. establishment.
    b. consolidation.
    c. investigation.
    d. job change.

20. Men and women differ in their work patterns in that
    a. men follow a greater variety of patterns.
    b. women are the natural providers.
    c. most women work in factories.
    d. most women still interrupt work to take care of children.

Posttest score _____

Pretest score _____

Improvement _____

ESSAY QUESTIONS

To develop an even better understanding of the material in this chapter, answer each of the following essay questions as completely as you can, referring to the text material to support your answer.

1. Describe the three systems that make up adult development: self as individual, self as family member, and self as worker.

2. Discuss the factors present in the transition from the family one is born in to the family one creates.

3. Differentiate between intrinsic and extrinsic factors of a job. Describe some of the intrinsic and extrinsic factors that you have experienced and explain which were most important to your reaction to the job.

4. Describe and compare the theories of mate selection suggested by Freud, Centers, Winch, and Murstein.

5. Describe the research on cohabitation. Based on the results of this research, would you recommend that someone enter into such a relationship?

6. Describe what in known so far about families with same-sex parents.

7. Describe the stages of parenting and give examples of each, from your own personal observations if possible.

8. Describe the vocational stages suggested by Havighurst. Do you think they are realistic? Explain your answer.

9. Explain the difference between formal and informal occupational preparation.

10. Compare and contrast the roles of men and women in occupations and as members of a dual-worker couple.

ANSWER KEY

Key Names

1. c	3. d	5. i	7. a	9. j	11. k
2. e	4. f	6. h	8. g	10. b	

Pretest

1. a	5. a	9. d	13. b	17. a
2. d	6. c	10. a	14. c	18. c
3. c	7. b	11. c	15. d	19. d
4. b	8. d	12. d	16. a	20. b

Programmed Review

1. intimacy, generativity
2. work, living, intimacy, young, middle
3. ecological, surroundings, environment, culture
4. self-actualization, lower, hierarchy, physiological, safety, belong, esteem
5. humanistic, worth, self-esteem, failure, anxiety, despair, regard
6. identity, assimilative, unchanging, accommodative, changeable, balanced, integrate
7. transition, emotional, attitudinal, functional, conflictual
8. intrinsic, extrinsic, satisfaction, motivation, involvement, identity, extrinsic
9. triangular, intimacy, passion, decision/commitment, love
10. parent, mate, instrumental, stimulus-value-role, appearance, conversations, roles, system, boundary
11. 90 percent, Cohabitating, one-third, commitment, fidelity, permanence
12. single, intimate, marriage
13. life, origin, marriage, birth, parenthood, school, birth, departure, death
14. identity, life, roles, relationships, generational, outside, parenting
15. parenting, work, envious, bond, time, communication, interests, conflict
16. support, pregnancy, adjustment, self-esteem, characteristics
17. parents, parenthood, image-making, nurturing, authority, interpretive, interdependence, departure, conflicts
18. common, mother, divorce, never-married, separated
19. earn, black, poverty, intergenerational, financial, social
20. financially, parenting, emotional, care, failing, time
21. same-sex, positive
22. occupational, choice, career, retirement
23. acquisition, identification, industry, identity, productive, productive, contemplating
24. status, paying, paid, choices, discrimination
25. learning, on-the-job, expectations
26. shock, unrealistic, frustration, anger
27. mentors, teaching, training, advancement, models, independent
28. consolidation, niche, alternative, advancement, stability, responsibility, prestige, mentor, autonomous
29. dominant, minority
30. women, 11 percent
31. variety, interrupt, children, wage
32. economic, interesting, challenging, self-direction, salary, future, advancement
33. physically, psychologically, self-esteem
34. risk, salaries, advancement

35. full-time, 20, money, self-fulfillment, dissatisfaction, conflicts, demands, hours, conflicts, crises
36. housework, child care, family
37. yes, no, no
38. no, yes, no
39. no, no, yes
40. yes, yes, no
41. yes, no, yes
42. no, yes, yes
43. yes, yes, yes

Posttest

1. a	5. b	9. b	13. c	17. d
2. b	6. c	10. a	14. b	18. c
3. d	7. a	11. c	15. d	19. b
4. c	8. c	12. d	16. b	20. d

15

Middle Adulthood: Physical and Cognitive Development

CHAPTER OUTLINE

Development in Middle Age
Prime Time or The Beginning of the End?
Midlife Crisis and Related Myths

Physical Continuity and Change
Changes in Capabilities
Menopause and the Climacteric
Sexuality in the Middle Years

Health and Disease
The Good News About Aging and Health
Major Diseases of Middle Adulthood
Cumulative Effects of Health Habits
Stress and Health
Ethnicity, Poverty, and Health

Cognitive Continuity and Change
Fluid versus Crystallized Intelligence
Experience and Expertise
Cognitive Skills in Context
Functional Changes in Cognition

KEY TERMS AND CONCEPTS

In order to be sure that you understand the vocabulary of this chapter, look up each of the following terms in the text and write out the definition. Because there are so few new terms in this chapter, take the time to go back and review some of the terms in the other chapters to be sure you have not forgotten any of them.

Climacteric
Command generation
Crisis model
Crystallized intelligence
Declarative knowledge

Fluid intelligence
Menopause
Osteoporosis
Procedural knowledge
Sensuality
Transition model

KEY NAMES

After reading the chapter, try to match the following individuals with their contribution to the field of psychology and then check your answers with the Answer Key at the end of this chapter. You will notice that some of these names were discussed in earlier chapters. I have included them here because they deal with middle adulthood as well.

_____1. Else Frenkel-Brunswick

_____2. Raymond Cattell

_____3. Roger Gould

_____4. Ronald Kessler

_____5. Richard Lazarus

_____6. Daniel Levinson

_____7. K. Warner Schaie

a. age 48 crisis

b. fluid/crystallized intelligence

c. gentle shift into midlife

d little hassles

e. seasons of life

f. stages of adult thinking

g. transformations

Try to answer each of the following questions without referring back to the text. Check your answers with the Answer Key at the end of this chapter and record your Pretest score in the space provided.

1. The "command generation" is a term used to describe people between the ages of
   a. 20 and 30.
   b. 20 and 40.
   c. 30 and 50.
   d. 40 and 60.

2. While the _____ model links the normative developmental changes of middle age to predictable crises, the _____ model rejects the idea that a mid-life crisis is a normative developmental event.
   a. crisis; transition
   b. normative; idiosyncratic
   c. non-normative; normative
   d. transition; idiosyncratic

3. Research in sensory functioning in middle adulthood has found that
   a. sensitivity to temperature decreases.
   b. visual acuity declines rapidly from 35 on.
   c. hearing loss is more common in men than in women.
   d. sensitivity to taste and smell remains high.

4. The heart pumps _____ percent less blood for each decade after adulthood.
   a. 2
   b. 8
   c. 16
   d. 25

5. Which of the following individuals believes that middle age is a transition period involving a redirection of goals?
   a. Freud
   b. Kessler
   c. Neugarten
   d. Super

6. The end of menstruation is called
   a. climacteric.
   b. menarche.
   c. menopause.
   d. middle age.

7. Two established long-term effects of menopause are
   a. changes in bone mass and genitals.
   b. night sweats and hot flashes.
   c. cardiac and respiratory disease.
   d. gray hair and wrinkles.

8. The disease associated with loss of bone mass is
   a. arteriosclerosis.
   b. arthritis.
   c. rheumatism.
   d. osteoporosis.

9. Hormone replacement therapy involves which two hormones?
   a. estrogen and androgen
   b. thyroxin and progesterone
   c. testosterone and androgen
   d. estrogen and progesterone

10. On the average, women experience their last menstrual period between the ages of
    a. 55 and 65.
    b. 45 and 55.
    c. 40 and 50.
    d. 50 and 60.

11. Research on weight gain in middle adulthood indicates that
    a. most people require drastic weight loss programs.
    b. a 5 to 10 pound weight gain is critical.
    c. it is healthy to gain a pound or so a year after age 40.
    d. adults should lose a pound a year after age 40.

12. Hispanic-Americans are more likely than whites to have all of the following diseases
    EXCEPT
    a. AIDS.
    b. hypertension.
    c. cancer.
    d. diabetes.

13. What percent of people maintain a stable level of intellectual performance into their seventies?
    a. 15 to 30
    b. 30 to 45
    c. 45 to 60
    d. 60 to 75

14. All of the following are parts of fluid intelligence EXCEPT
    a. analysis of problems.
    b. memorizing.
    c. inductive reasoning.
    d. perception of new relationships.

15. Which of the following increases during middle adulthood?
    a. figural relations
    b. inductive reasoning
    c. overall intelligence
    d. vocabulary

16. Novices differ from experts in that they
    a. have more procedural knowledge.
    b. have less declarative knowledge.
    c. more quickly and easily recognize relationships.
    d. organize their knowledge better.

17. For most middle-aged adults, the context for continued development of cognitive skills is the
    a. home.
    b. workplace.
    c. school.
    d. community

18. It is estimated that the knowledge of a computer scientist is obsolete within
    a. 2 to 3 years.
    b. 3 to 5 years.
    c. 5 to 7 years.
    d. 7 to 9 years.

19. According to Schaie, the _____ stage is entered in middle age.
    a. reintegrative
    b. achieving
    c. responsibility
    d. departure

20. By old age, the individual enters the _____ stage of Schaie's theory.
    a. achieving
    b. responsibility
    c. reintegrative
    d. executive

Pretest score _____

In order to test your knowledge of this chapter, fill in each of the blanks in this chapter review without referring back to the text. Check your answers with the Answer Key at the end of the chapter and then reread any sections in the chapter with which you had trouble.

Development in Middle Adulthood

1. Middle adulthood covers roughly the years from age _____ to age _____. People in mid-life are aware of being _____ not only from youngsters and young adults but also from the retired and elderly. The future no longer holds _____ possibilities.

2. In middle-age, physical activity may be slightly _____, but experience and self-knowledge allow people to _____ their own lives. They are able to make _____ with an ease and self-confidence that leads to this age group being called the _____ generation.

3. Frenkel-Brunswick sees the period of middle adulthood as one of _____ activity usually marked by both psychological and biological _____. Levinson found mid-life transition to be a time of moderate to severe _____ for both men and women.

4. For most people, there is a sense of _____ in middle age. It may be the _____ of life with respect to one's family, career, or creative talents, but there is also an awareness of _____ and a sense that _____ is running out.

5. While the _____ model links the normative developmental changes of the period to predictable crises, the _____ model rejects the ideal that a mid-life crisis is the norm. Development is marked by a series of _____ major life events that can be _____ and planned for.

6. Many of the studies on the crisis model are based on _____ populations rather than normal samples, and focus on white, middle-class _____. Some researchers question whether such male themes as anguish over _____ and over the inadequacy of one's _____ even apply to women.

7. Kessler believes that a mid-life crisis is the _____ rather than the rule, and that midlife is a transition period when people _____ youthful goals for more _____ ones. When facing trouble, mature people are likely to compare themselves to people who are _____ off. Those most likely to experience a mid-life crisis tend to avoid _____ and use _____ to avoid thinking about their changing bodies and lives. Mid-life crises are more common among the _____ than the poor or working classes.

Physical Continuity and Change

8. Vision tends to be fairly stable from adolescence to the 40s or early 50s when visual _____ declines. Hearing becomes less acute after the age of _____ and continues to decline. Hearing loss is more common in _____ than in _____. Taste and smell, and sensitivity to pain _____ at different points but sensitivity to temperature changes remains _____.

9. Reaction time drops off _____ throughout adulthood, and though motor skills decline, actual performance remains _____. Learning _____ skills becomes more difficult.

10. The nervous system begins to slow down after age _____ and the skeleton stiffens and _____ a bit during adulthood. Skin and muscles begin to lose _____ and there is a tendency to accumulate more subcutaneous _____. The heart pumps _____ less blood for each decade after adulthood, and by middle age, the opening of the coronary arteries is nearly _____ less than in the 20s. Lung capacity _____ as well.

11. The term _____ refers to the broad complex of physical and emotional effects that accompany hormonal changes in middle age. In women, this includes _____, the end of menstruation.

12. Menopause generally occurs between the ages of _____. Ovulation becomes _____ and then stops altogether, less _____ is produced, the _____ slowly shrinks, and there may be some reduction in _____ size. Research indicates that _____ and _____ are the only symptom probably caused by menopause. Night _____ may be extensive enough to cause insomnia.

13. In general, considerable research indicates that most women do not respond _____ to menopause. Many women feel _____ and more in _____ of their own lives. During this period of their lives women are more likely to be worried about becoming _____. The _____ context of menopause can also affect the woman's feelings about herself, her _____, and her actual _____ symptoms. Some researchers have suggested that the excessive focus on _____ and _____ in Western cultures may contribute to the symptoms that some women experience.

14. The estrogen loss that accompanies menopause results in changes in _____ mass and the _____. The loss in bone mass is _____ as great and more rapid in women, and bone _____ are more common in women as well. This may be associated with the disease, _____. The decrease in estrogen may also lead to _____ atrophy and a rise in the rate of _____ disease.

15. Hormone _____ therapy in the form of either _____ or _____ supplements or a combination of the two is sometimes used to treat the symptoms of menopause. It slows down _____ loss and reduces the incidence of _____ heart disease. There is an increased risk of _____ but the combination of the two hormones minimizes the risk and may increase the ability to prevent _____. Weight-bearing _____ also helps.

16. Unlike estrogen, _____ decline gradually over a long period of time. Men may suffer from symptoms caused by psychological stress such as _____ pressure, boredom with a _____ partner, family _____, or _____ of ill health.

17. Sexual activity in the middle years may slow down because of poor _____ or lack of _____. Sexuality is redefined to embrace the concept of _____ and both men and women require more _____ for sex. There is often an increase in sexual _____ and _____ among middle-aged men.

Health and Disease

18. The leading cause of death for U. S. adults in middle adulthood is _____. Throughout much of the lifespan, the death rate of men is _____ that of women of the same age. Men are more apt to work in dangerous _____, they are likely to be less concerned about their _____ than women, they are less likely to visit a _____, and they may have a higher _____ predisposition to disease.

19. Many health experts believe that by following a program of regular _____, lessened _____, and good _____, people can slow the aging process. Regular exercise can slow the deterioration of _____ tissue and reduce body _____, prevent deterioration of the _____ and combat some forms of _____.

20. Of the more than 2 million deaths in the United States in 1990, 20% were caused by _____-related illnesses. Among people between the ages of 35 and 64, smoking is responsible for more than _____ of all deaths. The groups disproportionately affected by the lure of cigarette smoking include _____ groups, people with the least _____, and those below the _____ level.

21. Stress plays a role in many of the _____ of middle adulthood. How an individual _____ and _____ an event plays an important role as well. Occasional exposure to stressful events may be an important stimulus to continuing _____ development. The effects of stressful events are _____. According to Lazarus, the effects of little _____ may be more serious than believed. Everyday hassles predict a person's _____ and _____ health far better than major life events. The frequency, duration, and _____ of stress determine whether or not we feel overwhelmed.

22. The heaviest burden of disease and death is borne by _____ groups and the _____. Statistics show that _____ people are more likely to die from heart disease, hypertension, cancer, diabetes, accidents, and AIDS and _____ have higher death rates from infectious and parasitic diseases, diabetes, hypertension, and AIDS. African-Americans and Hispanic-Americans tend to underutilize the _____ care system until they are in the midst of an emergency. _____ and lack of health _____ discourage them from taking advantage of health screenings and other early detection methods.

224

Cognitive Continuity and Change

23. Horn has suggested that there are _____ different kinds of intelligence. _____ intelligence includes _____, inductive _____, and the perception of new _____. It increases until late _____ or early _____ and then _____ gradually throughout adulthood. In contrast, _____ intelligence, which comes with experience and education, is based on the body of _____ and _____ accumulated over the years. It is the ability to find new _____, make _____, analyze _____, and use previously learned _____. People acquire crystallized intelligence through formal _____ and it often _____ over the lifespan.

24. It has been shown that between 45% and 60% of people maintain a _____ level of intellectual performance well into their 70s on various tests of intelligence. Losses during middle age are very _____. Skills that require _____ become increasingly difficult as people grow older, but intellectual activities that are well _____ and used _____ are maintained at high levels of efficiency.

25. Experts tend to have more knowledge, both _____ or factual and _____ or action information. This knowledge is better _____ in experts. They quickly and easily recognize _____ and link these to appropriate procedures and necessary responses. Among other aspects of expert performance are a continuous development of _____, knowledge and skills that are _____ to one area or field, knowledge that is highly _____, or _____-oriented, rapid _____ that minimizes the need for an extensive memory search, and generalized _____ and _____-solving skills.

26. For most middle-aged adults, the context for the continued development of cognitive skills is the _____. Adults with a high degree of occupational self-direction have a high degree of intellectual _____. This is especially true in fields marked by rapid professional _____.

27. There has been an increase of college students over age _____. This dramatic trend coincides with the recognition that humans are _____ learners. Studies show that the majority of middle-aged students are _____ about their work, attend classes _____ and get better _____ than other segments of the college student population.

28. Schaie has suggested that it is the _____ not the nature of intelligence that changes over time. The young adult is in the _____ stage. In middle adulthood, we enter the _____ stage. For some middle-aged people, this stage takes a different form called the _____ stage. In older adulthood, the uses of intellect shift to the _____ stage. Intellectual changes during the middle years mainly consist of _____ and emphasis in how _____ is applied.

Now try to answer each of the following questions without referring back to the text. Check your answers with the Answer Key at the end of the chapter and record your Posttest score in the space provided. Enter your Pretest score and subtract to find your improvement score.

1. Chronologically, middle age covers the period from _____ to _____ years of age.
    a. 40; 60 or 65
    b. 30; 50 or 55
    c. 35; 55 or 65
    d. 50; 70 or 75

2. Most researchers agree that middle age is a
    a. very definite crisis period.
    b. crisis period for men but not for women.
    c. period of transition but not crisis.
    d. crisis for women because of menopause.

3. The transition model of middle age
    a. sees this period as a time of unexpected crises.
    b. is based on a clinical sample, which may not be representative of the population in general.
    c. presents the period as one of trauma.
    d. describes the period as one of anticipated major life events.

4. Research in physical development of middle age has shown that
    a. reaction time drops off quickly in middle age.
    b. actual performance remains constant.
    c. motor skills remain constant.
    d. learning new skills is easy.

5. By middle age, the opening of the coronary arteries is nearly _____ less than it was in the 20s.
    a. one-quarter
    b. one-third
    c. one-half
    d. three times

6. The broad complex of physical and emotional effects that accompany hormonal changes in middle age is called
    a. climacteric.
    b. menopause.
    c. menarche.
    d. transition.

7. Kessler believes that mid-life crises are more common among the
   a. working classes.
   b. poor.
   c. unemployed.
   d. affluent.

8. Most women view menopause as
   a. the end of their usefulness.
   b. the beginning of old age.
   c. easy or moderately easy.
   d. the end of their sexual life.

9. In middle adulthood, _____ decreases dramatically, whereas _____ declines gradually over a longer period of time.
   a. estrogen; androgen
   b. progesterone; estrogen
   c. testosterone; androgen
   d. androgen; estrogen

10. For many adults, sexuality is redefined during the middle years to embrace the concept of
    a. intellectualization.
    b. intimacy.
    c. sensuality.
    d. independence.

11. The leading cause of death in the United States for adults in middle adulthood is
    a. accidents.
    b. cardiovascular disease.
    c. cancer.
    d. homicide.

12. Even past age 70, only _____ percent of people have symptoms of heart disease.
    a. 10 to 20
    b. 20 to 30
    c. 30 to 40
    d. 40 to 50

13. Habitual exercise in middle age can do all of the following EXCEPT
    a. reduce body fat.
    b. combat some kinds of arthritis.
    c. prevent deterioration of the joints.
    d. prevent cancer.

14. Among middle-aged people between the ages of 35 and 64, smoking is responsible for more than _____ percent of all deaths.
    a. 5
    b. 10
    c. 25
    d. 50

15. Both Hispanic-Americans and African-Americans are more likely than whites to die of all of the following diseases EXCEPT
    a. diabetes.
    b. parasitic diseases.
    c. AIDS.
    d. hypertension.

16. Which of the following does NOT belong?
    a. declarative knowledge
    b. procedural knowledge
    c. action information
    d. how-to information

17. Which of the following does not belong with the others?
    a. crystallized intelligence
    b. problem analysis
    c. inductive reasoning
    d. making judgments

18. All of the following professions are likely to suffer from "professional obsolescence" EXCEPT
    a. medicine.
    b. computer technology.
    c. law.
    d. engineering.

19. According to Schaie, the young adult is in which stage?
    a. achieving
    b. executive
    c. responsibility
    d. integrative

20. According to Schaie, for some middle-aged adults such as managers, government officials, and corporate executives, the responsibility stage becomes instead the _____ stage.
    a. achieving
    b. executive
    c. reintegrative
    d. obsolete

Posttest score _____

Pretest score _____

Improvement _____

228

In order to enhance your understanding of this chapter, answer each of the following essay questions as completely as you can, using the text as a source of material to support your answer.

1. When does middle adulthood occur? Base your answer on this chapter in your text and your own personal experience or the experience of people you know.

2. Is there a mid-life crisis? Discuss research on this issue.

3. Describe the physical changes of middle age.

4. Describe menopause and discuss the myths and realities that surround it.

5. What is the impact of poverty on health in middle adulthood?

6. What is meant by the command generation? Give some specific examples.

7. Compare and contrast fluid and crystallized intelligence and the patterns they follow throughout adulthood.

8. Describe Lazarus's theory of "little hassles" and stress.

9. What are the factors that differentiate between experts and novices?

10. Describe hormone replacement therapy and its advantages and disadvantages.

ANSWER KEY

Key Names

1. a	3. g	5. d	7. f
2. b	4. c	6. e	

Pretest

1. d	5. b	9. d	13. c	17. b
2. a	6. c	10. b	14. a	18. a
3. c	7. a	11. c	15. d	19. c
4. b	8. d	12. c	16. b	20. c

Programmed Review

1. 40, 60 to 65, separate, different
2. diminished, manage, decisions, command
`3. declining, crises, crisis
4. ambivalence, prime, mortality, time
5. crisis, transition, expected, anticipated
6. clinical, males, mortality, achievements
7. exception, trade, realistic, worse, introspection, denial, affluent
8. acuity, 20, men, women, decline, high
9. slowly, constant, new
10. 50, shrinks, elasticity, fat, 8 percent, one-third, decreases
11. climacteric, menopause
12. 45 and 55, erratic, estrogen, uterus, breast, hot flashes, night sweats, sweats
13. negatively, freer, control, widows, cultural, behavior, physical, youth, attractiveness
14. bone, genitals, twice, fractures, osteoporosis, vaginal, cardiovascular
15. replacement, estrogen, progesterone, bone, coronary, cancer, osteoporosis, exercise
16. androgens, job, sexual, responsibilities, fear
17. health, opportunity, sensuality, time, anxiety, dissatisfaction
18. cancer, twice, occupations, health, doctor, genetic
19. exercise, stress, diet, muscle, fat, joints, arthritis
20. smoking, 25%, minority, education, poverty
21. diseases, perceives, interprets, personality, additive, hassles, physical, mental, intensity
22. minority, poor, black, Hispanics, health, Poverty, insurance
23. two, Fluid, memorizing, reasoning, relationships, adolescence, adulthood, declines, crystallized, knowledge, information, relationships, judgments, problems, strategies, education, increases
24. stable, limited, speed, practiced, regularly
25. declarative, procedural, organized, patterns, competence, specific, procedural, goal, recognition, thinking, problem
26. workplace, flexibility, obsolescence
27. 35, lifelong, conscientious, regularly, grades
28. function, achieving, responsibility, executive, reintegrative, orientation, intelligence

Posttest

1. a	5. b	9. a	13. d	17. c
2. c	6. a	10. c	14. c	18. c
3. d	7. d	11. b	15. b	19. a
4. b	8. c	12. b	16. a	20. b

16
Middle Adulthood: Personality and Sociocultural Development

CHAPTER OUTLINE

Personality Continuity and Change
    The Tasks of Middle Adulthood
    Personal Reactions to Middle Adulthood

Family and Friends: Interpersonal Contexts
    The Generation that Runs Things
    Relationships with Adult Children
    Relationships with Aging Parents
    Introduction to Grandparenting
    Friendships: A Lifelong Perspective

The Changing Family
    Divorce and Remarriage
    Reconstituted Families

Occupational Continuity and Change
    Midcareer Reassessment
    Job Change and Stress

KEY TERMS AND CONCEPTS

To become familiar with the vocabulary used in this chapter, look up each of the following terms in the text and write out the definition.

Empty nest

Expansive women

Innovative women

Job burnout

Kinkeepers

Launching of adolescents

Men in midlife crisis

Myth

Protesters

Pseudo-developed men

Punitive-disenchanted men

Reconstituted or blended families

Role conflicts

Role strain

Traditional women

Transcendent men

KEY NAMES

After reading the chapter in the text, try to match each of the following individuals with his or her contribution to the field of psychology. Then check your answers with the Answer Key at the end of this chapter.

_____ 1. Terri Apter

_____ 2. Erik Erikson

_____ 3. Robert Havighurst

_____ 4. Robert Peck

_____ 5. Lillian Troll

a. conflicts of adult development

b. developmental tasks

c. generativity versus self-absorption

d. intergenerational relationships

e. types of midlife women

Now try to answer each of the following questions without referring to the text. Then check your answers with the Answer Key at the end of this chapter and record your score in the space provided at the end of this section.

1. Who was one of the first theorists to emphasize the second half of life?
   a. Erikson
   b. Jung
   c. Peck
   d. Maslow

2. According to Erikson, a person in middle adulthood must achieve a sense of
   a. generativity.
   b. identity.
   c. industry.
   d. integrity.

3. Which of the following occurs in middle adulthood, according to Peck?
   a. ego transcendence versus ego preoccupation
   b. body transcendence versus body preoccupation
   c. ego differentiation versus work-role preoccupation
   d. mental flexibility versus mental rigidity

4. The man who does not have a mid-life crisis but has found adequate solutions to most problems of life is
   a. pseudo-developed.
   b. punitive-disenchanted.
   c. transcendent-generative.
   d. a victim of mid-life crisis.

5. A man who has been unhappy and alienated for most of his life and displays signs of a mid-life crisis is called
   a. pseudo-developed.
   b. transcendent-generative.
   c. punitive-disenchanted.
   d. generative.

6. The overload of demands within the same role is called role
   a. conflict.
   b. reversal.
   c. strain.
   d. overload.

7. The period of the family life cycle in which the last child is launched is often called the
   a. stage of independence.
   b. empty nest.
   c. loss adjustment stage.
   d. college stage.

8. By middle age, the relationship between parents and their children becomes
   a. more strained.
   b. less relaxed.
   c. less involved.
   d. more reciprocal.

9. The primary parent-child relationship in middle age usually involves the _____ as caregiver.
   a. mother
   b. father
   c. daughter
   d. son

10. Fewer than _____ percent of aging parents share a home with their middle-aged children.
    a. 2
    b. 4
    c. 7
    d. 10

11. Grandparents who become the "anchor of stability" for their grandchildren are filling the role of
    a. being there.
    b. family national guard.
    c. arbitrator.
    d. family biographer.

12. The role of imparting and negotiating family values is part of the grandparenting role of
    a. being there.
    b. arbitrator.
    c. family national guard.
    d. family biographer.

13. Adults at all stages believe that the most important aspect of friendship is
    a. reciprocity.
    b. similarity.
    c. proximity.
    d. communication.

14. The most complex friendships occur among people in
    a. adolescence.
    b. young adulthood.
    c. middle adulthood.
    d. late adulthood.

15. Almost _____ percent of contemporary marriages involve the remarriage of one or both individuals.
    a. 20
    b. 30
    c. 40
    d. 50

16. Recently divorced men and women have higher rates of all of the following EXCEPT
    a. alcoholism.
    b. schizophrenia.
    c. physical illness.
    d. depression.

17. Which of the following family types does not belong with the others?
    a. reconstituted
    b. blended
    c. step
    d. extended

18. Most stepparents report all of the following as difficulties experienced in the stepparent-stepchild relationship EXCEPT
    a. discipline.
    b. sibling rivalry.
    c. children's personalities.
    d. gaining acceptance of children.

19. The first reaction to involuntary job loss is usually
    a. shock and disbelief.
    b. relief and relaxation.
    c. depression and loneliness.
    d. despair and grief.

20. The psychological condition of emotional exhaustion that affects people in the helping professions is called
    a. emotional exhaustion.
    b. stress.
    c. burnout.
    d. disillusionment.

Pretest score _____

235

To test your knowledge of this chapter, fill in each of the blanks in the chapter review without referring back to the text. Then check your answers with the Answer Key provided at the end of this chapter and reread any areas of the chapter that gave you problems.

Personality Continuity and Change

1. _____ was one of the first theorists to emphasize the second half of life. He believed that older people mainly need to find _____ in their lives.

2. According to Erikson, the basic issue facing people in middle age is _____ versus _____. People act within three domains: a _____ one, by giving and responding to the needs of the next generation; a _____ one, by integrating work with family life and caring for the next generation; and a _____ one, by contributing to society on a greater scale.

3. Peck proposes _____ issues or conflicts of adult development. As physical stamina and health begin to wane, people must make the adjustment of valuing _____ versus valuing _____ powers, stress _____ over _____ in human relationships, experience emotional _____ versus cathetic _____, and mental _____ versus mental _____. Three additional dimensions begin to occur in middle age including _____ differentiation versus _____ preoccupation, body _____ versus body _____, and ego _____ versus ego _____.

4. Although men's psychological well-being traditionally has been linked to their _____ role, Farrell and Rosenberg point to the importance of _____ relations at mid-life. The _____ man does not have a mid-life crisis but has found adequate solutions to most problems of life. The _____ man copes with problems by maintaining the facade that everything is satisfactory or under control. The man in mid-life _____ is confused and feels that his whole world is disintegrating and the _____ man has been unhappy or alienated for much of his life.

5. Traditionally, women have defined themselves more in terms of the _____ cycle than in terms of their place in the _____ cycle. Women tend to report major life transitions associated with the _____ of their children, the time when their children _____ home, and _____.

6. _____ women have relatively little difficulty shifting into the role of mature woman. _____ women who had pursued careers begin to reassess the work they have done. _____ women make marked changes in their goals in midlife, and _____ attempt to postpone midlife as long as possible.

7. Role _____ occurs when there is not enough time for all roles. Role _____ is associated with an overload of demands within the same role. Women react more strongly than men to the _____ changes of aging.

Family and Friends: Interpersonal Contexts

8. Middle-aged people act as a _____ between the younger generation and the older generation. They may _____ goals not achieved; they may have to acknowledge that some goals will never be _____, and more than any other group, the middle-aged must live in the _____. They take on the role of family _____ as they maintain family _____, celebrate _____, keep alive family _____, gather the family for _____ celebrations, and reach out to family members who are far away.

9. Redefinition of the parent-child relationship begins with the launching of _____ into the adult world. Adolescents on the verge of assuming responsible adult roles are best supported by parents who maintain the _____ but increasingly trust and respect their _____, decisions, and progress toward _____.

10. Parents who remain married can anticipate spending a lengthy period of time together after the _____ of the last child. This period is sometimes referred to as the _____ and can be difficult if partners have grown _____ over the years. Marital satisfaction in this period is not necessarily based on the same _____ of interaction as in earlier phases.

11. Adult children often feel the need to _____ themselves before they can see their parents in a _____ way. Middle-aged adults will need to adjust to the changing needs and roles of an _____ parent. When parents are in good health and can live independently, the relationship is often characterized by _____.

12. The primary parent-child relationship at this stage of life generally involves the _____ as caregiver. This relationship includes regular _____, shared _____, and a reciprocal exchange of _____. As parents age, role _____ gradually takes place between middle-aged people and the older generation.

13. According to Troll, surveys show that middle-aged children are likely to live relatively _____ to their parents and see or speak with them on a regular basis. Fewer than _____ of aging parents share a home with their middle-aged children. Most have regular contact with their grown children, which is likely to _____ when problems arise. The responsibility falls on the woman who may have to juggle the needs of her aging _____, her young adult _____, her _____, the _____ of her husband, as well as her own _____ and _____ needs. Most women manage to meet these responsibilities by eliminating time for _____.

14. The majority of Americans become _____ in middle age. They fulfill the roles of _____ as an anchor of stability to both grandchildren and parents, family national _____ by being available in times of emergency, _____ by imparting and negotiating family values, and maintaining the family's _____.

15. For older people, whose children are grown or who are widowed, _____ fills many vital emotional needs. Most middle-aged people report they have several close friends with whom they have been involved for at least _____. Women seem to be more deeply involved in _____ and consider _____ most important in their real friendships, while men tend to choose their friends on the basis of _____.

The Changing Family

16. Divorce is more likely in _____ adulthood. The breakup of a marriage is the culmination of a long process of emotional _____. The _____ usually raises the issue first. Women are often _____ with marriage sooner than men. Divorce is often associated with _____ about marriage.

17. Most people experiencing divorce perceive it as a kind of _____. For the partner who did not make the decision to divorce, there is often a feeling of _____. Even if the marriage was unsatisfactory, the final decision comes as a _____.

18. Recently divorced men and women have higher rates of _____, physical _____, and _____. Most divorced individuals experience considerable improvement and well- being within _____ of the final separation. Divorced women are likely to have greater _____. Divorced men have the highest rate of _____ among all single groups.

19. When divorced or widowed people with children remarry, they form stepfamilies, also known as _____ or _____ families. Second marriages are often characterized by more open _____, greater acceptance of _____, and more _____ that disagreements can be resolved. The current remarriage rate closely parallels remarriage rates in Europe and the United States in the _____ centuries. Contact with the former _____ often continues and may include shared _____, financial _____, and _____.

20. Stepparents should try to establish a position in the children's lives that is _____ from that held by the real mother or father. When asked what the greatest difficulties are in a stepparent-stepchild relationship, most stepparents mention _____, adjusting to the _____ and _____ of the children, and gaining the _____ of the children. _____ often have more problems than _____ in adjusting to their new roles.

21. Girls are likely to have greater difficulty forming a good relationship with their _____ than boys. Boys often have tumultuous, conflictual relationships with their _____.

Occupational Continuity and Change

22. A period of serious _____ reassessment or reexamination often occurs at mid-life. Levinson found that adults in their 40s may experience a shift in their _____ and _____ that leads them to consider changing the course of their careers.

23. Only a _____ of people make dramatic career shifts at midlife. Those who do are likely to feel that their abilities are _____ at their current job. Middle-agers may also change jobs because of _____.

24. People who are fired, laid off, or forced to retire from their jobs often face _____ problems that may outweigh their loss of _____. Individuals often react to career loss in ways that are similar to the _____ response triggered by the death of a loved one. The pattern of grieving begins with the initial _____ and _____, followed by anger and _____. Some people even go through a _____ stage, followed by _____, loneliness, or physical ailments. Once the grief reaction has passed, the jobless can begin to _____ the loss, develop a sense of _____, and attempt to _____ energies toward finding another job.

25. It is likely that the middle-aged individual has more of his or her _____ invested in the job and older people are more likely to face age _____ both in hiring and in training programs. Whatever job the worker is able to find is likely to be at a lower _____ and _____ than the previous one.

26. _____ is a psychological state of emotional exhaustion, often accompanied by extreme cynicism that develops among individuals in the helping professions. It applies to the effect on people who have worked hard and bent all of their efforts to reach a virtually _____ goal, and failed. The general cause of burnout is a lack of _____ in a work situation where great _____ has been expended and where high _____ originally predominated. These workers may turn on people they are supposed to _____, or withdraw from _____ involvement. They may experience physical _____, psychosomatic _____, low _____, mediocre _____, or absenteeism. Burnout can be avoided by learning to be _____, promoting _____ in job requirements, attempting to keep the rest of their lives _____ from work, and developing interests _____ of the job.

POSTTEST

Now try to answer the following questions without referring back to the text. Check your answers with the Answer Key at the end of this chapter and record your Post-test score in the space provided. Enter your Pretest score and subtract for your improvement score.

1. Who wrote *In Over Our Heads*?
   a. Adler
   b. Kegan
   c. Freud
   d. Skinner

2. What is the negative outcome of Erikson's stage for middle adulthood?
   a. isolation
   b. diffusion
   c. self-absorption
   d. despair

3. Which of the following is an issue or conflict proposed by Peck for middle adulthood?
   a. ego transcendence versus ego preoccupation
   b. body transcendence versus body preoccupation
   c. ego differentiation versus work-role preoccupation
   d. valuing wisdom versus valuing physical powers

4. According to Farrell and Rosenberg, the _____ man copes with problems by maintaining the facade that everything is satisfactory or under control.
   a. pseudo-developed
   b. punitive-disenchanted
   c. transcendent-generative
   d. mid-life crisis

5. The man in mid-life crisis, as described by Farrell and Rosenberg,
   a. has found adequate solutions to life's problems.
   b. copes by maintaining a facade of well-being.
   c. feels his world is disintegrating.
   d. has been unhappy and alienated for most of his life.

6. Women tend to report major role changes at all of the following points EXCEPT
   a. their marriage.
   b. the birth of their children.
   c. the launching of their children.
   d. menopause.

7. The person in the family who maintains family rituals, celebrates achievements, and keeps alive family histories is called the
   a. manager.
   b. kinkeeper.
   c. grandmother.
   d. social organizer.

8. Redefinition of the parent-child relationship begins with the
   a. birth of the last child.
   b. mother's going back to work.
   c. launching of adolescents into the adult world.
   d. parent's retirement.

9. Before they can see their parents realistically, adult children often feel the need to
   a. maintain especially close relationships with their parents.
   b. see their parents often.
   c. try to model their lives after those of their parents.
   d. distance themselves from their parents for a while.

10. Middle-aged adults usually have a relationship with their aging parents that includes all of the following EXCEPT
    a. economic dependence.
    b. regular contact.
    c. shared memories.
    d. reciprocal exchange of assistance.

11. As parents age, the relationship with their middle-adult children is best described as
    a. economic.
    b. role reversal.
    c. equally interactive.
    d. interdependent.

12. The middle-adult woman has been called the "woman in the middle." She copes by reducing the time and effort she puts into satisfying the needs of her
    a. aging parents.
    b. young-adult children.
    c. career.
    d. marriage.

13. It is estimated that well over _____ people in the United States are involved in parent care at any given time.
    a. 10,000
    b. 100,000
    c. one million
    d. five million

14. What is the second most common reason for women leaving the workforce?
    a. illness
    b. caring for ill relatives
    c. childbirth
    d. marriage

15. When grandparents' major role is responding in times of emergency, they are taking on the grandparenting role known as
    a. family national guard.
    b. being there.
    c. arbitrator.
    d. family biographer.

16. The final decision to divorce is usually reached
    a. by both partners at about the same time.
    b. by the wife first.
    c. by the husband first.
    d. very late in the marital dissolution.

17. In 1999, almost _____ as many individuals divorced each other as married.
    a. half
    b. a third
    c. twice
    d. two-thirds

18. Most people experiencing divorce perceive it as a
    a. relief.
    b. short-term setback.
    c. failure.
    d. long-term problem.

19. The current remarriage rate closely parallels remarriage rates in Europe and the United States in the
    a. 1930s.
    b. 17th and 18th centuries.
    c. 19th century.
    d. 1950s.

20. All of the following help to avoid or minimize burnout EXCEPT
    a. being realistic in one's approach to work.
    b. attempting to keep a part of one's life separate from work.
    c. enthusiastic and devoted attention to the job.
    d. developing interests outside of the job.

Posttest score _____

Pretest score _____

Improvement _____

ESSAY QUESTIONS

To expand your knowledge of this chapter, answer each of the following essay questions as completely as you can. Use the material in your text to support your answer.

1. Describe Peck's critique of Erikson's theory and indicate how Peck would change the theory.

2. Describe and compare the four general paths of development that Farrell and Rosenberg suggest occur in middle adulthood and the four types of midlife women described by Apter.

3. Compare the middle adulthood experiences of men and women using as resources the research cited in this chapter and people you know who are in middle adulthood.

4. Describe the empty nest syndrome. Do you think this occurs equally in men and women? Explain your answer.

5. Discuss the responsibilities or obligations of middle adults to their aging parents. How do they usually react to the need to care for their parents?

6. Is there such a thing as a generation gap between middle-aged adults and their children or between middle-aged adults and their parents? Explain your answer.

7. Describe the stereotypical image of grandparents in the United States and discuss how this stereotype is being violated with people in middle adulthood becoming grandparents.

8. Describe the issues to be dealt with when divorce occurs.

9. Discuss the problems encountered in stepfamilies, and explain the ways in which stepfamily members can ease the transition.

10. Describe the typical reaction to job loss in middle adulthood.

ANSWER KEY

Key Names

    1. e   2. c   3. b   4. a   5. d

Pretest

1. b	5. c	9. c	13. a	17. d
2. a	6. c	10. d	14. c	18. b
3. d	7. b	11. a	15. c	19. a
4. c	8. d	12. b	16. b	20. c

Programmed Review

1. Jung, meaning
2. generativity, self-absorption, procreative, productive, creative

3. seven, wisdom, physical, socializing, sexualizing, flexibility, impoverishment, flexibility, rigidity, ego, work-role, transcendence, preoccupation, transcendence, preoccupation
4. job, family, transcendent-generative, pseudo-developed, crisis, punitive-disenchanted
5. family, career, birth, leave, menopause
6. Traditional, Innovative, Expansive, Protestors
7. conflict, strain, physical
8. bridge, regret, reached, present, kinkeepers, rituals, achievements, history, holiday
9. adolescents, dialogue, judgments, maturity
10. launching, empty nest, apart, patterns
11. distance, realistic, aging, reciprocity
12. daughter, contact, memories, assistance, reversal
13. close, 10 percent, increase, parents, children, marriage, health, career, personal, themselves
14. grandparents, being there, guard, arbitrator, biography
15. friendship, six years, friendships, reciprocity, similarity
16. young, distancing, wife, dissatisfied, misconceptions
17. failure, rejection, shock
18. alcoholism, illness, depression, two or three years, self-esteem, remarriage
19. reconstituted, blended, communication, conflict, trust, 17th and 18th, spouse, custody, support, visitation
20. different, discipline, habits, personalities, acceptance, Stepmothers, stepfathers
21. stepfathers, stepmothers
22. career, values, goals
23. minority, underutilized, job burnout
24. emotional, income, grief, shock, disbelief, protest, bargaining, depression, accommodate, hope, redirect
25. identity, discrimination, salary, status
26. Burnout, impossible, reward, effort, hopes, help, emotional, exhaustion, illnesses, morale, performance, realistic, changes, separate, outside

Posttest

1. b	5. c	9. d	13. d	17. d
2. c	6. a	10. a	14. b	18. c
3. d	7. b	11. b	15. a	19. b
4. a	8. c	12. c	16. b	20. c

17

Older Adulthood: Physical and Cognitive Development

CHAPTER OUTLINE

Aging Today
Ageism and Stereotypes
Four Decades of Later Life

Physical Aspects of Aging
The Changing Body
Health, Disease, and Nutrition

Causes of Aging
Hereditary and Environmental Factors
Theories of Aging

Cognitive Changes in Advanced Age
Cognition in the Later Years
Cognitive Decline
Compensating for an Aging Mind

In order to enhance your knowledge of the vocabulary used in this chapter, look up each of the following terms in the text and write out the definition.

Ageism
Alzheimer's disease
Atherosclerosis
Cataract
Centenarians
Dementia
Filial piety
Free Radicals
Glaucoma
Hypertension
Infarct

Lipofusein
Nonagenarians
Octogenarians
Pathological aging factors
Senescence
Septuagenarians
Stochastic theories of aging
Strokes
Transient ischemic attacks
Vestibular system
Visual acuity
Wisdom

KEY NAMES

After reading the chapter in the text, try to match each of the following names with his or her contribution to the field of psychology. Then look up your answers in the Answer Key provided at the end of this chapter. Again, you will notice that some of these names are from previous chapters, but they have all contributed to an understanding of late adulthood as well.

_____1. Paul Baltes   a. four decades of life

_____2. Irene Burnside   b. model of wisdom

Try to answer each of the following questions without referring back to the text. Check your answers with the Answer Key at the end of this chapter and record your score in the space provided.

1. The widely prevalent social attitude that overvalues youth and discriminates against the elderly is called
   a. stereotyping.
   b. ageism.
   c. youth orientation.
   d. elder abuse.

2. The tradition of veneration and respect for the elderly found in China, Japan, and other Far Eastern countries is called
   a. filial piety.
   b. ageism.
   c. elder worship.
   d. discrimination.

3. People between 60 and 69 years of age are considered the
   a. very old-old.
   b. old-old.
   c. middle-aged old.
   d. young old.

4. Of the old-old, about what percent live in nursing homes or other institutions?
   a. 90
   b. 75
   c. 19
   d. 10

5. The kind of life that individuals have led and the illnesses and accidents they have experienced are sometimes called _____ aging factors.
   a. experiential
   b. accidental
   c. pathological
   d. external

6. Which of the following does not belong with the others?
   a. wrinkles
   b. brown areas of pigmentation
   c. age spots
   d. liver spots

7. The loss of flexibility in the lens of the eye is responsible for
   a. the decline in the ability to focus.
   b. nearsightedness.
   c. glaucoma.
   d. color-blindness.

8. Which of the following senses tends to remain stable as people age?
   a. taste
   b. smell
   c. vision
   d. hearing

9. Height decreases in late adulthood are due to all of the following EXCEPT
   a. compression of cartilage in the spine.
   b. muscle weakness in the back.
   c. changes in posture.
   d. loss of bone calcium.

10. The production of antibodies peaks during
    a. adolescence.
    b. childhood.
    c. early adulthood.
    d. middle adulthood.

11. The majority of deaths in those over age 65 are attributable to all of the following EXCEPT
    a. cerebrovascular disease.
    b. cancer.
    c. cardiovascular disease.
    d. upper respiratory disease.

12. Which of the following disorders is more commonly known as hardening of the arteries?
    a. osteoporosis.
    b. arthritis.
    c. atherosclerosis.
    d. Alzheimer's disease.

13. The elderly average approximately _____ hours of sleep a night.
    a. 5
    b. 6 to 6-1/2
    c. 7
    d. 8 to 8-1/2

14. An interruption in breathing that lasts for at least ten seconds and occurs at least five times per hour during sleep is called
    a. sleep apnea.
    b. psychophysiological insomnia.
    c. narcolepsy.
    d. insomnia.

15. Stochastic theories of aging include all of the following EXCEPT
    a. wear and tear.
    b. the action of free radicals.
    c. damage to DNA.
    d. biological clocks.

16. Biological clock theories of aging suggest that some sort of timer is associated with which part of the brain?
    a. amygdala
    b. cerebral cortex
    c. hypothalamus
    d. cerebellum

17. Compared to younger adults, older adults are more likely to
    a. do better on tests of recall.
    b. do better on tests of recognition.
    c. be less selective in what they retain.
    d. forget metaphors.

18. One of the primary causes of cognitive decline is
    a. strokes.
    b. failing health.
    c. poor formal education.
    d. poverty.

19. Among those over 85 years old diagnosed with dementia, approximately 50% have
    a. ministrokes.
    b. brain tumors.
    c. Alzheimer's disease.
    d. schizophrenia.

20. A common psychological reaction in old age is
    a. schizophrenia.
    b. Alzheimer's disease.
    c. obsessiveness.
    d. depression.

Pretest score _____

PROGRAMMED REVIEW

To test your knowledge of this chapter, try to fill in all the blanks in the following chapter review without referring back to the text. Then check your answers with the Answer Key at the end of this chapter and reread any sections of the chapter that gave you problems.

Aging Today

1. On the average, today's older adults have a lower _____ level than most of the population. An aggressive advocacy group for the aged has been the _____.

2. Neugarten uses the word _____ to describe the attitude of indifference and neglect towards the aged. Several studies have found that attitudes toward the elderly are often _____.

3. In many of the world's religions, elders are considered to possess great _____. In American Indian tribes, the old have traditionally been _____ as wise elders, the transmitters of _____, and a storehouse of _____ lore. In China, Japan, and other Asian countries, older people are venerated and respected in a tradition known as _____ piety. In colonial America, the _____ tradition of veneration for elders was a powerful cultural influence. Old age was viewed as an outward manifestation of _____ grace and favor, the reward for an extraordinarily upright life.

4. According to Census Bureau projections, by the year 2030, one out of every _____ people will be 65 or older. The decade from 60 to 69 marks a major _____. Income is often _____ by retirement, society frequently reduces its _____ of persons in their 60s, and many react to these expectations by slowing down their pace in a kind of _____ prophecy.

5. According to Burnside, the major developmental task of people in their 70s is to maintain the personality _____ achieved in their 60s. Many people in their 70s suffer _____ and _____. Friends and family may _____ at an increased rate.

6. Most octogenarians experience increased difficulty in _____ to and _____ with their surroundings. Most people over age 85 live in their own _____. Only _____ reside in nursing homes. People over _____ make up the fastest-growing segment of the U. S. population and _____ are the fastest growing segment worldwide.

7. People over 90 are _____ and are often _____, more _____, and more _____ than people 20 years younger.

Physical Aspects of Aging

8. The kind of life that individuals have led and the illnesses and accidents they have experienced are called _____ aging factors. Evidence of aging is seen in the skin, which becomes less _____. Age spots may appear as brown areas of pigmentation sometimes called _____ spots.

9. The senses become _____ efficient as a person ages. Hearing _____ are quite common. There is some decline in the ability to _____ on objects, which may be due to loss of flexibility in the _____ of the eye. The lens may become somewhat cloudy or develop a _____. Older people lose some visual _____. The sense of taste shows considerable _____ even into old age, but the sense of _____ often declines.

10. The structure and composition of muscle _____ change, and muscle function is affected by the changing structure and composition of the _____. Older adults are usually an inch or more _____ than they were in early adulthood due to compression of cartilage in the _____, and _____ changes in posture. The tendency to fall and fracture bones may increase because of changes in the _____ system. It takes longer for a muscle to achieve a state of _____, the blood vessels become less _____ and some become _____. Decreased lung function may reduce the _____ supply, and fine motor coordination and the speed of reaction time _____.

11. In the aged, there is decreased blood flow to and from the _____, and increased recovery time after each _____. The _____ capacity of the heart, lungs, and other organs also decreases with age. Many older people adapt more slowly to the _____ and have similar difficulty coping with the _____. The production of antibodies peaks during _____ and then starts to decline. The result is that by old age, people have less protection against _____ and _____.

12. When health problems occur, they are often _____, the most common being _____, _____ problems, and _____. The elderly are also prone to accidental _____. The increase in health problems reflects the body's decreased ability to cope with _____. The rates of death are higher for _____ than for _____, and whites suffer from a rate of cardiovascular disease that is _____ as high as the rate for Asians.

13. It is not unusual for older Americans to be both _____ and _____. Much of the problem lies in the overconsumption of _____, which, if not used, are stored in the body, even within the walls of the _____. This leads to a condition called _____, or hardening of the arteries.

14. Middle-aged and older people are advised to supplement their diets with _____. Because the muscle tone of the intestines decreases, _____ may occur. Nutritionists recommend the addition of _____ foods to the diet and plenty of _____.

15. Some researchers are convinced that as much as one-third of the elderly are hospitalized because of the overuse, misuse, or abuse of _____. For many elderly people, the problem may relate to changing body _____.

16. Older people average between _____ hours of sleep a night and experience significantly more _____ than younger people. There is an increase in stage _____ sleep and a decrease in stages _____ sleep. _____ sleep disorders occur in about one-third of all older people. Insomnia is related to recent _____ in the person's life. Poor sleep _____ includes sleep related habits and behaviors incompatible with sleep. _____ insomnia is sometimes linked to adjustment sleep disorders and poor sleep hygiene. Insomnia is also linked to a variety of _____ disorders, including major depression and anxiety. Sleep _____ is an interruption in breathing that lasts for at least 10 seconds and occurs at least five times per hour. Periodic _____ movements may cause brief arousal in the sleeper.

Causes of Aging

17. It is clear from studies of several species that the life span has a _____ component. _____ life adds several years, as does _____ versus single status. _____ has a consistently negative effect.

18. _____, or normal aging, refers to the biological process of aging associated with the passage of time that affects all people. According to _____ theories of aging, the body ages as a result of random assaults from the internal and external environment. These theories are sometimes called _____ theories and compare the human body to a machine that wears out. It is thought that as cells age, they have a harder time disposing of _____. Extra substances, particularly a fatty substance called _____, accumulate in cells, and pieces of molecules called free _____ react with other chemical compounds in the cell and may _____ normal cell functioning.

19. _____ theories of aging suggest that the programmed actions of specific inherited genes determine aging. It is believed that approximately _____ human genes determine the average life span of the human being. Biological _____ are associated with programmed aging. It is suggested that there is a pacemaker or timer housed in the _____ and in the _____ gland.

Cognitive Changes in Advanced Age

20. Most mental skills remain relatively _____. Many of the memory problems that some older people suffer are due to _____, inactivity, or side effects of prescription _____.

21. Older adulthood brings a decline in the _____ of both mental and physical performance. Older people have slower _____ times, _____ processing abilities, and _____ processes. Some of this slowness may be due to the fact that older people seem to value _____ more than younger people. Older people are sometimes slower because they have not _____ a particular skill lately.

22. Older individuals are able to pick up and hold slightly _____ sensory information than young adults. On average, they have a slightly shorter _____ span, particularly when _____ things are happening at once.

23. Studies of learning and recall show that older people often remember _____ items on a list or _____ details in a design. They are less _____ in organizing, rehearsing, and encoding material to be learned. Older subjects tend to do better on _____ tasks than on _____ and are _____ in what they retain, remembering what is _____ and _____ in their lives

24. _____ memory appears to remain fairly intact in older adults. They are better at recalling details of _____ events. The expert knowledge associated with _____ can be broken down into _____ knowledge, _____ knowledge, _____ contextualism, value _____, and _____. Wisdom is a cognitive quality founded on _____, culture-based intelligence that appears to be related to experience and personality.

25. According to Baltes, wisdom appears to focus on important and difficult matters that are often associated with the meaning of _____ and the _____ condition. The level of knowledge, judgment, and advice reflected in wisdom is _____. The knowledge associated with wisdom has extraordinary scope, depth, and balance and is applicable to _____ situations. Wisdom combines _____ and _____ and is employed for personal _____ as well as the benefit of humankind. While difficult to achieve, wisdom is easily _____ by most people.

26. Among the primary causes of cognitive decline are _____ disease and strokes. Most cognitive decline is not intrinsic to the aging process itself, but is attributable to such factors as failing _____, poor formal _____, poverty, or low _____, which are _____ causes of decline.

27. _____ refers to the confusion, forgetfulness, and personality changes that are sometimes associated with advanced age. It affects only _____ of those over age 65. The label _____ is too often attached to elderly people. Improper _____, as well as chronic insufficient _____ related to _____, anxiety, depression, grief, or fear, can distort thinking in all people.

28. Alzheimer's disease involves a progressive deterioration of _____ cells. Autopsies reveal a characteristic pattern of damaged areas that look like _____. The high incidence of the disease in some families leads researchers to suspect a _____ cause. In the beginning, little things are _____, then there is a sense of _____. The patient is unable to do the most simple _____ and familiar people are not _____.

29. Strokes or _____ are another cause of dementia. This form of cognitive decline is sometimes called _____ dementia. An _____ is an obstruction of a blood vessel that prevents a sufficient supply of blood from reaching a particular area of the brain. If these events are small and temporary, they are referred to as _____ attacks.

30. Older people often imagine that their _____ will be in the hands of luck, chance, or powerful others. Individuals who believe this often become less _____ and less in _____.

31. Other secondary factors causing cognitive decline are _____ fitness, _____ deficits, use of _____, prescription and over-the-counter _____, and disuse of _____ functioning.

32. A mechanism to coordinate gains and losses in an aging mind is selective _____ with _____.

Now try to answer each of the following questions without referring back to the text. Check your answers with the Answer Key at the end of this chapter and record your Posttest score in the space provided. Enter your Pretest score and subtract to find your improvement score.

1. In colonial America, the elderly
    a. were considered a burden to most people.
    b. were so scarce that no one was concerned with them.
    c. received veneration in the biblical tradition.
    d. were worshipped.

2. Most people in their 70s experience all of the following EXCEPT
    a. loss.
    b. illness.
    c. death of friends.
    d. institutionalization.

3. Nonagenarians are people in their
    a. 90s.
    b. 80s.
    c. 70s.
    d. 60s.

4. In late adulthood, hearing deficits are
    a. rare.
    b. common.
    c. infrequent.
    d. nonexistent.

5. The elderly may have trouble driving because
    a. they cannot hear as well.
    b. they are unable to remember the route they are driving.
    c. they have trouble ignoring irrelevant stimuli.
    d. they are no longer able to maneuver the steering wheel.

6. The elderly's trouble in distinguishing tastes within blended foods is mainly attributable to a decline in
    a. their ability to see the type of food they are eating.
    b. their sense of taste.
    c. their sense of smell
    d. their ability to chew.

7. In late adulthood,
    a. the heart needs less recovery time after each contraction.
    b. there is increased blood flow to and from the heart.
    c. the reserve capacity of most organs increases.
    d. the lungs have a reduced capacity for the intake of oxygen.

8. Among older adults, the most chronic conditions include all of the following EXCEPT
    a. arthritis.
    b. diabetes.
    c. heart conditions.
    d. high blood pressure.

9. Dietary problems in late adulthood include
    a. being underweight.
    b. underconsumption of fats.
    c. being undernourished.
    d. consuming too many vitamins.

10. The drug abuse, misuse, or overuse problems found in the elderly are probably due to
    a. changing body chemistry.
    b. the desire to avoid pain.
    c. poor medical practices.
    d. lack of medical care.

11. According to research on aging,
    a. rural life takes five years off life expectancy.
    b. being married adds years to life expectancy.
    c. obesity does not seem to have an impact on life expectancy.
    d. radiation is no longer a threat to life expectancy.

12. As cells age, a fatty substance accumulates, which is called
    a. free radicals.
    b. DNA.
    c. lipofusein.
    d. estrogen.

13. The normal aging process, not connected with the occurrence of disease in the individual, is called
    a. senescence.
    b. senility.
    c. dementia.
    d. lipofusein.

14. Theories suggesting that the body ages as a result of random assaults from both the internal and external environments are called
    a. learning.
    b. genetic.
    c. stochastic.
    d. environmental.

15. Theories of aging that suggest that the actions of specific inherited genes determine aging are called
    a. stochastic.
    b. wear-and-tear.
    c. preprogrammed.
    d. genetic.

16. Memory for remote events is called _____ memory.
    a. sensory
    b. secondary
    c. primary
    d. tertiary

17. Dementia affects about _____ of people in late adulthood.
    a. 1 percent
    b. 2-4 percent
    c. 5-10 percent
    d. 15 percent

18. In the early stages of Alzheimer's disease
    a. long-term memory deteriorates.
    b. hospitalization is necessary.
    c. adaptations are relatively easy.
    d. the person must have constant care.

19. All of the following terms apply to stroke EXCEPT
    a. artherosclerosis.
    b. multi-infarct dementia.
    c. transient ischemic attacks.
    d. ministrokes.

20. The model of the mechanisms older adults use in cognitive functioning includes all of the following EXCEPT
    a. coordination.
    b. selection.
    c. compensation.
    d. optimization.

Posttest score _____

Pretest score _____

Improvement _____

To enhance your understanding of this chapter, answer each of the following questions as completely as possible, using the text for material to support your answer.

1. Define ageism and describe the stereotypes that exist in the current United States culture concerning the elderly.

2. Describe the four stages of late adulthood.

3 Describe the various factors involved in physical aging.

4. Some doctors are convinced that as much as one-third of the elderly are hospitalized because of the overuse, misuse, or abuse of drugs. Explain this statement.

5. Describe the sleep patterns in late adulthood and factors that contribute to insomnia in the elderly.

6. Describe the typical cognitive abilities of someone in late adulthood.

7. Compare the memory functions of middle and late adulthood.

8. Describes Baltes' concept of wisdom and discuss how an individual would probably reach this stage of mental development.

9. Describe the various forms of dementia that can occur in late adulthood and what treatments, if any, are available.

10. Explain selective optimization with compensation.

ANSWER KEY

Key Names

    1. b   2. a

Pretest

1. b	5. c	9. b	13. b	17. b
2. a	6. a	10. a	14. a	18. a
3. d	7. a	11. d	15. d	19. c
4. c	8. a	12. c	16. c	20. d

Programmed Review

1. educational, Gray Panthers
2. ageism, ambivalent
3. wisdom, venerated, culture, historical, filial, biblical, divine
4. five, transition, reduced, expectations, self-fulfilling
5. integration, loss, illness, die
6. adapting, interacting, homes, 19 percent, 85, centenarians
7. nonagenarians, healthier, agile, active
8. pathological, elastic, liver
9. less, deficits, focus, lens, cataract, acuity, stability, smell
10. cells, skeleton, shorter, spine, osteoporosis, vestibular, relaxation, elastic, clogged, oxygen, decrease
11. heart, contraction, reserve, cold, heat, adolescence, microorganisms, disease
12. chronic, arthritis, heart, hypertension, falls, stress, women, men, twice
13. overweight, undernourished, fats, arteries, atherosclerosis
14. calcium, constipation, high fiber, water
15. drugs, chemistry
16. 6 to 6-1/2, awakenings, 1, 3 and 4, Adjustment, stresses, hygiene, Psychophysiologic, psychiatric, apnea, limb
17. hereditary, Rural, married, Obesity
18. Senescence, stochastic, wear-and-tear, waste, lipofusein, radicals, interrupt
19. Preprogrammed, 200, clocks, hypothalamus, pituitary
20. intact, depression, drugs
21. speed, reaction, perceptual, cognitive, accuracy, practiced
22. less, perceptual, two
23. fewer, fewer, efficient, recognition, recall, selective, useful, important
24. Tertiary, historical, wisdom, factual, procedural, life-span, relativism, uncertainty, crystallized
25. life, human, superior, specific, mind, virtue, well-being, recognizable
26. Alzheimer's, health, education, motivation, secondary
27. Dementia, 2-4 percent, senile, nutrition, sleep, illness
28. brain, braided yarn, genetic, forgotten, confusion, tasks, recognized
29. ministrokes, multi-infarct, infarct, transient ischemic
30. fate, competent, control
31. physical, nutritional, alcohol, drugs, mental
32. optimization, compensation

Posttest

1. c	5. c	9. d	13. a	17. b
2. d	6. c	10. a	14. c	18. c
3. a	7. d	11. b	15. c	19. a
4. b	8. b	12. c	16. d	20. a

18

Older Adulthood: Personality and Sociocultural Development

CHAPTER OUTLINE

Personality and Aging
   Developmental Tasks in Older Adulthood
   Continuity and Change in Older Adulthood
   Successful Aging

Retirement: A Major Change in Status
   Physical, Economic, and Social Conditions
   Deciding to Retire

Family and Personal Relationships
   When Parenting is Over
   Caring for an Ill Spouse
   Widows and Widowers
   Siblings and Friends

U. S. Social Policy and Older Adults
   The Demographics of Aging
   Frail Older Adults
   Lifestyle Options for Older Adults

Look up the following terms and write out the definition of each. Then review the key terms from the previous chapters dealing with adulthood. Many of those terms apply to this chapter as well.

Identity   Retirement maturity
Institutionalization   Status passage
Magical mastery   Widower's impotency
Parental imperative

KEY NAMES

After reading the chapter in the text, try to match each of the following names with his or her contribution to the field of psychology. Check your answers with the Answer Key at the end of this chapter.

_____1. Robert Atchley   a. assimilation and accommodation

_____2. Paul and Margaret Baltes   b. continuity

_____3. Paul Costa and Robert McCrae   c. ego transcendence

_____4. Erik Erikson   d. integrity versus despair

_____5. Daniel Levinson   e. life satisfaction

_____6. Robert Peck   f. neuroticism

_____7. Jean Piaget   g. transition

Try to answer each of the following questions without referring back to the text. Check your answers with the Answer Key at the end of this chapter and record your Pretest score in the space provided.

1. Sociologists call a change in role and position a
    a. status passage.
    b. role reversal.
    c. promotion.
    d. transition.

2. Which of the following is considered the most important factor in satisfaction and adjustment in late adulthood?
    a. class
    b. social interaction
    c. health
    d. adequacy of housing

3. When studying people who continued to have a positive outlook even when health was failing, Heidrich and Ryff found that _____ play(s) a critical role in adaptation.
    a. family ties
    b. income
    c. adequacy of housing
    d. social comparison

4. Erikson's stage for late adulthood is
    a. trust versus mistrust.
    b. intimacy versus isolation.
    c. integrity versus despair.
    d. generativity versus stagnation.

5. Which of the following is NOT an aspect of personality investigated by Costa and McRae in their research on the maintenance of personality throughout adulthood?
    a. extroversion
    b. neuroticism
    c. psychoticism
    d. openness to experience

6. Costa and McRae found that over a 30-year period between middle and old age, men showed a minor shift towards becoming more
    a. introverted.
    b. open to experience.
    c. neurotic.
    d. psychotic.

7. Using the TAT, Gutmann found in late adulthood a shift from
   a. neurotic to psychotic behavior.
   b. introversion to extroversion.
   c. active to passive mastery.
   d. masculine to feminine behavior.

8. Gutmann found that both sexes in late adulthood respond to the freedom from the
   a. need to look good.
   b. responsibility of caring for a home.
   c. worry over money.
   d. parental imperative.

9. According to Erikson, those who can look back and feel satisfied that their lives have had meaning will have a sense of
   a. trust.
   b. integrity.
   c. generativity.
   d. initiative.

10. Research by Levy showed that those who adjusted to retirement best were those who
    a. wanted to retire whether or not they were in good health.
    b. were in good health even if they did not want to retire.
    c. were in good health and wanted to retire.
    d. needed to retire because they were in poor health.

11. An individual's adjustment to retirement will be easier if the person has
    a. little education.
    b. few civic involvements.
    c. been devoted to the job and feel they have done their best.
    d. found satisfaction outside of the job.

12. About _____ of retired U. S. adults age 65 or older have social security as their major source of income.
    a. one-third
    b. one-half
    c. two-thirds
    d. three-quarters

13. In 1950, about _____ of all men over age 65 were still working; in 1995, about _____ of this age group still had a job or were looking for work.
    a. half; 12 percent
    b. one-third; 25 percent
    c. three-quarters; 50 percent
    d. one-quarter; 75 percent

14. What percent of elderly Americans now have great-grandchildren?
    a. 10
    b. 23
    c. 36
    d. 40

15. There are more than _____ times as many older-adult widows in the United States as there are widowers.
    a. three
    b. five
    c. ten
    d. twenty

16. The preoccupation with widowhood among middle-aged and older women is
    a. definitely abnormal.
    b. useless because most will not experience this state.
    c. firmly rooted in reality.
    d. extremely dysfunctional.

17. Compared to widows, widowers are
    a. more active in social organizations.
    b. more apt to become isolated.
    c. less prone to sexual problems.
    d. less likely to experience prolonged sexual inactivity.

18. Today most older people in the United States are
    a. white.
    b. black.
    c. Hispanic.
    d. Asian.

19. The fastest growing segment of the population is
    a. adolescents.
    b. adults in middle age.
    c. those between 65 and 75 years of age.
    d. adults over 85 years of age.

20. About _____ percent of people over 65 are in nursing homes.
    a. 4
    b. 10
    c. 25
    d. 30

Pretest score _____

To test your understanding of this chapter, try to fill in each of the blanks in the chapter review without referring back to the text. Then check your answers with the Answer Key at the end of this chapter and reread those parts of the chapter that gave you problems.

1. A major change in role and position is a status _____, and the effect that these changes have depends in large part on the _____ that an individual attaches to those events.

Personality and Aging

2. _____ refers to the reasonably consistent set of concepts that a person has about his or her attributes. Whitbourne states that the process of maintaining a consistent identity is like Piaget's process of _____. A balance must be maintained between _____ and _____.

3. Erikson suggests that older people ponder whether their lives have fulfilled their earlier _____. Those who can look back and feel satisfied with their lives will have a sense of _____. Those who see nothing but a succession of wrong turns and missed opportunities will feel _____. Wisdom enables the older adult to maintain _____ and an integrated _____ in the face of physical deterioration and even impending _____. Many look to their children and grandchildren as a _____ in whom traces of their own personality and values will live on.

4. Levinson views old age similarly to young adulthood and middle age in that there is a period of _____ that links the previous life structure to the incipient life structure of late adulthood. And Peck views old age in terms of the resolution of the conflict between ego _____ and ego _____.

5. Atchley suggests that _____ provides people with an identity, and people strive to be consistent in their behavior because it makes them feel more _____. These changes are in line with a relatively constant inner _____ that we use to define ourselves.

6. Costa and McRae classified adult men into _____, the amount of anxiety, depression, self-consciousness, vulnerability, impulsiveness, and hostility displayed; _____ versus _____, and degree of _____ to experience. People who rate high on neuroticism are the ones who tend to be _____; people who were extroverted were _____ and outgoing.

7. Gutman's research indicated that 40-year-old men tended to view their environment as being within their _____. Sixty-year-old men saw the world as more _____ and _____ and saw themselves _____ and conforming to the environment in what is called a shift from _____ to _____ style. Very old men move to _____ mastery and both sexes are liberated from the _____ imperative.

8. Life satisfaction and adjustment in older adulthood has little relationship to _____ itself. _____ is considered the most important factor, but money, social _____, marital _____, adequacy of _____, amount of _____ interaction, and _____ are also important. Life satisfaction in later adulthood is also determined by how older people define _____ functioning. Middle aged and older adults defined psychological well-being in terms of an _____ orientation and older subjects also pointed to the acceptance of _____ as an important quality. Researchers found that social _____ plays a critical role in adaptation, and with social _____ (the maintenance of meaningful _____, normative _____, and _____ groups) offsets the negative effects of poor physical health and has a positive impact on well-being.

9. African-American adults are more likely than whites to live in _____, have less _____ , be single _____, and experience substandard _____ care. Two key factors that are largely responsible for the staying power of many African-Americans are affiliation with a _____ and help from _____ and _____. They look to the church for a range of _____ services and rely on their church for _____ assistance.

Retirement: A Major Change in Status

10. The pattern of and adjustment to retirement are the result of physical _____, _____ status, the _____ of others, and the need for _____ fulfillment. _____ men who want to retire fare the best.

11. Most older Americans have sufficient _____ assets to live on. In terms of net worth, older adults tend to be _____ than young adults. However 10 percent of America's elderly live below the _____ line. _____ people are much more likely to be poor than those who are _____. Members of _____ groups are more likely to be poor. _____ are more likely than _____ to be poor.

12. An individual's lifelong _____ toward work also affects feelings about retirement. Disengagement is especially hard for people who have never found _____ outside of their jobs. The problems tend to be worse for the less _____, the _____ strained, and those with few _____ or _____ involvements.

13. Women who had a continuous work history over an extended period of their adult lives adapted more _____ to retirement. This was due to the fact that they had more _____ security and were better _____ for retirement.

14. Thompson suggests that preparing for retirement consists of _____, retirement _____, and retirement _____. An index of retirement _____ indicates whether the retiree has adequate savings and income, a place to live, and plans for further work or activities. If economic trends continue, _____ people may have the option of an early retirement.

Family and Personal Relationships

15. For most individuals in later adulthood, the direct responsibilities of _____ are over, and they are more satisfied with their _____ after the children leave home. Happy marriages that have survived into later adulthood have often adopted a style that is more _____ and _____. Traditional _____ roles seem to become less important.

16. Most older adults report having relatively _____ contact with children and grandchildren, and often provide their adult children with various forms of _____. Over 40 percent of elderly Americans now have _____.

17. Most older adults who need help tend to rely heavily on their _____. Caregiver wives often report more _____ than caregiver husbands.

18. There are more than _____ times more elderly widows in the United States than widowers. Older widows tend to survive about _____ longer than older widowers, following a spouse's death. Women of all ages are less likely than men to _____, partly because our society favors the pairing of _____ men with _____ women.

19. In the immediate aftermath of a spouse's death, there is increased _____, help, and perceived _____ obligations. In time, _____ relationships usually improve or remain close, but _____ relationships are less predictable and may be _____ affected. In these cases, the wife has often been the _____. Widowers are more likely to become _____ from the couple's previous social contacts, generally less active in _____ organizations, and prone to _____ problems following bereavement (a form of impotence known as _____ impotency). Widowers generally have greater _____, education, freedom from _____ problems, and access to _____ relationships than widows. But they have more trouble coping _____.

20. In later adulthood, many people report increased contact with and concern for _____. They are valuable companions for the kind of _____ that leads to ego integrity. They may also work together to organize and provide help to an _____ parent. Siblings are also important to a widow's recovery from _____.

Social Policy and the Elderly

21. Social policy that affects older adults is influenced by the _____ composition of the population. These policies are most important to the _____ elderly. The fastest growing segment of the older population is _____ years old and older, and data show that the oldest old may actually be _____ than people in the young-old age group. It is the sheer size of the Baby Boom cohort that is expected to drive up _____ costs.

22. In the 1970s, much public attention focused on the _____, ill _____, and inadequate _____ conditions of older people and the limited _____ services available to them. Critics of our social services have often warned that we sometimes consider _____ placement when other services might be more appropriate. The institutional care we give our older people varies widely in _____.

267

23. One in four individuals over age 65 can expect to be _____ to the point where institutionalization will be necessary. _____ for the elderly are an option. Retirement _____ allow older people to live together but they _____ them from the rest of the world. Polls show that most elderly people want to spend their postretirement years in their own _____ and preferably in their own _____.

POSTTEST

Now try to answer the following questions without referring back to the text. Check your answers with the Answer Key at the end of this chapter and record your score in the space provided. Then enter your Pretest score, subtract, and record your improvement score.

1. Gail Sheehy's interviews of adults in their 60s and 70s revealed that these people looked to a life full of
   a. limitations.
   b. potential.
   c. disabilities.
   d. boredom.

2. According to Whitbourne, the process of maintaining a consistent identity is a lot like Piaget's ongoing process of
   a. adaptation.
   b. conservation.
   c. egocentrism.
   d. centration.

3. Researchers have found that there is a trend away from _____ in the African-American culture.
   a. family
   b. friendships
   c. careers
   d. prayer

4. Levinson views old age as a period of
   a. stability.
   b. transition.
   c. crisis.
   d. depression.

5. Peck views late adulthood as a time for the resolution of the conflict between
   a. integrity and despair.
   b. continuity and stability.
   c. ego transcendence and ego preoccupation.
   d. emotional flexibility and emotional rigidity.

268

6. Atchley suggests that the changes experienced in late adulthood are in line with
    a. a sense of integrity.
    b. an inner core by which the person defines himself.
    c. a growth toward ego transcendence.
    d. other transitions in life.

7. According to Costa and McRae, neuroticism includes all of the following EXCEPT
    a. anxiety.
    b. depression.
    c. introversion.
    d. vulnerability.

8. Besides neuroticism, and extroversion/introversion, what is the third dimension measured by Costa and McRae in their study of adult men?
    a. openness to experience
    b. consistency
    c. psychoticism
    d. control

9. Researchers have found that very old men view life with
    a. active alertness.
    b. passivity.
    c. complacency.
    d. magical mastery.

10. According to Whitbourne, the process of maintaining a consistent identity involves use of both
    a. introversion and extroversion.
    b. stability and change.
    c. assimilation and accommodation.
    d. transcendence and preoccupation.

11. Erikson suggests that people in late adulthood are in the stage of
    a. integrity versus despair.
    b. generativity versus self-absorption.
    c. intimacy versus isolation.
    d. trust versus mistrust.

12. It is more likely that members of each of the following groups will be poor EXCEPT
    a. women.
    b. minority members.
    c. single people.
    d. married people.

13. All of the following are part of Thompson's suggestions for preparing for retirement EXCEPT
    a. decelerating.
    b. investments.
    c. retirement planning.
    d. retirement living.

14. The index of retirement maturity is based on all of the following measures EXCEPT
    a. adequacy of savings and income.
    b. a place to live.
    c. health.
    d. plans for further work or activities.

15. Marital satisfaction in older couples is enhanced by
    a. an emphasis on traditional gender roles.
    b. children remaining home for longer periods of time.
    c. a career for each partner.
    d. an egalitarian and cooperative marriage.

16. In the immediate aftermath of widowhood, which relationship is most likely to be unpredictable?
    a. father-child
    b. old friendships
    c. mother-child
    d. grandparent-grandchild

17. In later life, social networks are
    a. nonexistent.
    b. more diverse.
    c. more constricted.
    d. more numerous.

18. Siblings are valuable companions for the kind of reminiscing that leads to
    a. ego integrity.
    b. trust.
    c. industry.
    d. initiative.

19. Research has shown that health care costs will rise over the next 25 years because of the
    a. extensive medical care needed by the oldest old.
    b. new technology being used.
    c. a scarcity of doctors.
    d. sheer size of the Baby Boom cohort.

20. People who end up in nursing homes are more likely to be
    a. married.
    b. childless.
    c. single.
    d. under 65.

Posttest score _____

Pretest score _____

Improvement _____

ESSAY QUESTIONS

To further expand your understanding of the material in the text, write out the answers to the following questions as completely as you can. Use the material in the text to support your answers.

1. Describe a pattern of successful aging.

2. Contrast the experience of aging in the African-American community with that of the white culture.

3. Compare the theories of Erikson, Peck and Atchley in relation to late adulthood.

4. On what basis did Costa and McRae evaluate the personality of adult men? What trends did they find?

5. Describe the sex differences in coping styles in late adulthood.

6. How does the stage of integrity versus despair in Erikson's theory relate to the previous seven stages of his theory?

7. What conditions affect a positive adjustment to retirement? What can people do to prepare themselves for this transition?

8. Describe sex differences in reactions to retirement.

9. What happens to a couple's marriage and their relationships with their children after their grown children leave home?

10. Describe the impact of siblings on the life of older adults.

ANSWER KEY

Key Names

1. b	3. f	5. g	7. a
2. e	4. d	6. c	

Pretest

1. a	5. c	9. b	13. a	17. b
2. c	6. a	10. c	14. d	18. a
3. d	7. c	11. d	15. b	19. d
4. c	8. d	12. c	16. c	20. a

Programmed Review

1. passage, meaning
2. Identity, adaptation, assimilation, accommodation
3. expectations, integrity, despair, dignity, self, death, legacy
4. transition, transcendence, preoccupation
5. continuity, secure, core
6. neuroticism, extraversion, introversion, openness, hypochondriacs, assertive
7. control, complex, dangerous, accommodating, active, passive, magical, parental
8. age, Health, class, status, housing, social, transportation, positive, "other", change, comparison, integration, roles, guidelines, reference
9. poverty, education, mothers, medical, church, family, friends, social, practical
10. health, economic, attitudes, work-related, Healthy
11. financial, wealthier, poverty, Single, married, minority, Women, men
12. attitude, satisfaction, educated, financially, social, political
13. easily, economic, prepared
14. decelerating, planning, living, maturity, fewer
15. parenting, marriages, egalitarian, cooperative, gender
16. frequent, assistance, great-grandchildren
17. families, stress
18. five, 50 percent, remarry, older, younger
19. contact, kinship, mother-child, father-child, negatively, kinkeeper, isolated, social, sexual, widower's, income, health, more, emotionally
20. siblings, reminiscing, ailing, bereavement
21. demographic, frail, 85, healthier, Medicare
22. poverty, health, living, social, nursing home, quality
23. disabled, Day centers, communities, isolate, communities, home

Posttest

1. b	5. c	9. d	13. b	17. c
2. a	6. b	10. c	14. c	18. a
3. d	7. c	11. a	15. d	19. d
4. b	8. a	12. d	16. a	20. c

19
Death and Dying

CHAPTER OUTLINE

Thoughts and Fears of Death
Denial of Death
Preoccupation with Death

Confronting Your Own Death
Death as the Final Stage of Development
Stages of Adjustment
Alternate Trajectories

The Search for a Humane Death
Hospices
The Right to Die

Grief and Bereavement
Grieving
Bereavement in Cross-cultural Perspective
Rituals and Customs
When a Child Dies

Completing the Life Cycle

KEY TERMS AND CONCEPTS

In order to increase your knowledge of the vocabulary used in this chapter, look up each of the following terms in the text and write out the definition.

Active euthanasia
Anticipatory grief
Assisted suicide
Bereavement overload
Chronic grief
Grief work
Hospice

Living will
Medical power of attorney
Passive euthanasia
Right to die
Submissive death
Suicidal erosion

KEY NAMES

After reading the chapter in the text, try to match each of the following names to his or her contribution to the field of psychology. Check your answers with the Answer Key at the end of this chapter.

_____ 1. Eric Erikson

_____ 2. Robert Kastenbaum

_____ 3. Jack Kevorkian

_____ 4. Elizabeth Kübler-Ross

a. assisted suicide

b. integrity

c. path to dying

d. stages of adjustment to death

Try to answer each of the following questions without referring back to the text. Then check your answers with the Answer Key at the end of this chapter and record your Pretest score in the space provided.

1. All of the following seem to be common reactions of western technological, youth-oriented societies towards death EXCEPT
   a. avoiding it.
   b. denying it.
   c. being preoccupied with it.
   d. understanding of it.

2. Today, death is most likely to occur in
   a. a hospital.
   b. the person's own home.
   c. a hospice facility.
   d. a nursing home.

3. When Kübler-Ross studied hospital personnel's reactions to dying patients she found that
   a. patients were encouraged to discuss their death openly.
   b. family and friends were encouraged to help the patient determine what to do with the time they had left.
   c. efforts were made to keep patients from discussing their feelings.
   d. the professionals were well trained to handle the situation.

4. Burt has just found out that he has terminal cancer, but he is positive that the test results are wrong. Burt would be in which stage of adjusting to death?
   a. anger
   b. denial
   c. acceptance
   d. depression

5. Mrs. Margolis has known that she is dying for some time now, but has promised God that if she can just live to see her youngest daughter married, she will donate her organs to research and attend church whenever she is well enough. Mrs. Margolis is in which stage of adjustment to death?
   a. bargaining
   b. denial
   c. acceptance
   d. anger

6. Mr. Constanzi is quietly awaiting his death. He is in which stage of adjusting to death?
   a. anger
   b. acceptance
   c. depression
   d. denial

7. Who suggested that the elderly go through a life review?
   a. Erikson
   b. Peck
   c. Kübler-Ross
   d. Butler

8. Which of the following is the term for letting oneself die?
   a. submissive death
   b. passive euthanasia
   c. suicide
   d. mercy killing

9. Which of the following does not belong with the others?
   a. mercy killling
   b. euthanasia
   c. grief work
   d. right to die

10. The Hospice concept is that death is
    a. something to be fought at all costs.
    b. something to be avoided.
    c. a natural stage of life.
    d. not going to occur until advanced old age.

11. Positive steps to bring about a premature death is called
    a. active euthanasia.
    b. passive euthanasia.
    c. partial euthanasia.
    d. suicide.

12. All of the following are accurate statements about the living will EXCEPT
    a. it is concerned with avoiding the use of heroic measures to maintain life.
    b. it applies to cases of irreversible illness.
    c. it is legally binding.
    d. those who observe its terms are protected.

13. Short-term adjustments to personal loss are called
    a. depression.
    b. anticipatory grief.
    c. mourning.
    d. grief work.

14. The shock phase of the grieving process lasts
    a. only a few minutes.
    b. for several hours.
    c. for several days.
    d. at least two years.

15. The grief that is experienced during a prolonged illness is called
    a. anticipatory grief.
    b. grief work.
    c. mourning.
    d. depression.

16. Those who experience the loss of several friends or family members in a year or two may experience
    a. grief work.
    b. anticipatory grief.
    c. bereavement overload.
    d. massive manic depression.

17. In Egypt, mourners are encouraged to
    a. deny the existence of death.
    b. express their grief through emotional outpourings.
    c. attend the Todos Santos.
    d. get into therapy as soon as possible.

18. Failure to recover from a loss is called
    a. chronic grief.
    b. anticipatory grief.
    c. bereavement overload.
    d. mourning.

19. It used to be customary for a widow to wear
    a. white.
    b. gray.
    c. black.
    d. navy blue.

20. When a child dies,
    a. siblings may experience feelings of guilt.
    b. doctors see the death as punishment.
    c. parents may be particularly confused.
    d. siblings recover rapidly.

Pretest score _____

To further test your knowledge of this chapter, fill in each of the blanks in this chapter review without referring back to the text. Then check your answers with the Answer Key at the end of this chapter and reread the sections in the chapter with which you had problems.

Thoughts and Fears of Death

1. Several authors have suggested that our Western technological, youth-oriented society has a curious habit of _____ and _____ death while, at the same time, being strangely _____ with it.

2. In earlier periods in history, death was a _____ event. It usually occurred at _____, with family members present. The details of preparing the body for burial and the final rituals were _____ and _____ events. In the late 20th century, most people die in _____, and the body is presented for final viewing in a _____ home.

3. Denial is a common mechanism for coping with _____. Some researchers believe that our cultural _____ against death is weakening.

4. When Kübler-Ross began her study of the dying process, she met with considerable _____ and _____ from hospital staffs. Once a terminal diagnosis had been made, both nurses and doctors often paid less _____ to that patient. Patients were discouraged from _____ their feelings about dying. Medical professionals who understand the dying process are better able to set _____ goals for good outcomes and help the individual die with _____, express final _____ to family and friends, and face death in the manner _____ with his or her lifestyle.

5. Psychoanalytic theory asserts that anxiety or fearfulness at the prospect of one's own death is _____. Several studies have found that older adults are less _____ about death, that those with a strong _____ in life fear death less, and that some elderly people report feeling _____ at the prospect of their own death. When young people are asked how they would spend their six remaining months of life, they describe activities such as _____ and trying to accomplish _____ they have not yet done. Older people speak of _____ or _____ and other inner-focused pursuits. They talk of spending time with their _____. Participants did report fear of a _____ and painful dying process.

Confronting Your Own Death

6. According to Butler, people often spend their last years conducting a life _____. At no other time is there as strong a force toward _____ as in old age. The process often leads to real _____ growth; individuals can resolve old _____, reestablish _____ in life, and even discover new _____ about themselves.

7. Kübler-Ross identified _____ stages in the process of adjusting to the idea of death. In the _____ stage, the person does not acknowledge the possibility of death and searches for other more promising opinions and diagnoses. Once the person realizes he or she will indeed die, there is _____, resentment, and envy. The person in the _____ stage looks for ways to buy time. When all else fails, _____ takes hold. In the final stage of _____, the person accepts and awaits his or her fate quietly. Not all people go through the _____ and only a few go through them in this particular _____.

8. In no illness are reactions to the dying process more influenced by the nature of the illness than in _____, a disease that is often sexually transmitted and thus surrounded by strong _____. The prolonged dying process makes _____ and forgiveness difficult.

9. The commonly accepted ideal trajectory is to be healthy to age _____ or more, put one's _____ in order, and die _____ and without _____. Surveys show that far more people prefer a _____ death.

10. The greatest number of suicides occurs among people over age _____. Four times as many _____ as _____ commit suicide, and the rate for men steadily _____ with age. These statistics do not take into account the more passive forms such as _____ death or letting oneself die, and suicidal _____ through excessive drinking, smoking, or drug abuse.

The Search for a Humane Death

11. We are good at providing _____ care to dying patients, but extremely poor at dealing head-on with their _____ and _____. They are _____ from their loved ones in a sterile environment; _____ are made for them; they are often not told what their _____ are for; and if they become upset, they are often _____. Doctors and other health care professionals are starting to be more _____ with dying patients. The current view is that dying patients should be given some measure of _____ and be permitted to state how much _____ they want. When people are put in nursing homes or hospitals prematurely, they feel that they can no longer _____ their own lives and respond by giving up the _____.

12. The notion that dying people should maintain some control over their lives and their death gave rise to the development of _____ for the dying. They are designed to help terminally ill patients live out their days as fully and _____ as possible. The first hospice for the dying was started in _____. Most hospice programs are part of comprehensive _____ organizations, which usually include an _____ unit, _____ programs with a variety of _____ services, medical and psychological _____, and ongoing medical and nursing services that relieve _____ and control _____.

13. The hospice concept views death as a normal and natural _____ of life to be approached with _____. Their first aim is to manage _____. They try as much as possible to _____ the dying person's rights in regard to _____ about death.

14. _____, or mercy killing, was practiced in ancient Greece and perhaps even earlier. Positive steps to bring about a premature death is called _____ euthanasia, and in our society the act is considered _____. _____ euthanasia involves no positive action but merely the withholding of life-sustaining procedures. The _____ informs the signer's family or others of the signer's wish to avoid the use of heroic measures. It is not legally _____, but it does _____ those who observe its terms from legal liability for doing so.

Grief and Bereavement

15. Short-term adjustments to the death of a loved one include initial emotional reactions to the personal loss or _____ work, and the practical matters of _____ arrangements, _____ matters, and _____ procedures. Long-term adjustments include the changes in _____ patterns, routines, roles, and activities necessary to cope with the social _____ left by death.

16. The survivor needs to _____ the reality of the loss and to realize that the loss causes some _____, and he or she must rechannel the _____ energy previously invested in the deceased. Those who do suggest a pattern note that initial reactions often include _____, numbness, denial, and disbelief. There may be _____ or attempts to _____. In the second phase, survivors may experience _____ grief, with a _____ or pining for the lost person. If there has been a long illness first, survivors experience some _____ grief.

17. Models of stress and coping note the value of strong _____ supports in negotiating a crisis. About 40 percent of the comments made by widows about post-bereavement social relationships were _____. Support from _____ seems more helpful than _____ support.

18. Older people who experience the loss of several friends or family members in a short span of time may experience bereavement _____. These affects have been felt recently by the _____ and _____ communities hit by AIDS. Depression is a serious risk during post-bereavement, especially for _____. So is _____ abuse.

19. Stroebe and her colleagues explored the universality of grief responses and found that responses are _____ and _____ defined. While the modern Western view of grief requires that people engage in proper grieving by _____ from their grief quickly, many non-Western cultures stress a continuing _____ with the deceased. In Japan, mourners have a home _____ dedicated to family ancestors. In Egypt, mourners are encouraged to _____ their grief through _____ outpourings.

20. _____ grief is a pathological mourning process. In the Leiden Bereavement Study, there were found variations in bereavement based on the _____ of the relationship before the death, the nature of the _____, whether there was an opportunity to _____ the death, and the practical _____ the bereaved received from others.

21. It used to be customary for a widow to wear _____ and refrain from _____ activities for several months or a year to symbolize her presumed _____ distress, and the culture allowed for a long _____ period. Funerals and memorial services can impart a sense of _____, decorum, and continuity. They can _____ the values and beliefs of the individual.

22. When a child dies, many of the aspects of grief and bereavement are _____. The brothers and sisters of a dying child may be particularly _____ and death is often seen as a _____. Many siblings do not disclose their secret _____, feelings of _____, or misunderstandings. Often the medical caretakers become involved in the child's hopes for _____ and will also experience feelings of _____ and anticipatory _____. A crisis of _____ is not uncommon for survivors following the death of a child.

23. During the festival of Todos Santos, Mexicans stop to remember and respect the _____. Todos Santos stems from Mexicans' belief that death is a _____ element of the life cycle. At the center of the celebration are community altars that welcome _____ to return. Each family has its own altarpiece, known as an _____, to honor and remember deceased family members. From this festival, children learn that death is a _____ part of life and is not to be _____.

POSTTEST

Now try to answer each of the following questions without referring back to the text and check your answers with the Answer Key at the end of the chapter. Record your Posttest score in the space provided. Enter your Pretest score, subtract, and record your improvement score.

1. In past centuries, people usually died in
   a. hospitals.
   b. their homes.
   c. nursing homes.
   d. hospices.

2. Studies have found that concerning death, the elderly are
   a. more likely to fear a prolonged dying process.
   b. afraid of dying more than younger people.
   c. preoccupied with dying.
   d. obsessed with the deaths of friends and family.

3. Kübler-Ross found that medical personnel often deal with death through the use of
   a. intellectualization.
   b. repression.
   c. denial.
   d. projection.

4. According to Erikson, people will be low in anxiety about dying if they have a sense of
   a. despair.
   b. acceptance.
   c. denial.
   d. integrity.

5. According to Kübler-Ross, the second stage in the reaction to impending death is
   a. denial.
   b. anger.
   c. bargaining.
   d. acceptance.

6. A person mourns for the losses that have already occurred and for the death that will occur in the stage of
   a. denial.
   b. anger.
   c. depression.
   d. acceptance.

7. Kastenbaum advocates an approach to death that
   a. allows people to follow their own path to dying.
   b. helps people to progress through the stages of grief in proper order.
   c. helps people to avoid feelings of anger and depression.
   d. emphasizes open expression of grief.

8. The first hospice was started in 1967 in
   a. the United States.
   b. Germany.
   c. England.
   d. China.

9. All of the following are part of the most commonly accepted ideal trajectory for dying EXCEPT
   a. being over 85 years of age.
   b. sudden death.
   c. accidental death.
   d. absence of pain.

10. Suicidal erosion is accomplished by all of the following EXCEPT
    a. excessive drinking.
    b. smoking.
    c. refusal of medical help.
    d. drug abuse.

11. Most hospices are
    a. private organizations.
    b. part of comprehensive health-care organizations.
    c. volunteer organizations.
    d. not permitted to operate as they would like.

12. Euthanasia was practiced
    a. as far back as ancient Greece or even earlier.
    b. only in the 20th century.
    c. only in oriental societies.
    d. in the United States on a regular basis until recently.

13. Who is the most outspoken advocate of assisted suicide today?
    a. Freud
    b. Kervorkian
    c. Birren and Birren
    d. Kübler-Ross

14. Which of the following is an example of passive euthanasia?
    a. giving a person an overdose of medication
    b. using a death machine such as Dr. Kervorkian's
    c. removing a respirator from a dying patient
    d. not resuscitating a patient who goes into cardiac arrest

15. All of the following are part of the Harvard Criteria for determination of a permanently nonfunctioning brain EXCEPT
    a. active reflexes.
    b. being unreceptive and unresponsive.
    c. a flat EEG.
    d. no circulation to or within the brain.

16. Those who suggest a pattern of grieving indicate which of the following as the first stage?
    a. active grief
    b. shock
    c. yearning
    d. preoccupation with the deceased

17. In the second stage of the bereavement reaction, people may experience all of the following EXCEPT
    a. shock.
    b. preoccupation with thoughts of the deceased.
    c. yearning.
    d. active grief.

18. Support from which individuals seems to offer the most help during bereavement?
    a. family
    b. spouse
    c. peers
    d children

19. In which country are mourners encouraged to focus on their grief and engage in cathartic emotional outpourings?
    a. Japan
    b. United States
    c. Mexico
    d. Egypt

20. In which country is the festival of Todos Santos held?
   a. England
   b. Spain
   c. Mexico
   d. France

Posttest score _____

Pretest score _____

Improvement _____

ESSAY QUESTIONS

To further expand your knowledge of this chapter, answer each of the following essay questions as completely as you can. Use the material in the text to support your answer.

1. Describe the process of denial as a defense mechanism and discuss its application to dealing with death and bereavement.

2. Describe how current cultures, including that of the United States, deal with death.

3. Explain Kübler-Ross's research in death and dying and describe the changes that have occurred because of her work.

4. Describe the life review suggested by Butler. What is its value?

5. Discuss the difference between suicidal erosion and submissive death and how they relate to euthanasia.

6. Describe how the timing of death affects the dying trajectory.

7. Is there such a thing as a humane death? Explain your answer.

8. Describe the purpose of hospice, and the services offered the dying and their families.

9. Discuss the suggested stages of bereavement and whether or not they fit your experiences with bereavement.

10. How does the death of a child differ from the experience of the death of any other loved one?

ANSWER KEY

Key Names

1. b   2. c   3. a   4. d

Pretest

1. d	5. a	9. c	13. d	17. b
2. a	6. b	10. c	14. c	18. a
3. c	7. d	11. a	15. a	19. c
4. b	8. a	12. c	16. c	20. a

Programmed Review

1. denying, avoiding, preoccupied
2. familiar, home, family, community, hospitals, funeral
3. stress, taboo
4. resistance, denial, attention, discussing, realistic, dignity, sentiments, consistent
5. normal, anxious, purpose, calm, traveling, things, contemplation, meditation, families, prolonged
6. review, self-awareness, personality, conflicts, meaning, things
7. five, denial, anger, bargaining, depression, acceptance, stages, order
8. AIDS, emotion, acceptance
9. 85, affairs, suddenly, pain, sudden
10. 45, men, women, rises, submissive, erosion
11. health, worries, thoughts, isolated, decisions, treatments, sedated, honest, autonomy, medication, control, struggle
12. hospices, independently, England, health-care, in-patient, home-care, home-based, consultation, pain, symptoms
13. stage, dignity, pain, respect, choices
14. Euthanasia, active, murder, Passive, living will, binding, protect
15. grief, funeral, financial, legal, life, void
16. accept, pain, emotional, shock, anger, blame, active, yearning, anticipatory
17. social, negative, peers, family
18. overload, gay, minority, men, drug/alcohol
19. historically, culturally, recovering, bond, altar, express, emotional
20. Chronic, meaning, death, anticipate, support
21. black, social, emotional, adaptation, order, reaffirm
22. intensified, confused, punishment, fears, guilt, recovery, failure, grief, values
23. dead, natural, ancestors, ofrenda, natural, feared

Posttest

1. b	5. b	9. c	13. b	17. a
2. a	6. c	10. c	14. d	18. c
3. c	7. a	11. b	15. a	19. d
4. d	8. c	12. a	16. b	20. c